MIDNIGHT
OIL

MIDNIGHT OIL

V. S. PRITCHETT

VINTAGE BOOKS
A DIVISION OF RANDOM HOUSE
NEW YORK

FIRST VINTAGE BOOKS EDITION,
November 1973
Copyright © 1971 by V. S. Pritchett

*All rights reserved under International and Pan-American
Copyright Conventions. Published in the United States
by Random House, Inc., New York. Originally published in the United States by Random House, Inc., in
1972, and in Great Britain by Chatto and Windus,
London, in 1971.*

Library of Congress Cataloging in Publication Data

Pritchett, Victor Sawdon, 1900–
  Midnight oil.
  1. Pritchett, Victor Sawdon, 1900   I. Title.
[PR6031.R7Z52 1973]   828'.9'1203 [B]   73–4012
ISBN 0–394–71952–2

Manufactured in the United States of America

TO
DOROTHY

Whence is thy learning? Hath thy toil
O'er books consum'd the midnight oil?

—John Gay

MIDNIGHT OIL

INTRODUCTION

◆◆◆

This is the year of my seventieth birthday, a fact that bewilders me. I find it hard to believe. I understand now the look of affront I often saw in my father's face after this age, and that I see in the faces of my contemporaries. We are affronted because, whatever we may feel, time has turned us into curiosities in some secondhand shop. We are haunted by the suspicion that the prayers we did not know we were making have been only too blatantly answered.

I have before me two photographs. One is, I regret, instantly recognizable: a bald man, sitting before a pastry board propped on a table, and writing. He does little else besides sit and write. His fattish face is supported by a valance of chins; the head is held together by glasses that slip down a bridgeless

3

nose that spreads its nostrils over a mustache. He is trying to find some connection with the figure in the other picture taken fifty years ago. He knows that the young fellow sitting on the table of a photographer's in Paris, a thin youth of twenty with thick fairish hair, exclaiming eyebrows, loosely grinning mouth and the eyes raised to the ceiling with a look of passing school-boy saintliness, is himself. The young one is shy, careless, very pleased with himself, putting on some impromptu act; the older one is perplexed. The two, if they could meet in the flesh, would be stupefied, and the older one would certainly be embarrassed.

The embarrassment is the subject of this book. To write about one's childhood is comparatively simple. One's life has a natural defining frame. One knows who one is; in childish egotism, one supposes people have a relationship only with oneself. But after the age of twenty, the frame is uncertain, change is hard to pin down, one is less and less sure of who one is, and other egos with their court of adherents invade one's privacy with theirs. One's freedom is inhibited by their natural insistence on themselves; also, the professional writer who spends his time becoming other people and places, real or imaginary, finds he has written his life away and has become almost nothing. The true autobiography of this egotist is exposed in all its intimate foliage in his work. But there is a period when a writer has not yet become one, or just having become one, is struggling to form his talent, and it is from this period that I have selected most of the scenes and people in this book. It *is* a selection, and it is neither a confession nor a volume of literary reminiscences, but as far as I am able I have put in my "truth."

I am not sure whether I should describe myself as an egotist or an egoist. The distinction is subtle and important; I am forced to use the personal pronoun and would do anything, if I could, to avoid it in a book like this. I am not a public figure. I would almost prefer to use the pronoun "we" rather than "I"—and I do not mean in the editorial or royal sense—and there is a strong argument for doing so. For a writer is, at the very least, two persons. He is the prosing man at his desk and a sort of valet who dogs him and does the living. There is a time when he is all valet looking for a master, i.e., the writer he is hopefully pursuing.

When I got out of the train in the early spring of 1921 at the Gare du Nord, I was all valet: the master was no more than a wish or a dream, and it would be a long time before the two would be united to each other. To find the writer, the valet had decided that he must break with his family and with everything and everyone he knew and go to France—a common opinion in the twenties. In my case this would be a remedy for what I foolishly thought was my fatal disadvantage: lack of education. I had little romping notion of "seeing the world"; in a disorderly way, I quite seriously wished to be taught. The petty aspect of the drama could be detected by the anxious way I kept on touching three of my pockets as I followed the porter who was carrying my heavy leather suitcase to the barrier. I had £20 divided among them. This sum, one could tell from my frightened eyes, had got to last forever, and the word "forever" was like a sustaining tune running through my head. If it did not last forever, I would be back in London with my tail between my legs; back on a stool in the leather trade. They used stools in those days.

Two things stick in my mind when I look back upon that arrival. First, the sight of Sacré-Coeur on its hill just before the train got in. White and Byzantine, this prosperous church looked like some harsh oriental bird with a large eye just below the dome—as it appeared in the afternoon light—a hard eye that cynically regarded the sins of Paris and made no comment. The second sight was alarming until I got used to seeing it all over the walls of Paris: the huge word *Défense,* followed later by the words *Loi de* and some nineteenth-century date. I would have to live carefully.

The bid for freedom was not as bold as I needed to think it. I would not have got away so easily if a Mr. Hotchkiss, a member of my father's church in Bromley, an outer suburb of London, had not happened to be in Paris doing the books of an Anglo-French company. He met me at the barrier and carried me off in a taxi while the Rue La Fayette rocked alongside, and the disturbing dome of Sacré-Coeur reappeared up the hill in side streets. We arrived at the Hotel Chatham. I was a little ashamed that Mr. Hotchkiss carried a Baedeker. He was a man with heavy plodding boots and a long face, like Jouvet's, who knew his way about. He had the not-uncommon English art of pretending to be stupid and then giving a shy, comic side-glance; a dry affectionate fellow, but with his cranky side. He stayed at the Chatham because English painters used to stay there, years before. He used to be a Tolstoyan. He had given that up now, but I had seen the Complete Works in his house, and I had one memorable chat with him in Bromley about Russian literature; when I left I wished, for a while, that he were my father. The idea had to be dismissed: his wife was a shouting woman (from South Africa, I believe) who sounded as if she were calling the cattle in. You could hear her far down the street, where no one shouted. We used to say, "There goes Mrs. H. calling the cattle off the veldt." If she caught me coming back from the station in Bromley she would make me carry a pile of broken boxes containing damaged fruit she had bought cheap in Covent Garden; and, on our way, her quick eyes would look for bits of wood in the

6

street or in peoples' front gardens. If she saw any, she would give one of her shouts and make me run in and get it. Very humiliating if you were wearing a bowler hat. She was a good-natured woman, but economical. Her husband was a frugal man too.

We dined at Duval's that evening. Mr. Hotchkiss told me that the Duval restaurants belonged to the Paris of Arnold Bennett. They were safe respectable places and, he said, inexpensive. The waitresses were middle-aged women who wore long starched white aprons that came up to their chins, and had been chosen for their plain faces. Here I saw my first pepper mill, ate my first *omelette fines herbes,* drank my second glass of wine. Mr. Hotchkiss drank a glass, too; he would not have dared to drink a glass in Bromley in the presence of a member of our sect. It was forbidden. He carefully calculated my share of the cost of the dinner at Duval's, and I admired his scrupulous behavior. My father would have largely put the amount down to expenses and charged someone else for it, in a generous way, which would lead to trouble the next day. But Mr. Hotchkiss went one better. We got out into the Rue de Rivoli, where I was taking in yet another breath of the Paris night air. It was like one's first cool smell of the sea, but a sea made lightly of Gauloises, coffee, scent and castrol. As we stood there a lady of the French Red Cross, who was collecting money for the French wounded in the 1914 war, shook her collecting tin at us. Mr. Hotchkiss's big droll eyes went dead with patriotism.

"Noos avongs no blessays ah noo," he said, and walked off.

"Money is all they think of," he said.

Fifteen years later when my father's business went bankrupt, my father shrewdly called in Mr. Hotchkiss to "wind up" the firm, and when the job was done refused to pay him the usual fee, on the grounds that they belonged to the same church. Mr. Hotchkiss, who had admired my father for years, could not believe this betrayal and wept when he told my brother about it. Soon after, the poor good man died.

I was shocked by the accent of Mr. Hotchkiss. I was already an accent snob, hot on vowels and the French "r." We walked back to the hotel, and outside a gaudily lit shop-window a girl accosted us. My heart raced, my body iced and then became boiling hot, for she looked like a pink-faced angel with eyes like blue crystals. Her eyes and voice made my skin prickle.

"Did you see that girl?" I said, swaggering, putting on an air of experience, to see how she would affect a member of our church.

"You'll see a lot," he grunted. I had grown a year older.

My father's friend lived for tasks. In England, in his spare time he liked making brass rubbings of the tombs in Norman churches. On our second day I went up in his esteem by saying I must find a cheaper hotel to live in. Eagerly he found me a much cheaper hotel near the Champ de Mars, and then we went to the Invalides and, reading from the Baedeker, looked down at Napoleon's tomb. He discussed Tolstoy's opinion of Napoleon and Napoleon's Paris. He was a good guide.

I was sure that my father would have told Mr. Hotchkiss that I was being sent to Paris for a few weeks to "learn the language" and go into the textile trade. So I told Mr. Hotchkiss that this was not so. I was going to stay "forever" in Paris, or at any rate I was going to travel from country to country all over the world, and I said I intended to be a writer. Mr. Hotchkiss said thoughtfully that this was exactly what I should do.

"But Father is against it," I said.

Mr. Hotchkiss thought a long time and then said: "You should do what you want to do." The next day, after taking me up the Eiffel Tower, Mr. Hotchkiss left.

In our family, as I have told in *A Cab at the Door* we lived an isolated life. No friend ever came to the house, not even Mr. Hotchkiss. Father always said he had no time for people. We had to ask permission to see our friends, and that was rarely given; and if it was, we had to dress up in our best clothes. "Is your own family not good enough for you?" was the piercing question. My earliest pleasure was therefore in being alone; and to be alone in Paris, knowing nobody, was an intoxication: it was like being on the dizzy brink of knowing everybody. I felt I was drinking the light of the city and the words I heard spoken by passers-by. After Mr. Hotchkiss had gone, I walked to the Place de la Concorde and there by the bridge in the shade of the warm trees looked over the stone wall into the river. I was instantly under a spell. The water looked still, yet it rustled like a dress. I had never seen water and stone in such pleasant conversation, the stone moonish, shading to saffron like the cheese of Brie, the water womanish and velvet. My solemn young eyes were seeing order and feeling united. I was so moved that I could feel myself grow into a new being. I repeated to myself my vow—for I was at the vowing age—never to leave France, and I was so entranced that tears came to my eyes. I walked from bridge to bridge along the Seine, past the acacias, the poplars and the planes that leaned with a graceful precision over the water, each tree like the stroke of a painter's brush. The orderliness of the trees, the gravely spaced avenues, rearranged my mind. My English feeling was for Wordsworthian nature; here nature had been civilized. I was shocked and converted in an hour, and though later in life I have often lapsed, the conversion has remained.

It was exasperating that I was followed by a couple of boys who jeered, "Look at the Englishman, oh yes, oh yes!"—exasperating because at school I had won a prize for French, but could hardly tell them I had read Molière, Bernadin de Saint-Pierre or Balzac; that given time I could tactlessly recite from Victor Hugo's *Les Châtiments*, beginning with

> *Waterloo, Waterloo morne plaine*

and was in the middle of Anatole France. It was annoying. Language and the sound of words had been my obsession from childhood; the pursed or the open subtlety of French vowels, the nasal endings, the tongue slipping along over silk and metal, the juiciness of the subjunctive, made my own lips restless. My ear was good, if my grammar was bad. As I walked I repeated to myself the names of the shops: *quincaillerie, boulangerie, bouquiniste;* even the horrific words *voies urinaires* plastered over the buildings, and any phrase I overheard. But the word that had an overwhelming beauty for me was *cinquième:* my room was on that floor in the hotel. What significance *cinquième* had! Its meaning was liberty.

I did have two introductions to people in Paris. My father had had ambitions to extend his business into the perfumery trade, and in fact he had once set fire to the top floor of his premises in Middle Street while experimenting with essences, boiling them, I suppose. Anyway that narrow street was soon glorious with fire engines: a District Call, he boasted when he came home bandaged. He had given me an introduction to a scent maker and also to a Christian Science lady. The scent man lived in the Faubourg Poissonnière. He asked me to lunch at his flat. (I was to spend nearly two years in Paris, but I think I was briefly invited only three times to the house of a French family.) This gentleman had a reddish mustache, and lived in a spacious and dowdy place of polished floors and gilded furniture. The floor polish had a sickly smell. All the family were at lunch. His wife, a cheerful woman, stood scooping out soup at the end of the table and passed it to her two daughters, their husbands and her son and the rest of us. One of the sons-in-law was a young officer in the army, full of wine and butter. He was in uniform. They were all shouting and laughing most of the time, especially at me. I could not understand much of what they said, and my grammar made them throw down their table napkins and shout with merriment. At every half-sentence they corrected my genders. I was unlucky enough to defend myself by saying I had trouble with my *gendres*. Screams of laughter. Lunch was a withering lesson at school.

The father stopped them at last and said: "There is only one solution. You must get a 'sleeping dictionary,'" and this started the warm-eyed girls off again.

"Do you know what that is?" the father asked me.

"Yes."

"Ah," shouted the soldier. "He is making progress already." This started the girls again.

After lunch the son took me into a small salon with gilt cabinets in it. He was a pale boy with red hair and a large Roman nose. "My father is right," said the son. "My mother arranged a mistress for me."

I heard my voice say coldly: "We do not do such things in England." I was astonished by my hypocrisy.

"Don't you believe it," the soldier said. "I was with the English during the war."

I couldn't bear the condescension in the son's long naked

nose. His voice seemed to come down it. One of the young daughters overheard us and said to her sisters: *"Il est féroce, cet anglais."*

But the city was evidently made for me. It was built for Art and Learning, whereas my London was built for government and trade. At home I was a tolerated joke, "the professor." One foggy morning when I'd been with my father in Cheapside, he had stopped to talk to a customer in the textile trade who asked what I was going to do. My father said: "He says he wants to be a journalist."

The man replied: "Give him a copy of Compton Mackenzie's *Sinister Street*. That will cure him." Because of this I have never read that famous novel.

In Paris, I thought, a conversation like that could not take place. Here one was driven into displaying a talent. One would even be mocked for not doing so.

And how the streets and gardens of the city *helped*: the names were an encyclopedia of French history and classical instruction. In the parks the statues of heroes and goddesses, busts of painters, dramatists and writers, gesticulated among the nursemaids and the children, and shared the place with the birds. In the next few days the old age that had rounded my shoulders in London—the James Barrie-Edmund Gosse stoop—slipped away from me.

The Christian Science lady lived near the Champ de Mars. She was a pleasant woman, busy and contented in the knowledge that she had had the final revelation about God and man, particularly on the practical side. I met her carrying a long roll of French bread under her arm into her house. A sort of virginity had been restored to her in the crisis of middle age. It turned out that she had once been married to a Frenchman, a problem which had been successfully prayed away to another address. She had lived in Paris most of her life. She took me out to lunch in Passy at a pretty and very private garden restaurant which, she said, was unusual among Paris restaurants. The owners were noted for their moral standards and cleanliness. We ate in the garden, and I was given a glass of Vichy water. This drew out the buried Calvinist.

"The war was the final manifestation of French decadence," she said. ("Manifestation" was a word often used by our sect. It was followed by another favorite: "mesmerized.")

"They are mesmerized by sensuality. Their food is the cause of it—cooking in butter, the sauces, apéritifs and above all their strong coffee and wine. These stimulate their sensual appetites and make the French the most unspiritual race on the earth. They are far from God as we know him 'through Science.'"

I said I liked sitting in the cafés.

She corrected me: "French people of good family *never* go to cafés."

This lady was kind, but one soon came up against a blank wall in talking to her. The effect of these opinions was to make me want to eat more sauces and drink more wine. I kept quiet about this, but went with her to the Christian Science meeting because there, she said, someone might know of a job, for my £20 was running out; to stay in France I would have to earn my living. She said the editor of a Paris newspaper was an admirer of the *Christian Science Monitor* and very interested, as they said, "in Science." I was astounded. What influence our religion had! My doubts must be wrong!

Every small experience played on my wavering mind. The meeting of twenty-five people was held on Sunday morning in the room of a small dancing academy for young ladies in a genteel quarter. The waxed floor, the large black-framed mirror on the wall, the piano rather chipped with its ill-tuned

notes, would send my mind wandering through the prayers
and readings to the imaginary Mademoiselle counting out the
steps: *"Un, deux, trois, quatre—attention, Marie-France"* in
some refined Edwardian tinkle. Even our First Reader, who
read the Lord's Prayer in the primmest of good French,
sounded rather as if he belonged to the eighties of last century
than to 1921; and indeed, young and American, he suggested,
as many polite Americans did at that time, a society fixed in
the past. The sensation of joining a previous age of gentility
was a novelty to me who had been brought up in vulgar
England and in a family where manners were unknown, where
everyone shouted, and no one had any notion of taste, either
good or bad. We lived without it. And after the meeting, the
amount of bowing and hat-raising that went on suggested a
social life which I was entering just as, of course, it was mad-
deningly on the way out. Too late. Too late. I longed, for my
first two or three weeks in Paris, to be in this sense a bourgeois,
if only to have something to give up.

In Paris the congregation were gayer and slacker than
ours in Bromley, for they were a mixture of tourists glad to be
out of England or America, business people, or French and
Italian Protestants, who said it was a liberation to get away
from the Lutheran and other churches. They seemed to be the
happiest people on earth: the Divine Mind fizzed like some
harmless *vin mousseux* and stimulated the yes-yes-yes of the
Americans. One or two of these had started or inherited small
banks in the United States which were booming, and the
Divine Mind had so arranged it that in Paris one got more
and more francs for the dollar every month on the falling
exchange—an exchange that fell because of the decadence and
sexual indulgence of the French, their obsession with food and
wine, their neglect of plumbing, and the disastrous fact of

being Latins with the long, now happily decayed, influence of the Roman Catholic Church behind them. It amuses me to read nowadays that the twenties were a decade of wit and license. I had fallen not among sinners, but among the good.

I told everyone I spoke to that I wanted to be a writer. Or a painter. I had brought a box of watercolors with me. Two men in the group took this very kindly. One was the Reader —whose French was so good—a well-off, handsome and ascetic American of about thirty-five; his father was a small banker who had lived in Paris before the war.

"I was an abstract painter." He smiled wearily at his folly.

"Can I see your pictures?"

"No, I've given it up."

Abstract painting was on the right lines, he said; it was more "mental," less of the flesh and the senses than the traditional thing. It alarmed me to hear he was one more of those intelligent men who had given up literature and art for our religion. Shyly, tolerantly, he looked back on those mistaken Bohemian days. My resistance to the idea of becoming a purely spiritual being hardened. Still, he forgave me for hankering after the life he had, with evident struggle, put aside. He was a fanatic beneath his irony and gaiety. He had mortified the flesh. There was a rumor that he had attained the ideal, and lived in a state of blessed virginity with his wife.

The other man was totally different: a gaudy and fleshy Americanized Londoner called Shaves. He sang louder than anyone else when the hymns started. I shall have more to say about this touching and ludicrous man, who when he laughed looked like someone shouting in agony for help. He was in his forties. Once in the street after the meeting he could not hide his relief—he was made to go to church by his wife—and started to bawl out bits of opera while his wife and three young children tried to stop him. He was unquestionably common.

> *"La, la, la, di, da, dah! Oh, my old coat,*
> *My old coat tried and trusted*

—Know it? *Bohème!* Cecil Chavasse, Metropolitan Opera, New York. My father. Ever hear him? What a voice!"

He scrutinized me. I'd never heard of his father. He gave me his look of vulgar appeal, then he committed a crime. Christian Scientists are told not to smoke or chew tobacco, for Mrs. Eddy belonged to the tobacco-chewing age in the U.S.A. Mrs. Nathaniel Hawthorne had felt as she did about it. Mr. Shaves pushed a cigarette into a small holder, stuck it at an angle of 45 degrees in his mouth, and sailed off under his straw hat like a Cockney tripper at Southend. His wife put on the Christian Science smile of seeing and hearing no evil.

Nothing came of the Christian Scientists. After three weeks my money was nearly gone. I was desperate. I tried to get jobs on English newspapers. In a fatuous moment I went to *Le Figaro* and asked the girl at the desk, as best I could, if I could get a job as a reporter. I tried banks, tourist offices. I read with bewilderment French advertisements. Then one evening of panic I saw an advertisement in the Paris *Daily Mail:* a photographer wanted an assistant. I could hardly sleep that night. I brought the full force of Christian Science prayer to work. A success! At eight the next morning I rushed off to the place on the Boulevard des Italiens. It was a photographer's shop. The manager said: "I suppose your parents sent you over to study?" "No," I said. "I have to earn my living." I got the job.

I was a good young man, but the good have their dubious moments. I went to the nearest post office and sent a telegram to my father. I knew he would be pleased. But it was also a message of defiance. Letters had been coming from him every other day, advising me to make a daily list of my expenses, asking what I was doing about my laundry, and so on, pointing out that I must, when in doubt, refer any detail to himself and the Divine Mind; and from then on there would be half a page on its operation, on the need to make the most of this experience until I came home, to see what would "unfold" for me in a few weeks. He had a very neat hand which ran one word into the next, so that his letters were like one long sentence. I was not to regard these letters, he said, as lectures. A letter came back at once in answer to my telegram, asking me to say whether the photographers were a sound firm; was the salary paid by the week or month? The advice to put down my daily expenses was repeated. He always did this himself and, I believe, this was one of the reasons for his chronic insolvency. The mere act charmed him into extravagance. These letters touched me, but my weeping days were over, and I was angry. I sent him a rude letter saying I did not want his advice every day, and that I was quite able to manage my own life. This must have hurt him and—so unreasonable is guilt—I felt guilty in standing up for my independence. But not for long.

I started work on a misty morning. The shop was in an arcade and was the Paris branch of an English manufacturer of photographic plates and papers. At first I had thought the boss was French, for he had the black long curly mustache and frisked-up hair of a French barber of the period, and wore a tight jacket and boots with high heels. In fact, he was a London sparrow brought up in Marseilles. His sallow skin looked as though it had been painted with walnut stain and he spoke

French fast, but with an entirely English pronunciation. His "combiangs" and "ker voolay voos" raced through the tongue of Molière like a rusty lawn-mower. He pointed out that on the small salary he was paying me I should have to leave my hotel and find a cheaper room.

That morning, I saw my job was a comedown after the leather trade. First of all, the situation of the shop was wrong. Du Maurier, Murger and W. J. Locke and Anatole France would have dropped me if they had known I was earning my living on the Right Bank within five minutes of Thomas Cook and American Express: that I was in Paree and not Paris. My mind split: here I was copying, in pencil, lists of stock on half-sheets of flimsy paper, hour after hour, in the dark back office of the shop, but my other self was across the river among the artists. The other workers in the shop were, first, the salesman: he was a heavy, black-haired, scowling young Highland Scot, a handsome man with gray, threatening eyes and a very soft voice. He had run away from home at fifteen and, disguising his age, had fought in the artillery in the 1914 war. He was a broken-nosed army boxer, too. Toward the end of the war he had been blown off his horse and received a chunk of high explosive in his bottom, and spoke of this with gravity. He had married a Frenchwoman, and I imagined a pert little midinette; but one day she stood in the arcade outside making signs to him, and I saw she was a plain, short woman, middle-aged and enormously fat. They lived in Montmartre, and he spoke of her cooking reverently. He was a magnet to all the women who came to the shop. They became helpless or frantic at the sight of him; he would stand close to them and look down into their eyes, unsmiling, and speak in a low voice, with slow, pedantic deliberation.

The rest of the staff were a nimble little guttersnipe from Montmartre called Pierre, and a gangling, hot-faced Breton. I was the clerk; they were messengers and packers. I checked the stock in a storeroom opposite the shop and packed as well. After a month, when suddenly my awkward French became fluent, I had to serve the customers and deal with the dozens of cash on delivery forms at the post office. By this time, if the boss had left, I had to type out short letters to the customers, on an old English typewriter. I bought a book on French commercial correspondence. I was the hero of Pierre, the Montmartre boy, who jumped about as he watched me type with three fingers and helped me salt-and-pepper the letters with the proper French accents.

The customers were mainly from firms of photographers in Paris, but many came up from the provinces bringing with them—to my mind—all that one thought of as the provincial bourgeois. Madame Bovarys came in to see the Scot. Their voices—and his—would drop to murmurs. Sometimes the two would disappear into the street together, and the Scot would be away for half an hour; the office boys, particularly the Breton, danced about him when he came back trying to get details out of him. What was she like in bed? The male photographers had an artistic appearance which I admired. They wore hard-crowned black hats with wide brims, and a loose black bow dangling from the collar. I longed to dress as they did, but the artistic dress was beyond my income.

For some time I was the office joke. The French boys could not pronounce my name. I became M. Shwep or Machin-Shwep, occasionally M. Victor, and their clown. We all got on well. There is that picture of me sitting on the counter of the shop, wearing the tweed jacket and flannel trousers—a uniform unknown to the French in the twenties, for most Frenchmen wore black then—and my juvenile grin. I grinned most of the time, for I was careless of the future, living from day to day, free to do as I pleased. I finally became acceptable to the French boys when in the evenings we left the shop and all walked arm in arm along the boulevard, practicing the girl auction invented by the Breton.

"How much to sleep with this one? A thousand, five hundred, a hundred, twenty, ten?" they shouted as the girls came toward us.

One day I had a triumph.

"Monsieur Shwep—how much?"

"Twenty-two francs fifty," I said.

They were ravished by this superb office joke. Twenty-two francs fifty was the well-known price of one of the photographic papers we sold. How easily the office humorist is born.

But the Scot was the hero of the shop. It was he who was worshiped as we trailed after him to the bistro round the corner. His unsmiling face imposed. His drinking amazed. His betting at Auteuil and Longchamps was famous. We marched back to the shop after lunch, the Montmartre boy singing:

O! o! o! o! o!
Monsieur Mac boit pas d'eau.

The boss was frightened of the Scot, who towered over him. Mac's gestures were as slow as his speech. His arm came up as if judging for an uppercut when he talked to the boss, whose eyes began to flutter and his feet to edge back. Sometimes, when one of the Madame Bovarys came into the shop and the magnetizing stares and monosyllabic invitations began, the boss would come out to stop them, but his courage always failed; and with ceremonious impudence Mac would say that in view of the importance of the lady as their best customer from Lille or Dijon, he thought he would go out for half an hour with her for a drink. One lunchtime when we were at the bistro and he was talking to the barman about some horse race or other, one of his women (who could not get a word in) became annoyed. She made a dart at his fly and pulled his cock out. The Scot turned slowly to her with admiration. He buttoned up, and our procession marched back to the shop. Mac went straight to the boss, and in the sad manner of some old Scots preacher he told the boss what had happened.

"I thought it might be advisable to warn you about the bistro," he said, "in case you should find yourself in a similar situation."

I left my room on the *cinquième* at the hotel. I now lived in a cheap room in Auteuil, a fashionable quarter, but my room was in the poorer part of it, where servants, shop assistants and small employees lived. I had given up trying the Latin Quarter, for thousands of Americans had swarmed in and put up the prices. I had been forced to reject a tiny room in the Mont Saint Geneviève because the place stank. In Auteuil I found a good cheap room on the ground floor in the flat of a war widow who went out to work every day as a charwoman. She was a sad woman in her thirties who came from Tours, and she was very religious, a strong Catholic, and very proud of the pâtés of her region. A priest used to bring her little boy back from school at the weekends; nuns visited her. The flat had two rooms. Mine was nearly filled by a large bed and a washstand, and looked out on a yard and dirty wall.

When she was at home Mme. Chapin wore a black overall from chin to feet, and felt slippers. She had a lamenting voice, and sounded like one of the Fates. On Sunday mornings, usually when I was naked and washing in cold water, for there was no bathroom, she would come in with my laundry and stand there telling me bits of her life.

"Oh, that filthy war," she would say again and again. "My husband would have been the chief mechanic at the garage if he had not been killed."

Paris was a wicked city of heartless people, she would groan, as I tried to cover myself with the little wet towel. And there was a good deal of "Such is life," in my mother's fashion. Mme. Chapin worked for a rich cocotte up the street.

"A life of luxury—but with women like that, a false step, a suspicion, and the man who keeps them throws them into the gutter."

On Sundays she dressed in her best black, and now her face would seem rounder, and her yellowish eyes would become warm and seductive. Her pale, dressed-up little boy would stare at me.

"Ah, my son," she often said to him. "Look at the gentleman. He works. Work—follow his example, my son." And they would go off to Mass. I got to know Mme. Chapin very well.

"I feel safe with you," she said after a month. "It was not the same with my Polish lodger. I never felt any confidence with him, but with you it is different."

I was hurt. One Sunday, when Christmas came, she came in dressed up in her black as usual with her boy. She was going on her annual visit to her sister, who had come to stay at the Ritz. This sister was a kept woman and lived with a motorcar manufacturer. The rich sister gave her discarded dresses to sell, and the boy was given a book or a toy. When Mme. Chapin came back, she fell back on her stock epitaph, standing still as stone in the doorway, in her mournful voice: "With those women, one false step . . ." She seemed more like a man than a woman to me.

It did not occur to me until forty years later that this annual visit would make a good story. I moved the two sisters to London and, in the manner of writers, changed or added to what I could guess of their characters. I gave Mme. Chapin a husband. I think that what prevented me from writing the story before was my knowledge of her real life. It was not until I had given her an imaginary husband and transferred her to another place that she took on the reality of fiction and one, I think, that dignified her. It is part of the function of the novelist to speak for people, to make them say or reveal what they are unable to say, to give them a dignity, even the distinction of being comical, though she was not comical in my story. But in those Paris days I could not easily think of what to write about, and I did not know that the creative impulse is often ignited when scenes and people from the almost forgotten past are struck like a flint against something from the present. Her one happiness was knowing the "saintly Brothers" who took charge of her son.

At lunchtime I usually ate a crusty roll and butter, and by six o'clock, after the long wait in the queue at the post office with the parcels, I was torn between hunger and the whole of Paris. I walked down to the Tuileries, crossed the Pont des Arts into the Latin Quarter and then began a torturing study of the grocers, the butchers and the menus of restaurants. I was reading Rabelais by now and his joy in the belly, his lists of sausages and pâtés and his cries of *"à boire"* half fed me. The sight of snails, cheeses, garlic sausages and the oily *filet d'hareng* worked on me until I had to give in. In the next two years I ate my way through the cheap streets of Paris. I sat alone, read or watched people. I was no longer a shop assistant when I left at six o'clock. I became a gifted student, a writer, a painter "studying life." The noise of these restaurants made me happy. I had no friends, but the crowd seemed to be my friends. There was a stout, shouting fellow in a place in the Rue de Seine whose voice was rich and greedy; he had a peg leg, and when he came in he used to unstrap it and hand it to the waitress, who stood it in the corner. Now, where in London, I thought, would you see a sight like that? Afterward I sat in cafés in the Boulevard Saint Michel and watched the students at their game of squirting soda water at one another and joined in their singing.

> *Ton honneur sera perdu*
> *Comme les autres*
> *Tu feras ma pauvre fille*
> *Comme less autres font*

One day a sewage cart passed and the students rushed from the café, took off their hats, and with bowed heads walked in funeral procession behind it.

One evening I discovered that the artists met in the Rotonde and Dôme at Montparnasse, and there I sat over a glass of coffee or beer for the rest of the evening, hoping that some of their genius would rub off on me. One night, there was a violent thunderstorm. I had switched from Rabelais to Plato. What with the lightning, and the wine inside me, I was exalted. After these speechless evenings I would walk across that part of Paris, through Grenelle, to the room in Auteuil, and I would either go exhausted to bed or sit up trying to write, while my landlady groaned in her sleep in the room next door.

Most writers begin by imitation. I had the examples of Stevenson, Chesterton, Belloc and—for his practical hints— the clever short sketches of Barrie. In French there were the essay-like writings of Anatole France. Naively I supposed that these writers were all learned men who had read enormously at the university, and that until I had read pretty well as much, I would not be able or even entitled to write at all. I passed my Saturdays looking over the book shops of the Boulevard Saint Michel or the boxes of the *bouquinistes*. I saw that I had not only English literature but the whole of French literature standing between me and the act of writing. Books were cheap. I was used to going without a meal, if necessary, to buy them. I bought indiscriminately. I had got a history of French literature; then the Rabelais; Balzac with his gluttonous appetite for the names of pieces of furniture, door knockers, lamps, the names of trades and products, pushed me to the dictionaries, but the *Contes Drolatiques* were cheerfully licentious; at any rate, in print, I would be a sexual adventurer. I read Lamartine, Vigny and witty Beaumarchais; out of duty to my dead cousin Hilda I read Victor Hugo *and* the Pléiade; I mixed the sermons of Boileau with the titillations of *Manon Lescaut;* Chateaubriand was given up for the adulteries and seductions of Maupassant, or the ballads of Villon. What could I possibly get out of such chaotic reading? How far did my understanding reach? Not far at all, but I did seize the nature of these writers in some of their pages, for something stuck in the confusion of my mind as I sat reading by the light of Mme. Chapin's oil lamp. The row of books along the high flyblown mirror over the marble mantelpiece in my room got longer and longer, and the smell of the lamp was made aromatic by the smoke of Gauloises.

There was another reason for hesitating to write: a love of painting, the old hangover from my painting days at Rosendale Road School and *Modern Painters*. I spent afternoons in the galleries and stood unnerved by the pictures of the Post-Impressionists in the shops. The smell of paint itself excited my senses. I gazed with desire at the nudes. The attraction of painting was that a work could be instantly seen—no turning of the page—and each brush stroke "told" to the eye. I lived by the eye: the miles I walked in Paris fed the appetite of the eye above all, so that I could imagine everything in the city was printed or painted on me. One warm Saturday I took my watercolors to Saint-Cloud and sat down to paint a group of trees. Other painters, stout men with beards, were painting Cézanne-like pictures of Prussian blue avenues. I squeezed and dabbed my paints, and after a couple of hours got up to study the running muddle I had made. I was angry with my incompetence. I sneezed. The grass was damp, and within an hour I was down in a café trying to kill a heavy cold with hot rum and lemon. It lasted a dreadful fortnight in which I moved to Russia and read *Anna Karenina*. My career as a painter was over; but, all the more, pictures seemed to tell me how I ought to write.

The question was, What to write about? I found I simply wanted to write anything. I used to go and look at the Sorbonne: obviously I was not a man of learning. I gazed at Racine's face: dramatic verse was beyond me. I had read that one writes because one has something to say. I could not see that I had anything to say except that I was alive. I simply wanted to write two or three sentences, even as banal as the advertisement on a sauce bottle, and see them in print with my name beneath them. I was at the bottom rung.

Suddenly I had a stroke of luck. I saw in the Paris *New York Herald* a note asking their readers to send in jokes. I realized I had been giggling for some weeks over one. After an hour or so of struggle I wrote it out. I had been standing outside the Opéra with a young Englishman I had met, studying the playbills. He said, "Let's go there tomorrow night." I said, "We can't. There's nothing on." He pointed to the notice. "Yes, there is," he said. "They're doing *Relâche*." I sent this to the paper. The next day it was published with my full name and address underneath it. (I resented that they put in my address, exposing me as an amateur.) They did not pay me. This was my first published work. I kept it a long time. It taught me one thing. If one had nothing to say one could at any rate write what other people said.

I was unable to progress from this point. I went back to the English writers I then admired: the Georgian poets, people like Stevenson, Chesterton, Belloc, Max Beerbohm. What was their common characteristic? It was obvious. They walked. Even Max Beerbohm had walked one morning. Walking started the engine inside them and soon came the words; but they walked on the "open road," not simply about city streets.

So, when the weekend was fine I took to the road. Paris was small in 1921. It ended at the fortification where the Métro stopped. There were not a great many motorcars about, and I often walked out to Saint-Cloud, to Saint-Germain and to Versailles, to Marly; and once, on a longer holiday, to Chartres, to see the blue glass and the withered kings. I came back white with dust and with a full notebook. I was being Stevenson without the donkey, or *The Beloved Vagabond*, with knapsack, garlic sausage to eat in a field by the roadside or at some cheap restaurant where, sweating and tired, I found my head spinning with the wine I drank. (*A boire!*) I think I was never happier. On longer journeys—to Pontoise and Poissy—I came back by train. Later on I found a young Englishman who came into the shop one day and talked about a writer called Lytton Strachey. My friend worked at the Bourse, and we went on a tramp in the real Bellocian tradition. We made a vow. We vowed we'd cross the Loire. We walked to Orléans and crossed the river. The country was dull, the pavé roads were straight and monotonous, the villages were not pretty; in the nights the bullfrogs barked in the pools of the plain; the wide riverbed of the Loire when we came to it was all stones, and the water had dwindled to little pools between them. We were twice pulled up by astounded gendarmes who thought we were tramps and asked us why we didn't take a train. We said it was *pour le sport,* a phrase that was just coming in. "You are mad," they said as they got back on their bikes, with that heavy swing of belts and leggings, and continued the interminable moralizing of the gendarmerie.

This young man was intelligent. He too felt liberated by being in Paris and hated that he had to go back into the family stockbroking business in London. He was a more sensible reader than I; he introduced me to the works of the new writers: Keynes, Roger Fry and Clive Bell. I envied him because he had been to an English public school; he envied me for wanting to be a writer. I said if I could not manage to be a writer I would still not return to England. He said I was right. He added he had an uncle who owned a mine in Morocco and that the uncle might give me a job as a labor manager there! On and off, after that, I would see myself dressed in breeches, gaiters and open-necked shirt by the lift of some rattling mine. I was always weather-beaten in these pictures. This dream became so real to us that he wrote to his uncle, who wrote back and said, alas, he had sold his mine. Another fantasy of ours arose because he had acted in *A Midsummer Night's Dream* at school: we called ourselves Pyramus and Thisbe, a joke that seemed sidesplitting to us. When he laughed, his wide mouth curved up almost from ear to ear and his eyes closed into long curving slits. He was very shocked by the screaming greedy frenzy of the brokers at the Bourse, a noise that could be heard streets away, even in the Boulevard des Italiens. After we had been friends for some time, an American at the Christian Science meeting said: "I suppose you know he is Jewish? I thought I ought to warn you."

This was my first meeting with anti-Semitism. I did not know he was Jewish; but it made me reflect that, especially in my school life, the only boys who took my desire to write seriously were Jewish.

But what was I to write about? My collected works were on the little bamboo table at Mme. Chapin's. There was my major work, done three or four years back: three pages on the Reformation and Renaissance meeting in the works of Milton. There was half a page describing the clock in our dining room at home. There were two more half-pages on my brother's hairy friend and another two on a man in the leather trade who was always quoting Shakespeare as we turned over the sheepskins on the warehouse table. And there was my latest work: the joke. I must hurry. I have already told how I had read in Barrie's *When a Man's Single* that the thing to do was to write on the smallest things and those near to you. There is a straw caught on the window ledge. Will it fall or will it stay? There was an essay, he said, in things like that. What was nearest to me? My room, Mme. Chapin groaning next door. Nothing there. And then, by a trick of memory, my mind went back to my first room in Paris. There was a barracks near my new room and at night I would hear the bugle, as I used to hear the bugle at the Champ de Mars. The beautiful word *cinquième* sounded at once in my head. My nights there came back to me. I set about evoking the rough blue cloth on the table, the attic window, the carpet worn by so many predecessors till it was as thin as a slice of ham, the bugle call, even the notices on the door: "No strangers in the room after eleven" and "After eleven a supplement for electricity will be charged": and how the light flicked off at that hour. I began to write. Mme. Chapin's groans supplied a tenant for the room next door at my old hotel. I wrote for two hours. On other nights

I rewrote several times. I added some sentimental moralizings.

At the photographer's I stayed late and typed the thing. I sent it to a London paper, and not to lose time I finished two more and sent them. They went to two weekly reviews, *The Saturday Westminster* and *Time and Tide* and to the *Christian Science Monitor*. There were weeks of iron silence. Then, within a month or two of one another, the three papers accepted them. There! It was easy to be a writer. Outwardly cool and with a curious sense of being naked and exposed, I hummed inside with the giddiness of my genius.

I cannot describe my shamefaced pride. There was no more "I want to be a writer." I was a writer. Editors thought so. I told the boys and the Scot at the shop. The Scot had his nation's regard for the written word. The wet-mouthed Breton gaped and punched me in the back. Pierre astonished me. He was always picking up Montmartre songs and about this time his favorites were one about the rising price of Camembert, and a topical one about Deschanel, the Prime Minister who had fallen out of the train on his way to the lavatory, a song with a chorus of innuendo:

> *Il n'a pas abîmé ses pyjamas*
> *C'était épatant, mais c'était comme ça.*

He stopped and put on a small act: "M. Shwep, the great Balzac," he sang and danced around me. He had picked up the name from the street. At his age boys know everything.

I told Mme. Chapin. She congratulated me, but hers was a face of little expression. Mournfully, after reflection, she said the man who kept the woman for whom she worked was a journalist. I could not tell her how her groans had helped me to write and I felt, when I saw her, how strange it was when she stood bringing in my shirts that part of her led a ghost life in what I had written. She asked to borrow the first article. She wanted to show it to the priest who came on Saturdays with her boy.

A week later the priest returned it. "Ah," he moralized. "At that time you were on the *cinquième*. Now you are on the ground floor."

There was, to judge by the amusement in his eyes, another meaning to this sentence; like every Frenchman he loved a *nuance*. I read and reread this article again and again and then, as happens to writers, I was impatient with it and disliked it. I had my first experience of the depression and sense of nothingness that comes when a piece of work is done. The satisfaction is in the act itself; when it is over there is relief, but the satisfaction is gone. After fifty years I still find this to be so, and that with every new piece of writing I have to make that terrifying break with my real life and learn to write again, from the beginning.

Sometimes when I wanted to hear English voices I went to an English tearoom in the Rue de Rivoli. The place was crowded with tall pink Englishmen in light gray herringbone suits, their summery wives and pigtailed daughters. I was sitting there one day, when a man of about fifty with a foppishly drooping mustache and a very correct out-of-date appearance asked if he might sit at my table. He appeared to be a Frenchman. I was being very French by now and I was abashed when he said a few things in English. His gray eyebrows were brushed up, his large eyes rolled mockingly: under his mustache large, wet wolfish teeth were showing.

"Are you on holiday?"

"No," I said.

"Ah," he said. "Then you are at the Sorbonne."

"No," I said. "I live here." I was always proud to say I *lived* in Paris.

"Ah"—again. "Your family live in Paris?"

"No, in London. I work here."

"How interesting," he said. "May I ask what is your occupation?"

"I work at a photographer's shop."

The waitress came up and he said to her, "I shall have a *mille-feuille* and a cup of tea," and to me he said: "I am an Inspector of Schools in England. It's a great bore. I have to get away to France. England is intolerable, don't you find?" he said. "Why did you choose photography?"

"I didn't." It never took long for this to burst out—"I am trying to be a writer."

He ignored this and now began cornering me in the English fashion. Where did I live in England? Where did I go to school? I told him.

"Oh, Alleyn's school. I inspect it. I know the headmaster. A grammar school," he said severely. He put his head on one side; his teeth and eyes became playful.

"And so you are going to be a writer? What are you reading? May I see?" I was reading *La Rôtisserie de la Reine Pedauque*. "Ah, Anatole France. A failure, don't you think?" he said. "Do you like it?"

I said I did.

"But it's pastiche," he said. "He gets it all out of books. Horrible man. He really is second-rate. So affected. His style is beastly."

Anatole France second-rate!

"He only wrote one good novel—*Le Lys Rouge*. Do you know that? That has form—nothing more."

I tried to think what "form" was. All I could remember

of this novel was the chapter in which the lover sees the pink nipple of his mistress's breast through her thin chemise, an incident that put me in a desperate state one hot afternoon in the Rotonde café. In England a girl had once let my hand play with her breasts and she had said, "You are a funny boy. Why do you do that?" This was nothing to the scene in *Le Lys Rouge*.

"Yes," I said. "I've read it."

"It's his only book. One used to see him—but no longer. Not after the Madame X business. Really he behaved appallingly. We're not on speaking terms," he said. "A mean little bookseller—but what do you expect!"

Good heavens! He knew Anatole France! Here I was, in the English tearoom, and with one who was at the center of French literary life.

"When one remembers what she did to get him into the Academy, and he treats her like that!" His eyes appeared to be denouncing me too. "And you admire his work!"

"And what is he—what are you going to write?" he said. "A novel? I never read English novels. Hardy, George Eliot—unbearable," he grimaced with suffering. "I only read French novels. Ah, not a novel. Then—what?"

The word "what" presented me with an endless wilderness. I, the one true friend of Anatole France, blushed and was wary. I began to hate this man's foolish mustache and his feline manner. I now played my trump card.

"I have had an article accepted by the *Christian Science Monitor*," I said. "And by two reviews."

The effect was awful.

"Oh," he said, as if he had got me pinned down at last. "You are not a follower of the Eddy, are you?"

"My father is. I am," I said.

"But, my dear boy," he said sharply, "you have horrified me. Why? Don't you know—well, I mean, the lies! She died drugged to the eyes."

It was not in the official *Life,* but people said this.

The awful thing about his horror was that it was playful. But now he became stern. "I must tell you," he said, austerely dismissing me, "I am an Anglo-Catholic. Do you know what an Anglo-Catholic is?"

I had heard of this religion.

"Never, never," he said, as if speaking of the intellectually unspeakable, "confuse that with the Roman Catholic." He paused. "Promise me."

"Oh, no," I said. I remembered now I had once been to an Anglo-Catholic church with my cousin when I was a boy in Ipswich. She had put on such airs during the service about my ignorance of ritual. This was the time when she said she was going to marry an earl: the church, the smell of incense, instead of the smell of peppermints and hair oil that came off the Dissenters I knew, made me feel I was among near-earls. It was uncomfortable. Until that moment I had been in love with my cousin. It was very humiliating. I could never get into the right set.

"You should read other writers," he said.

I was on my metal. I picked out ones that sounded impressive. "I've read Montesquieu," I said, "Boileau . . ."

He said, nodding with grim mockery: "And you are going to be a journalist?"

I was being stripped of all my pretensions, and I could see he was amusing himself by drawing me out. I did not know how to stop him. It occurred to me that he was the devil. I did not want to be reduced to nothing. I hated being questioned. I said something about having to get back to the shop, and got the waitress to bring me my bill. I was getting my money out of my pocket when he said: "I would like to ask you a favor. I always ask it of people I like. I have enjoyed talking to you. Will you let me look into your eyes?"

I was too startled to refuse.

"Ah, no, wide," he said.

"Ah," he sighed. He shook his head. "It is a virgin. Charming. You mustn't mind if I call you "it." I grew up in Italy. It's an Italian habit. Do you come here often? Perhaps tomorrow?"

"Sometimes," I said. I was in a rage.

"I have a great friend who is a journalist who might help you. I might persuade him to come and meet you."

I got away. He had made a fool of me. I was furious that he thought I was a virgin. So I was—but he did not know how far I had gone! I walked sulking up the Rue de Richelieu to the shop to hear the blessed words *"M. Shwep. Combien pour coucher avec?"*

The next day I did not go to the tearoom. I wanted vengeance, and in the evening when a prostitute stopped me in the Rue Stanislas while I was looking at a book-shop window and said: "Will you come with me?" I said coldly: "What for?"

She was taken aback. "What! You do not know what for?"

"Oh *that!* It doesn't interest me," I said. And walked away.

"Dirty swine!" she called after me.

After that I felt I was even with life.

I recovered. I went to the tearoom the following day. After all, he knew Anatole France.

He was sitting at the same table. "I hope you didn't come

yesterday. I was not here. I have been having the most awful trouble, really it is too shocking. I just come to Paris for ten days and my whole holiday is ruined."

He raised his hands and stared at me accusingly.

"Ruined!" he said.

"Disaster!" he said.

He contrived to look older, even more out of date. His eyes stretched until I thought the eyeballs would shoot up to the ceiling, and that he was commanding me to watch them go.

"One expects nothing of human nature—but of a lifelong friend!" He still accused. Slowly the eyeballs came down from the ceiling and he considered me.

"Will it tell me its name?" he said. The crushing "it" business had began again, but I could now laugh inwardly at the word.

"My name is Ralph," he said. "Do you know how to pronounce that? If you are going to be a writer you must pronounce it correctly Rafe. Say it."

"Rafe," I humored him.

"Never, never, never Ralph. That is middle class. Will you remember that? Rafe. Now perhaps we can be friends?"

I made a note of this.

"Rafe Shaw."

I have changed the name. But it was a plain name. I had not read *Burke's Peerage*, but I read the newspapers. I could see heavy black headlines. I could see columns and columns about a scandalous action for divorce. A small hyphen connected the name Shaw with another enormously territorial, dotted with tiaras and coronets, that swirled from mansions to castles, from embassies to yachts, from grouse shoots to palaces. Mother had said at the time, upset: "It's a good thing poor Queen Victoria is dead."

Mr. Shaw said nothing about this, but we were soon in and out of the embassy in Rome when he was a boy.

"Ah, Victor, the Italians have heart!"

What had happened to "poor Oscar"; the dreadful Queensberry would be "in-con-ceiv-able" in Italy. The Shaws were an aristocratic tree, shedding its leaves in all capitals from Petersburg to Athens; in Rome they had bloomed; but the ashy appearance of Ralph and his occupation showed that one branch had been, as it were, struck by lightning. But think of my case. I was rising. First Anatole France; now High Society!

"It is going to be a writer," Ralph said irritably. "In human nature it will find the depths. There is nothing more dreadful than seeing the character of a human being changed by money. But dreadful! A friend for life suddenly inherits two millions. Two million pounds. Oh yes. Left to him by the richest Duchess in the world. And it ruins him."

On a wage of thirty shillings a week I struggled to show despair.

"It's happening now. In Paris. A lifelong friend. I was going to bring him to meet you. But I couldn't. He has destroyed his character. I can hardly bring myself to speak to him. Victor, he has become suddenly *mean*, a miser. Avaricious. A millionaire and he won't spend a penny. One is expected to pay for his lunches, even his cab fares. He cheats porters and waiters of their tips—there are scenes everywhere—all over Paris. It is horrible. After twenty years I cannot bear to be with him. I told him I shall stay at the Récamier. I simply cannot bear to see what this has done to him."

There was one of those curdling pauses, and then the eyeballs shot up, and when they came down they rolled.

"And, Victor, he has married!" I have never heard the word pronounced with more disgust. "A widow. A second-rate

37

singer. I am asked to dine with them tonight. I doubt if I can stand it. I tell you this because, of course, he belongs, dear boy, to the profession you wish to adorn."

I was glad of the "you."

But the "it" returned.

"One could arrange perhaps for it to meet him," he said, "but one couldn't bear to, not at the moment. One cannot stay in the room with her. She stinks. She stinks like a polecat."

"Stinks!" he said. "And they keep the windows closed," he went on. "Think of me tonight." And he got his bill and carefully counted out coins from a little purse.

"And now," he said, "it must go back to its photographer's and tomorrow to the solaces of Mrs. Eddy. I am going to London on Tuesday. Will it have dinner with me on Monday?"

"Yes," I said. After all, I was sorry to lose contact with High Society.

"Ralph," he corrected me.

"Ralph," I said.

"Remember. We are friends."

On the Monday I called for Ralph at his modest hotel. The vulgar bells of Saint Sulpice, he said, deafened him. We took a tram to a place beyond Saint-Cloud. The forest was carved black by the full moonlight. We dined in a garden, and scores of nightingales were sounding like bells in the trees.

"Now I must give it a reward and tell it the full horror of the polecat. An intelligent man, a scholar, groveling before a grasping creature like that! Imagine being in bed with her, Victor! Now, tell me what it did. Now why did it go to the Sainte Chapelle? What a place! Did it go with a girl?"

"No," I said.

"I think it ought to meet some clever girls. I wonder now.

The Shaw girls are in Paris. They're staying at the Embassy."

He considered me. As I say, I read the papers. Whatever the Shaw girls did was in the papers, usually on yachts, in night clubs, getting engaged and getting disengaged. Articles on the Bright Young Things always mentioned them. They wore very little.

"Yes," he mused. "No. I wonder. Very good for it. They've got brains. But no," he went on. "It wouldn't do. All they think of is horses."

We sat drinking Burgundy, and over the brandy, High Society drifted away on the air. I was glad. The Shaw girls terrified me. As they drifted off, Ralph said suddenly: "Yes, I can see why you like France. I wonder if you are the short Mediterranean type? No, I think not. The head tells one everything. Turn your head sideways. I wonder . . . would you allow me to touch your head. I want to measure it."

At this he put a finger on my forehead and then the fingers of his right hand upon the back of my head.

"Ah, as I thought. The long flat-topped head—Celtic. Yes, it is a long-headed Celt. Not a trace of the Anglo-Saxon. It's name is Welsh." I had often been told that; but my name is Teutonic.

"Long-headed Celt. Will it allow me to follow an Italian custom, and kiss it?"

I could not move; I was also a little drunk. I saw the large eyes close and the damp mustache brushed my cheek as it passed and he kissed the top of my head. I sat speechless.

"Well, we must get our tram," he said.

I had scarcely heard of homosexuality. As far as I knew there was none at school. So Ralph's kiss seemed to me insulting and ridiculous. I put on a stupid, sulky, stolid look. The tram bumped into Paris. We said goodbye.

In the following year he wrote me one or two short

schoolmasterly notes; and once or twice he came to Paris for a week or two and I would have lunch with him; but he made no more Italian gestures. He did not ask about my writing. I enjoyed his scandalous tales and his stern remarks about literature. He was my first aesthete. When, after two years, I left Paris and was passing through London on my way to Dublin, where I had got a job as a newspaper correspondent, I called on him at his flat in Lincolns Inn. I did this out of curiosity, but also because I wanted to show him I was not now as naive as I must have once seemed.

He came to the door of his chambers wearing a black velvet jacket and looked at me like a cross aunt dealing with a rude nephew. He told me it was very ill-mannered to call upon people without first writing to ask if I might do so. I knew this, and I suppose my rudeness was, in a clumsy way, a young man's revenge. Still, he allowed me to come in. The walls of his flat were yellow with the backs of hundreds of French novels. The place was elegant. With him was an already celebrated young actor who was having a success in a Galsworthy play. I had evidently interrupted a long joke, for they resumed it. It was about a woman sex-maniac who was on trial and, running through the alphabet, they were inventing perversions. When he heard of my job in Ireland he did not congratulate me.

I left with the actor, who had to go to his theater.

I never saw him again, nor did he or I write. A few years later I ran into the actor, who said he had no recollection of meeting Ralph. No one had. When I was fifty I met the two Shaw girls. They had never heard of their relation. They had both married authors. I began to think Ralph did not exist. Perhaps he was a kind of Corvo. He is one of the mysteries of my life in Paris; the only certain thing is that he was an Inspector of Schools.

1

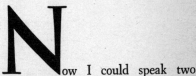ow I could speak two kinds of French fairly well. The first was polite. On my free Sunday afternoons I used to sit on a hard upholstered chair and have conversations about literature with a severe and very old French lady in Auteuil. She was a friend of my landlady's priest and approved only of the greatest writers—Racine and Corneille—who were correct in style and in morals. She pulled me up at every sentence, and I had to be wary of the grammar and pronunciation I had picked up from Pierre and the Breton at the shop. A mild phrase like *sans blague* annoyed her. My afternoons with the old lady were painfully polished exercises.

My desire to appear to be French took an extravagant turn. For a long time Pierre and I had admired each other's footwear. He wanted me to send to England for shoes like mine. I admired his boots. "Let's swap," I said. We measured our feet and, one evening in the shop, we swapped. He wore boots laced to the top from the small black patent toecaps. The boots had yellowish uppers that looked like a pair of old banana skins and very high, small, black heels. Tipping forward in his boots—which pinched a bit—I was forced out of my natural rushing walk into a small mincing step. I was very much struck by this when I saw myself in the mirrors of shops. The next thing was to get a wide-brimmed black hat with a round crown of the Bohemian kind worn by the photographers. On a youth as short as I was, these hats looked like umbrellas. I could not afford them. I settled for one with a high crown, pinched in the middle at the top, black and with a wide-ish brim. It made me look tall—more hat than suit. A pipe was the next thing. I would pass a shop in the Boulevard Saint Michel, where there was a pipe with a ten-inch stem. I used to visit this pipe nearly every day, yearning for it. At last I got paid for one of the articles I had written and bought the pipe. I filled it with rough French tobacco which blazed up like dry hay, and was soon sick in the street. This long pipe was impossible out of doors, for it was easily jogged down my throat if someone bumped into me; and it nearly dragged my teeth out. I returned to cigarettes: Gauloises or an English cigarette called Pirate, which blistered my tongue. I smoked all day long except in the shop. I took to doubling and trebling the usual amount of coffee I drank because Balzac had done this. On my way to the shop I passed his house in the Rue Raynouard, which reminded me of this; and there was another reason for drinking more coffee: I wanted to get a dark complexion. I had seen a man of thirty-five or so sitting on the terrace of a café; a tired, cynical *boulevardier* who had the dark olive look I wanted. His hair was receding. I cut a chunk of hair on the left side of my head to get this superb effect of a dissolute life.

I began to go to cheap cabarets. There were two popular places in Montmartre called Le Ciel and L'Enfer. In L'Enfer one was greeted by a smelly young wit dressed as the devil who mocked each customer. I slipped in behind two middle-aged women and so escaped his joke. But to the ladies he shouted: *"Oh, voilà deux nourisses de Saint-Germain-en-laye —en lait."* This joke came out every time I went there. I picked up a lot of songs and swapped them with Pierre.

"You can see M. Shwep has a mistress," said the Breton.

"I have," I said.

"Where does she live?"

"In my quarter. Auteuil."

"That is chic." They were awed.

"Is she English?"

"Yes."

"Ah," said the Breton, giving me a slap. "You come from Great Britain. I come from Little Britain. We understand each other. You're cunning; you've kept it very quiet."

I had invented this, of course.

That summer the Bohemian crowd in Montparnasse had thinned. They put on fisherman's shirts in fisherman blue, or loud red-and-white checks, and went off to the South of France. I could not afford such a journey, but in September when my fortnight's holiday came, I took the train to Rouen. My brother came over from London with a friend. I had longed to sleep *à la belle étoile* in the manner of Stevenson. I warned my brother and his friend of this, but they arrived in Rouen wearing bowler hats, without knapsacks, ground-sheets or blankets. The hats disgusted me; I made them leave them in the railway cloakroom. A heavy lunch, beginning with oysters, and washed down with cheap wine put us in a better temper. The friend wanted to get to Paris, but we forced him to walk northward. We were aiming for Dieppe: an hour or two after leaving Rouen, clouds piled up, then a heavy rain came on as we got to a large forest where we sheltered. We sat under trees, eating bread and sausage and then pressed on into the forest. Soon the wet darkness came, the footpaths confused us, and we had to find our way by striking matches that went out almost as soon as they were struck. The expedition was losing its high literary quality and soon sank to the coarse level of *Three Men in a Boat;* for when we decided to lie down for the night my ground-sheet and blanket had to serve for the three of us. So our night passed in a vulgar struggle with the blanket: now my brother pulled it his way, and the other youth pulled it off both of us. The rain, spouting through the trees, came down on us in lumps. At about three in the morning we could stand this no longer. We got up, and finding a path we groped mile after mile, until daylight, when at the edge of the forest we could smell apples. We were among the Normandy orchards and dogs barked at us. But no one was about. The rain stopped, the sun came out and we found a lane and staggered along it. We fell asleep as we walked, like drunks; we had to hold one another up. Eventually we gave in and lay down on a wet grass bank by the roadside. Two hours later we woke up: we found we had rolled off the bank and were sleeping in the road. One of Maupassant's peasants croaking along with a wagon had to stop to get by us. He did not say much. I was shabby, but the respectable clothes of my brother and his friend, though mud-spattered, must have saved us from suspicion. The fine rain came on again. We went through a sodden cornfield to a river, where we got out of our clothes and stood naked among the boulders, waist-deep in rushing cold water; then we wrang out our clothes, dried ourselves on our shirts and went on to a village. No villagers were about, but there were carters at the inn: we wisely drank a lot of cognac. My companions wanted to stay, but I was fiercely for the road; we found another village inn kept by a decent couple. Seeing an advertisement for a drink called Amourette, we plumped for that. The landlady dried our clothes and gave us a huge meal with two bottles of Normandy cider. Strong as Devonshire cider is, Normandy cider is much stronger; it flew into us as innocently as lemonade and suddenly made us incapable. The man and his wife couldn't stop laughing at us and the end of it was that we slept in a bed that night. The roads of Normandy are exposed, hedgeless and boring. We slept out again, in a field and once in a barn. Outside Dieppe we visited a castle from tower to dungeon; in the town we guzzled, but slept out on a cliff outside. I tried to make coffee on a methylated spirit stove, and when we lay down we spent a cold night watching the lights of the fishing boats in the Channel. Then for several days we walked back to Rouen by some roundabout route through some pretty places. I enjoyed this journey, as a young animal does, but except for games of *billards* with village people in the inns and a dance with some railway workers and their girls, the expedition was not up to the standard of Borrow, Stevenson and Belloc. There were no heroic invocations or poetic jollities; only grunts and wondering if our money would hold out. Jerome K. Jerome, as I say, haunted it. It worried me that as a traveler I was evidently tame. I also saw that to travel well one must travel alone.

The secret of happiness (they say) is to live in the imagination. I had many imaginary lives, building up every day and dissolving at night. I lay in bed reading, occasionally putting a date on the page of say *Le Père Goriot* and wondered what I should be doing in years incredibly far ahead—say 1930 or 1940. A strange woman with large dark eyes and wearing a long red velvet robe used to console me sexually. I fancy she must have been an idealized version of that disturbing second-hand clothes dealer my father had taken us to see in the Edgware Road when I was a boy. She had worn red velvet too. Late one night, having waited in a café near the Etoile for the orchestra to get round again to the "Danse Macabre" by Saint Saëns, I walked up the Avenue Hoche. Two girls jumped out at me, and one called out: *"Où allez vous, Monsieur le Marquis? Où couchez vous?"*

"Chez la Marquise," I said, shooting up into High Society, this being near the mansions of the Avenue Hoche. What wit! I was a marquis.

And I had found a marquise, a young girl. At any rate, her mother was having a quarrel with a Baroness, an Italian-American. This girl was training in Paris to be an actress. I met her at the time of my acquaintance with Ralph Shaw: and my tales about him went down well with her mother, who was very snobbish. ("Who were his people?" she kept speculating.) Our meeting had a headlong, unreal quality that lasted throughout our friendship. I had not been near the Christian Scientists for some time. (One or two complained that my breath almost knocked them down with the smell of wine), and I found they had moved their meeting place because their numbers had trebled. The new meeting place was a fashionable night club off the Champs Elysées, which was closed on Sundays. Two or three of the few men in the congregation used to go there at eight in the morning to remove the tables and the bottles, open the windows to get out the smell of wine and stale tobacco, and turn about twenty *gravures libertines* to the wall. On the platform where the band had played the night before, the Readers now read from Mrs. Eddy and the Bible, in that curious game of swapping texts which dissenting Protestants play.

Here I saw a graceful, but militant, well-tailored woman with straw-colored hair come in with a girl so strange and exquisite that my eyes filled with tears. Her body was slight, but she had a fine forehead and black hair that had the soft gleam of oil in its waves. Her long eyelashes hung over large blue eyes and she had very heavy short eyebrows. She wore a big bow in her hair so that the effect was of being half girl, half heavy-headed, thin-legged butterfly, rather than anything human; yet the artifice was not complete. Her lips and her round chin could hardly keep still for amusement. As the two passed where I was sitting I could see the maddening dark hair of her armpits under her sleeveless summer dress, and there was a breath of musky scent that put me in a frantic state. It melted into sadness, for I had the sensation (when she sat down two or three rows in front of me and I gazed at every move of her shoulders) that she had passed into an unattainable foreign distance. The older woman—her mother, I was to find out—could not have been more than thirty-seven. She was a pretty woman, with a small, decided chin and the proud collected eyes of a cat, and all through the service she kept turning to look at her daughter's hair and her face, as if the girl were some adored doll. Afterward, a middle-aged Italian was talking to them and gazing as intensely as I was at the daughter, and the mother looked at him mockingly as if she were saying: "Yes, of course, you have fallen for her. Everyone does. Isn't she dazzling? I invented her. You're not dangerous. But she is. She's mine." And, indicating the rest of us with a nod, "How she shows up these awful people."

I went away desperate. I had heard the mother's voice: they were rich, inaccessible English.

The next Sunday I went again in order to suffer. But after the service the mother was caught up in a conversation with a grand and sullen looking woman, and the daughter was alone. I was impelled by a force I did not know existed in me. I worked my way through the chairs to her. We looked at each other. I smiled. She smiled. I knocked over a chair. She laughed. We started talking fast. She had a low warm voice and everything that came spitting out of me made her laugh more. I had an inspiration. I pointed to the pictures with their backs turned toward us.

"I wonder what's on the other side of those pictures. Shall we try to see?"

"Oh yes." Enthusiasm!

"Come along." I dared her. "I'll turn one round."

"Please!" she said.

We made our way to the wall. I reached for a picture. It was very large, and I could not turn it more than a few inches; a heap of dust fell into my eyes.

"You see!" she said. "You must not get so excited. You *are* funny." Funny: the word haunted my efforts with girls. I was in love. And—I could not believe it—we instantly seemed to be living in each other's eyes.

Her watchful mother came smiling toward us, and I put on my best behavior. "We wanted to look at the pictures."

"And he got covered in dust," the girl said.

We walked out of the building talking. I was determined not to let them go. They had heard about this church from "the Baroness," the mother said. They had come, the mother said, to have a word with her. She asked me questions in an amused, drawling voice, looking me up and down. I was wearing my French hat, but I had put on my best suit.

"Where are you having lunch?" the mother said suddenly. "Are you free today?"

It was a miracle. We walked into the Champs Elysées, and once she turned to her daughter and muttered: "The Baroness was impossible."

"Poor Mummy," the girl said in a sorrowful voice and slowly shook her curls. And to me: "The Baroness is dreadful."

I was in the middle of a play.

"We come from Mexico," the mother said in a grand, drawling voice. The Baroness: Mexico: High Society.

We went off to a flat they had rented near the Rue Notre Dame des Champs that looked down on the Bal Bullier.

"I have brought Judy to Paris because she is going on the stage. It is possible, of course, nowadays for *ladies* to go on the stage," Mrs. Lang drawled on.

"I am going to be a writer," I said.

The girl clapped her hands. "You will write plays for me!" she said.

The mother smiled at me. "Isn't she a child?" she laughed.

By four o'clock that afternoon, in the impetuous laughing way of strangers who meet outside their own country, we had told one another what is called "everything" about ourselves. It was in fact a meeting not of three people, but of six—ourselves and our fictions. I have said that it was like being in a play, but really it was more like being in a puppet show. The girl was her mother's doll.

"You shall be cousins," said the mother when she had questioned me about my family. (I had, I must admit, moved them up in the world.) "He must be part of the family, mustn't he? You must call me Tia, that is Spanish for Aunt. Jolly good pals." There was a man-to-man touch about Mrs. Lang.

"Oh yes," cried the girl to her mother. "He's like your pony, that wicked pony of yours who took you to assignations."

"Really, Judy!" said Mrs. Lang. "Assignations—what a word!"

"Oh, but he did! It used to stand under Mummy's window waiting for her to climb down and dash off to marvelous parties."

Mrs. Lang said fondly: "You can't remember. You were only six in Puebla."

"It was the only way she could get out," said the girl. I saw Mrs. Lang galloping across the landscape, in the moonlight, to some hacienda. It was a thrilling sight.

"Married to that brute"—the brute was her elderly husband—"when I was sixteen, it was the only way. Her grandmother was Spanish—look at her hair," said Mrs. Lang in her offhand way.

Whenever I saw Mrs. Lang after this, I imagined her on a wild horse. Her life seemed to come out of a novel. The "brute" had been shot in the Revolution—"a good thing too" —and here she was fighting to get her money (for he had a big estate) out of the Mexican government. They had refused to hand it over; but now, after years, they had promised to pay up and so she had come to Paris. I was captivated by Mrs. Lang, especially by her strange strawlike hair, her cold eyes and her lazy laughing manner. I could see her sitting in her Mexican house which had once been a convent. She gets up and sticks a hatpin into a scorpion (or is it a tarantula?) that is going to drop on Judy's bed. Some nights a dozen hatpins impale the bodies on the wall. In the morning the maid collects them. I saw Mrs. Lang get a revolver out from under her pillow and shoot at the hand of a thief that comes stealthily round the handle of the door one night. Was it a thief or was it the ghost of a nun? Mrs. Lang was open-minded but she was (she said) a devilish good shot.

·   ·   ·

I left the house at five and walked down to the Boulevard Saint-Germain, then along the river, all the way to Auteuil, but I seemed to float. What I had so often dreamed had magically happened. I was in love, and although Judy and I had done nothing but laugh together, surely she was in love too? I was to meet them the next evening at a small restaurant. No one was happier than I to be able to lend Mrs. Lang fifteen francs toward paying the bill: she had foolishly left her purse in her other handbag. This evening Mrs. Lang told me that Judy was engaged to be married—engaged since the age of twelve: but the marriage would not take place until she became an actress.

"They'll give their eyes for her," the mother said. "The moment the lights go up . . ."

"Glorious lights, Puck!" Judy exclaimed. That was the name they gave me: they hated Victor as much as I did.

"She will make a fortune."

"Oh yes! And you will be famous and write a play and I will act in it," she said again.

Engaged? For a second I was jealous, but dismissed it. We had years before us.

So began—what? A love affair? Hardly. The sketch or outline of a love affair. A fantasy. I could never quite bring myself to believe Judy was human. But when the Breton at the shop had asked if I had a mistress and I had said "yes," it was Judy I was thinking of. After leaving the shop I would hurry up to the flat and would hear of her dangerous career. She was seeing theater managers in Montmartre, of all places; or she was having tea with that Italian; or considering posing as a model—"But only for the face," Mrs. Lang said. How reckless the rich English were. And then Judy's talk was a mixture of mischief and the unbelievable. She would say,

"Monsieur began to get—you know? Hot? He looked awfully hot." Or Monsieur wanted to make "assignations" or was "a bit *gallant*." And to me: "Your heart is like one of those hotels, you know?" And the mother said proudly: "Isn't she dreadful?" Where was I? Hadn't I read this somewhere—in Wilde? Was she an ingenue? Now when I think of our chats and our walks, I understand that Mrs. Lang and her daughter were both acting Edwardian roles. The mother could have appeared in any of the plays of the period.

The comedy of it all excited me and my vanity was flattered when men turned to look at Judy as we walked down the street. I discovered I was a natural flirt—as the word then was —and since the word "gallant" was a favorite of Mrs. Lang's, I was as gallant as anything with her daughter. A new faculty: what a pleasure it is to discover this when one is young and coming out of one's shell. And there was a darker side to this: I feared the accusations, the solemnities, the jealousies of adult love. I was "in love" with a girl who was really a child, though she was older than I. Was I a child, too? The doubt was wounding.

Paris had put a spell on me. Mrs. Lang and Judy were part of that spell. Mrs. Lang often had to go and see someone or other about her Mexican affairs (she said), and Judy and I were left in the evenings or on a Saturday or Sunday afternoon to ourselves. We wandered along the Seine, laughing and inventing fantasies. One afternoon we went out to Saint-Cloud and sat in the park. The girl started collecting snails from the grass, and we put a wall of stones round them.

"Look at our children," she said. She said this at the moment when I was wondering whether to break the spell and kiss her. But there are *voyeurs* in Saint-Cloud on Saturdays. I could hear one crawling on his hands and knees nearer and nearer to us. I got up in a temper and found the man.

"How dare you spy on us!" I said.

A sullen man stood up. "Who is spying? I have as much right to be here as you."

My imagination and temper went up in the air together. "I shall report you to the British Ambassador for molesting his daughter."

"Go on!" sneered the man.

I can't think what made me say such an absurd thing. I advanced upon him and he walked backward from me, swearing. I watched him till he went off.

"What was he doing?" Judy said.

"They spy on lovers." It was the nearest I came to saying I loved her.

"Whatever for?" she laughed. "You were very funny."

We went back to my room. This agitated me. The sight of the big double bed was like something large and human, and we behaved very respectfully before it. She looked at herself in the big mirror and for long afterward I used to remember her face reflected in it. I had bought some cherries, and we threw them into the branches of the tree in the yard so that they looked as if they were growing there. Mme. Chapin came in. She was delighted my "cousin" was so pretty, and often asked about her eagerly. I had gone up in Mme. Chapin's estimation, and she became almost fond.

What puzzled me was that the desire I had felt for Judy when I first met her would vanish when she was present; it was only when she was away that it returned.

I was now—mysteriously to me—the chief acknowledged, imaginary lover of Judy among her friends, who were mostly students, and I had no rivals. It was agreed we were both extraordinary and I certainly played on that. There was only one critical figure: this was a tall Danish girl who took an austere interest in Judy and me. She had straight hair and greenish eyes and was a big-boned girl who lived with a professor's family and was writing a philosophical thesis. She was the daughter of a sea captain. Those greenish eyes gazed at Judy and then at me greedily. One weekend we all went off to Fontainebleau together, taking a cheerful English youth with us. We walked through the forest, but he and I walked faster than they and so the girls were far behind most of the day. We stayed in a cheap hotel. The moon came up, the nightingales belled all night and I could not sleep. I shared my room with the young man, who made a whistling noise when he slept. The girls were next door. I longed to be with Judy and lay tortured by the moonlight and the nightingales. The next day the girls were always together and I was jealous. Judy had to go home when we got to Paris and I did not go with her. I was left with the Dane.

"I thought you always went with Judy."

"Not always," I said.

"I think you should have gone with her," she said. "She is unhappy."

I could guess the cause of Judy's unhappiness: the habits of the adventurous Mrs. Lang. The Mexican stories were true, but the Mexican money was a dream. The puzzle was to know whether Judy understood her beauty was used by her mother; knowing that it attracted us all, the gambler took to borrowing money from everyone Judy met. The Baroness had been at the beginning of this career. Now I who had had a struggle with an overwhelming father saw Judy in a similar case. The Danish girl soon told me the rest.

"We both love Judy," she said. "We ought to tell her. She must get away from her mother."

"I am not in love with Judy," I said. And I wasn't. The nightingales singing all night had sung it all away.

"Judy is sleepwalking and so are you," said the girl.

So love turned into fascination. Mrs. Lang, keeping up a fight for her dream, forgot about Mexico and took a job as a governess. Judy went from family to family looking after children. When she had time off I would go to fetch her. I felt great tenderness for her, but she would not speak of her troubles. Then, in a bad crisis in their affairs—for Mrs. Lang quarreled with her employers, usually about some slight to "an English lady"—they moved to (of all places) the Avenue Hoche, my marquis street.

I went there and a butler at the front door sent me to the servants' quarters. There, in the ironing room and treated with the contempt the French keep for their inferiors, the mother and daughter were living. We went out to a cab drivers' restaurant. The following week the mother went to work with a family in Dieppe, leaving Judy with me. I was living in her daydream; she was living in mine and, taking my opportunity, the disciple of Belloc and W. J. Locke, made her walk most of the way to Triel down the Seine. It was a hot, happy day. I remember the smell of hay and drinking wine and eating lunch under a tree. I remember I fell asleep, for I was woken up by Judy laughing at me. We traipsed on to an hotel at Triel and there I wanted to stay with her; but we were tired, I had just enough money left to take us back to Paris by train. So I said nothing. In fact, having been paid for two of my articles and having, unfortunately, boasted to Mrs. Lang about it, the clever lady had soon got most of it out of me.

The next week a message commanded Judy to join her mother in Dieppe. I saw Judy off at the Gare Saint Lazare. We were not sad. We still seemed to be living in each other's eyes. At twenty, one is lighted-hearted. It had all been gayer than love. A lesson, too: altogether Mrs. Lang had had from me what seemed the enormous sum of £10.

2

Now I look back on the tragic figure of Mr. Shaves I see he was not a born banker. He shared a corner of the bank with three other men. The other clerks looked like repressed rips, especially when they talked to women at the counter. Shaves was an indigestible pudding of suppressed virtues. The other clerks wore black or dark gray suits; he wore either a coca-brown or gray one with holiday stripes on it. There was a buttonhole in his jacket. His glossy, buttery hair frisked in curls of gray at the ears, he had a smoker's stained mustache; and very often he sat sideways at his desk lost in the sheer wonder of gazing at his trouser legs, his colored socks and his shoes. Only by an effort of will, recollecting his duty, would he suddenly sit straight at his work. Then he put on an absurdly mean expression.

Shaves was short and had puddled impudent eyes; he looked vulgar. His powerful voice had made the worst of American and English speech. I learned my first American phrases from him, leading from "Whad d'ya know?" on to "I'm through" and "I can't make it." Hollywood made them current in England eventually. He was a rumbustious English patriot who saw himself, after twenty-five years in the United States, fighting a dogged one-man war against that country. "Jesus," he would say, "you can have Paris and New York. I'm through with them. I can't take them."

The bank was a "whore-shop." In twenty-five years he had picked up every cliché going in suburban America. When he cashed my first check, he said: "You're a writer? You come from Bromley? Whad d'ya know! I was born in Lewisham."

He spread his arms: I thought he was going to embrace me. He had found what he was longing for, an ally.

"This'll interest you," he said, and from the counter he took a circular. On it was printed

The Boulevard Players Present

Fanny's First Play

By George Bernard Shaw

Among the cast of players was Basil Chavasse.

"I'm playing Gilbey," he said. "Ever seen it? That's my stage name."

"No," I said.

He was indignant; then he lit up. In the next quarter of an hour he ran through his favorite scenes. One I was to hear time and time again: "Remember how it goes—Gilbey says:

" 'We've done what we can for the boy. Short of letting him get into temptation of all sorts he can do what he likes.

What more does he want?' And Doris comes back with 'Well, he wants *me!*' Can you beat it?"

In the middle of this, Basil Shaves had passed the check, and collecting the money himself gave it to me.

"He's a Britisher," he called around to the office. He asked me to come and see the Shaves family in Neuilly.

The Shaves lived in a small villa, built in a mixture of red brick, yellow brick, and dotted with tiles; it looked like a colored crossword puzzle. There was a high noisy iron gate with spikes on top—French suburbanites fortify themselves—and as we crossed the pebbled stretch to the steps between dusty shrubs, Mr. Shaves said: "See that? No grass. You never see a decent lawn outside of England."

There were two very young children. Mrs. Shaves was a short woman with a heavy blob of white hair and a duck-like bosom which she seemed to carry about as if it were a personal tragedy. She made a soft noise like a carpet sweeper when she walked. There was a slender fair-haired daughter with her mother's pretty blue eyes and delicate voice, a child of nine. There was also a son with exactly her boyish pouting lips. The family gathered protectively around the husband and father. They laughed as he darted at once to a piano in the sitting room the first time I went there, banged out a tune, and wagging his head from side to side, started to sing. His voice had some quality that brought home the London streets. He swung round on the piano stool and called to me: *"Pagliacci—*know it?"

Mrs. Shaves said: "Basil's father was a singer."

"Cecil Chavasse, Metropolitan Opera House, New York." He had told me this when we had first met.

"Victor is too young," she said, tenderly. Shaves was annoyed that I was too young. His mean look came on for a moment.

"Basil's father. Chavasse was the stage name," his wife said.

"Berlin, Vienna, Brussels, New York, all over America. Australia. Italian opera," said Basil Shaves.

One of those marital interludes of competitive story-telling began.

"It was after the Australian tour that he brought Basil and the family from London to New York," Mrs. Shaves said complacently.

"I was twelve."

"All the famous singers used to come to my father's house," Mrs. Shaves said. "That is how Basil and I met." The Paris furniture, she took care to explain, was not theirs. All her best French furniture was at her sister's in New York.

"Her father was a connoisseur," said Mr. Shaves, admiring her family.

"My mother was French," Mrs. Shaves said, in a distinguished way.

"Yeah," said Mr. Shaves. There was a reverent pause and then Mr. Shaves switched back to *his* father. "Cecil Chavasse," he said. "A tragedy."

"A tragedy," said Mrs. Shaves in a firm voice.

"After the Australian tour he was billed to sing in Chicago. It was in December. Jesus, can it be cold in Chicago; the inside of his coat froze. He got laryngitis, his voice went. He couldn't sing. The voice went like that."

"They got a specialist from Vienna," said Mrs. Shaves, in her refined hoot.

"It went on for months," said Mr. Shaves. "He never sang again."

"At the height of his career," said Mrs. Shaves. "That's the trouble with the theater. A little thing—and you're finished. At fifty-one. It was terrible for Basil," said Mrs.

Shaves. "He was only sixteen. At that age you are impression-able. And for the family—his mother and two sisters."

"Father always lived," said Mr. Shaves. "We were at the Waldorf—suddenly, not a cent. He was a spender. Champagne dinners, open house and"—Mr. Shaves lowered his voice—"there were women. We were down to living in a couple of cheap rooms in Brooklyn," Mr. Shaves said.

Mrs. Shaves shook her head sadly.

"They put me into the bank. I wanted to be an actor," said Mr. Shaves. "The Rooters were looking after mother. Her sister," he jerked a proud thumb at his wife, and said with awe, "married a Rooter."

I was lost.

"Bankers. Own the bank," he said. Mr. Shaves's awe increased, and he gazed at his wife.

In all the time I knew Mr. Shaves his astonishment, his pride and his despair at having pretty well married into the Rooters always came out. He had married above himself. Mrs. Shaves was high above him—socially, intellectually, morally: *she* could have married a Rooter, too, instead of an unsuccessful clerk. He had ruined her.

We sat down to a meal. When Mrs. Shaves brought the casserole to the table and steam rose from it, Mr. Shaves said: "Victor understands what I mean. He's a writer. I ought to have left the bank. I'm an actor."

He looked at the food as if it were part of a plot against him. "I ought to have starved," he said. He was accusing us of preventing the starvation of an artist. The children lowered their eyes and giggled.

After dinner Mr. Shaves went to the piano, singing out a few lines from an aria, and then changing to another and another. "Do you sing?" he called to me. "Come on. I'll find something."

"I can't sing."

"You've never tried. Here, how about this? 'Cutts of the Cruiser What-not.' Know it?"

"Oh, Basil, please not that. Haven't you a French folk song? I'm sure Victor would like that," said Mrs. Shaves.

Mr. Shaves stuck a finger in an ear, burrowing there, in thought.

"Basil," said Mrs. Shaves.

He pulled his finger out of his ear. He had vulgar habits. "Come on, all of you." And he banged out a tune and sang:

> *"I'm Cutts of the Cruiser What-not*
> *A cruetty salt of the sea . . ."*

He paused. "That's good—a cruetty salt."

> *"When homeward bound*
> *My old ship runs aground*
> *I love it—I shriek with glee."*

Soon he forced all of us, except Mrs. Shaves, to sing it.

When I left, Mrs. Shaves said to me: "I am so glad Basil has found a friend."

A tussle was going on in the Shaves family. It had begun in 1914 in New York when the war broke out. Firmly kept away from the theater by his wife and his relations, he now saw his chance. He became violently patriotic, went off to Canada and got himself into the army; he expected to be sent to London. Instead he was sent to the weariest of the campaigns in that war: the stalemate in Salonika. His age was even then against him: something in his appearance, the mustache, no doubt, suggested Bairnsfather's Old Bill in the shell-hole; but Shaves was an old Bill in the regimental kitchens

throughout this war. When the war was over he went back to
New York and the bank. He got his wife to pull strings with
her relations and to get his transfer to London. No American
in 1919 wanted to go to London. They couldn't believe him.
They sent him to Paris. His wife may have had a hand in this:
Paris was far from Shaftesbury Avenue. Mr. Shaves admir-
ingly agreed, but set about getting his transfer to London.
Mrs. Shaves thought his part with the Boulevard Players
would divert him from this. On the contrary, it aroused his
desire to throw up everything for the stage. How complex are
human maneuvers: to get Mrs. Shaves out of Paris, he conveyed to her that he was exposed to moral danger there. Paris
was a sink, the office was a brothel. Once I stayed the night
in their house, and when we went off to our jobs in the morning it was touching to see his wife and his children standing
on the doorstep to see him off. Their smiles were anxious,
protective and wistful, as they saw the breadwinner light up
his cigarette and under the halo of smoke go bravely out, his
shoulders sagging, to face the sins and temptations of the
wicked city.

These things came out in my occasional walks with him
when I ran into him on the boulevard.

A walk with Mr. Shaves was always embarrassing. Once
out of the bank he looked like a tourist doing "gay Paree,"
with a foolish smile on his face. He waltzed along, humming
a tune out of one side of his mouth. His cigarette holder went
up and down according to his moods. What I dreaded was
that he would stop walking; for when a thought struck him
he would start to sing—as he thought—quietly. "La, da di da,
la la"—a bit of Italian opera; if it was a favorite bit, he would
go on far more loudly, making a sweep with his arms, "La di
da di plonk, plonk, plonk da-a-a-a"—in some finale, and utter
his common phrase: *"Figaro*—know it?" Or *"Tosca*—get it?"

We would continue our saunter. But sometimes he stopped with indignation: his moral nature gave him his mean expression.

"See that? No, there. That waiter looking at that woman —mentally undressing her. Victor, that's what I can't stand about this place. I've got to get my transfer."

Yet if a pretty girl passed us, his face would become dreamy: "Look at those breasts," he would say. But if the girl happened to look at him he would put on a stern look; if she looked at me, he would say, warning me: "They're brazen."

Outside a newspaper kiosk near the Palais Royal when, in a fit of showing off, I had stopped to buy *Le Crapouillot,* a gossipy paper about the arts and the theater—he started spouting his favorite lines from *Fanny's First Play,* the ones about the cockatoo. He was running over the scene with Knox. I have looked them up.

> "My Uncle Phil was a teetotaller. My father used to say to me, Rob, he says, don't you ever have a weakness. If you find one getting hold of you, make a merit of it, he says, your Uncle Phil doesn't like spirits but he makes a merit of it and is Chairman of the Blue Ribbon Committee. I do like spirits; and I make a merit of it, and I'm the King Cockatoo of the Convivial Cockatoos. Never put yourself in the wrong."

He came out strongly with the last lines:

"Convivial Cockatoos, Victor! Can you beat it?" A load of tourists were going into the hotel there. One or two looked cross because they thought he was shouting at them.

"What I've got to show is the change in Gilbey's character," he said, and he walked worrying under the arcades of the Rue de Rivoli.

∙   ∙   ∙

The bond between us, as he saw it, was that we were fellow artists, both at the beginnings of our careers.

I did not see much of him and then, in August, when so many shops and restaurants put up their iron shutters that the streets look blind, and when the Seine has its white August gleam, Mrs. Shaves's sister, the genuine Rooter, came over from New York, looking like something out of a bazaar. She soon put on the fashionable tawny, orange make-up and became parrotlike—Mrs. Shaves never had more than a dab of powder on her face—and took the family off to Britanny, leaving Mr. Shaves behind. I saw him sagging in the Café de la Paix. He was lost without them all. This brought out his confessional side. One Saturday afternoon we walked together. A walk with Mr. Shaves was like walking with someone undressed. We paused in fascination at Maxim's. What wickedness went on there! Up the Champs Elysées we strolled under the trees. We came to a stop at a café opposite Fouquet's, where we sat and where his look alternated between the showy and the agonized. The quickness of his fantasy and its sudden extinction gave one the impression that he was shady. He was not. He was tormented. Enthusiastically tormented. There was his enthusiasm for the affection of the two sisters. He sunned himself in it, congratulating himself on being adjacent to it.

"I have a lovely family," he said. But a cloud came over the sun. The sister-in-law had taken the whole family to Fouquet's to dinner the night before their holiday.

"I ought to have starved. Father starved when he was young." This theme returned.

"I ought not to have gone into the bank." This lead on to "ruin."

"I could not ruin them."

Looking for money in his wallet, he found a photograph. "She"—he showed me his wife's picture; she was a slender young woman at that time—"could have had anything she wanted. I have ruined them already."

There was remorse in this but out came the sun again, and his foot wagged faster and he hissed a tune and rolled his head from one side to the other, in time with it, happily. It was, I gathered, a kind of coup to have "ruined" someone who was almost a Rooter, a liberation.

He said: "The Thousand Islands—ever heard of them? You haven't heard of the Thousand Islands? Well, whad d'ya know! On the Saint Lawrence—that's where we spent our honeymoon. It took me six months to break the hymen. It all dates back to that—then the war—I was away. I came back. She wants something higher, Victor. She says I'm holding her back from God. Her sister's the same. That's my problem —I can't make it. I'm not pure, Victor!"

He looked at me with dreadful appeal.

"I sometimes undress and look at myself in the mirror. I get a funny pleasure out of looking at myself."

"Tolstoy used to do that," I said.

"What—Tolstoy the writer?" said Mr. Shaves, amazed. "Yes."

"Well, whad d'ya know!" He became furtive. "You know —the way my hair grows, everything about my body, interest me. I sometimes sit in a bus and imagine everybody there without a stitch on—nude. No kidding. I enjoy it. You say Tolstoy was like that?"

He sat like some steaming nudist beside me. He had put on weight in the last month or two, he said, his chest was over-developing; it worried him. Do men get like women? It was funny the pleasure you get from scratching your backside, almost like going to bed with a woman. That was why the Rooters got him into the bank: he'd got into a small touring company going to Detroit when he was sixteen, and a girl in the company was very kind to him. The company was broke and she let him lie beside her, naked, in her room. No, he never touched her. They just looked at each other. Innocent. But the family found and got him back to New York; he was too obviously following in father's footsteps.

Mr. Shaves, in confessions like these, would seem to swell. He was the Flesh, a man encumbered by his physical person. He saw the very pores of his skin through a kind of sensual magnifying glass: I often saw him hold up his hand and look at it with secretive wonder. Even in his walk, the roll of his gait, one could see he was bewildered by the obligation of carrying this warm throbbing load of flesh and tissues around, singing to himself as he went (I suppose) to distract his mind from it.

I sometimes saw Basil Shaves sitting at lunchtime with friends in one of the cafés on the Boulevard des Italiens. He had the gift of admiring his friends. He was casting himself for their lives. One day he called to me as I passed. I went to his table.

"This is Victor, he's a writer," he said.

I met a tall talkative Englishman, with sandy sidewhiskers, a military type; and a silent burly Frenchman. They said they were in the shellac trade. The Frenchman asked me, in French, what I was doing. Fatal question to a young man like me: I told him, at length.

"Tell him about that office boy, and Mac. Go on," said Shaves. "Tell him about your father," Shaves said. I had an audience.

The listening Englishman said to the Frenchman: "Just what we want, don't you think?" And to me: "Do you want a job?"

The Frenchman nodded. At the end of half an hour I

found myself in the shellac trade at double my salary, employed as a commercial traveler. The minds of businessmen—as Walter Bagehot says—live in a sort of twilight: the Englishman had taken me on because he had read Maupassant; the Frenchman because I had never played Rugby football. He had been one of the first to introduce Rugby football to France.

The Englishman had been a Staff Officer during the war. He was a bookish man, a connoisseur of pictures and would-be Bohemian. His voice was icy and excitable. The Frenchman was dour and quiet.

The office—I was glad to find—was far from the despised *grands boulevards,* in the old Temple quarter on the edge of the Marais and the old bourgeois Paris of Balzac. It was in a small seventeenth-century building in the Rue Vieille du Temple. The staff were a grumpy French virgin who had been educated in an English convent, and who soon needled me about the looseness of English morals; and a sad French salesman called Léger, an anxious, penny-counting man with a large family. He and the typist believed I was the son of a rich Englishman who had put money into the business and despised me. They were shocked by my light-headedness. He and the typist had a facility for hackneyed quotations. They talked like a French edition of *The Reader's Digest.* When I told Léger about my writings he said—but with sinister overtones: *"Le journalisme mène à tout."* The girl said, with disapproval: "I see you are a follower of Montaigne rather than Pascal."

She said that the English boss was going too far in discounting bills and putting unsold goods down to a varnish maker who had some connection with the firm; and by her look I saw she thought I was in the maneuver. Her tale was nonsense. The girl was in love with the boss, who could not bear her. She tried to interest him by putting on a sulky look and saying men were always pinching her breasts in the Métro.

I tried to smile away her sulks first of all; then I tried to dazzle. Another failure. I fell back on bickering; she liked that.

The job in the shellac and glue trade was very suited to me. It was more interesting than work at the photographer's. I was out of the office all day, calling on ironmongers, paint makers, furniture shops and sealing-wax factories, all over Paris and the suburbs. The glue buyers would hold my sample of glue up to the light, then they would give it a lick as if it were toffee. "Yes, very good, but we've got plenty." I never sold any glue, but we had interesting conversations. I always carried a book with me; some wanted to know what it was, and it was surprising among these tradesmen to find how many had views on Balzac, Hugo, Dickens and so on. I had a pleasant afternoon with a sealing-wax man, chatting about *Manon Lescaut*, a tale that put me in an erotic daze; he bought nothing, but twelve years later, when I was a known writer, I came across my old boss in London. He had given up shellac in the 1929 crash and was running three pubs near Leicester Square, and told me that the sealing-wax man had become one of the firm's best customers. I don't think this was true: my boss had the romantic belief in his own intuitions. I scarcely tried at all, for I was writing one or two more sketches and thinking of nothing else. The typist and Léger were scornful when I came back without orders every day.

The opportunity to go, with a purpose, into innumerable streets and corners of Paris—particularly in the old part where the big middle-class houses had been chopped into rooms for tailors, printers, cabinetmakers and all the petty trades—had for me the excitement of real travel. And, since I carried with me my little rustling samples of shellac, I felt I had a working right to be there. I strongly wanted to belong to this world of small trades. A man who made varnish became a human being to me. I would admire the way he fingered the flakes of shellac or studied my copal gum. My boss was an enthusiast and was sure that I was just the bright young man the business needed; so did the French Rugby player. They took me out to smart restaurants. In spite of the story of my violent difficulties with my father—for I was always talking about this—the boss, I found, had convinced himself that, handled the right way, my father would buy me a partnership in the firm: he saw money in me. Nothing could possibly have made me present my father as a man willing to pour out money on his son: rather the reverse. Like so many Englishmen, like myself indeed, the boss was a daydreamer. Carried away by what I told him, he instinctively reversed it to suit his dream. In time he saw there was no hope in me and he became doubtful. He was a hard-working man and was surprised that I would not work on Sundays.

Presently there was a disaster. Léger, the salesman, had had a temporary triumph. He had sold a large quantity of copal gum, and he sat working out his commission to the last centime.

But the copal (it turned out) was adulterated with gravel and quantities of cinder and dust; there was a row. The stuff— tons of it—was returned to the yard of the varnish manufacturer near Saint Denis to be sorted. The salesman, who was nearly out of his mind, was told to sort the stuff, and I had to work with him.

The week was hot. It was a long way to the factory, which was in a street that might have been painted by Utrillo. Léger told me to get there at seven in the morning. He was eager to get the job done. I managed to arrive on the first morning at half past seven, but the following days I found it hard to wake up, and I was an hour or more late. The tons of gum were stacked in a yard against a wall and looked like a heap of gray marbles. Our task was to shovel the gum and pass it through sieves: a cindery dust fell through and often left large stones which we had to throw out. We sieved and shoveled until six or seven every evening. The dust choked us, sweat soaked us and, all the time, Léger was muttering about the swindle and groaning about his commission which diminished with every shovelful. He groaned about his wife and family and the recklessness of the boss and sneered when I came late: "You don't care. Your father's a rich man." The drains of the neighborhood had gone wrong, and gangs were digging up the road for half a mile and the air was sour with the stink of cess. At midday we went to a rough restaurant where the roadworkers crowded in. We sat down at long tables. The laborers shouted and swore, swallowed their food and then, having drunk a bottle of wine apiece, fell asleep, some of them with their faces in their plates. They looked a savage lot, most of them, naked to the waist. There was one from Marseilles who bawled out the sailor's word for red wine: *"Encore du pousse-au-crime."*

Back to work we went in the long afternoons. At the end of the day, Léger and I stripped off our filthy shirts and went to the pump in the yard. I pumped water over Léger's back and he pumped it over mine. One or two women from the factory came to jeer at us.

After a week of this the heap wasn't much smaller. We got careless. "Leave the stones in," shouted Léger in a rage.

We got used to the jeering girls. Léger uttered a few well-known proverbs about women—not relevant to our situation. There were two or three more women every day and they came nearer to us. Their jeers became dirtier.

"Want to push your trunk upstairs?" a big one shouted at Léger.

"Whore," shouted Léger.

It was a mistake. He had just stripped and was under the pump. The big woman strode forward, got a quick grip of his trousers at the back and pulled them down his thin hairy legs, to his ankles. The women screamed with laughter. Léger thought I had done this and, blinded by water, grabbed a bucketful out of the trough and emptied it on me.

It soaked me and, seeing my state, one of the girls copied the big one, pounced on me from behind and the fat one pulled down my trousers too.

"Look at his little toy," the big one called out.

The owner of the factory had heard the shouts and found Léger and me trying to pull our sodden trousers up. The women ran off.

Léger behaved badly about this. He was getting his revenge. We sat steaming and soaking in the bus going back into Paris, which was crowded with workers. "They pulled his trousers off," he called out, indicating me to the passengers in the bus every now and then, as new passengers got in.

Worse, he told the boss, and said I had started the water-throwing. He said he would rather finish the job himself. I was always late.

"What indecency," the typist hissed at me in the office. "Like all the English. I know what the English girls at the convent were like. I've seen it with my own eyes."

The boss had lost money on this transaction and saw that after all these months I had sold little. He said he would give me one more chance. He was buying a consignment of ostrich feathers, and I was to sell them in the Faubourg Saint Honoré.

I felt insulted and mystified by this new job. Everything connected with the dress trade depressed me. I liked the dirtier occupations. But feathers! A world of women! The milliners and dressmakers, I found, always seemed to be at the top of high buildings. Some stout or waspish woman would either shut the door in my face or tell me no one used ostrich feathers any more now. One said cuttingly: "Go to the Folies Bergères." I gave up trying. Léger was sarcastic and so was the girl. The boss had forgotten his loss and had had a sudden success with shellac. "Nothing as usual?" he said, with a short laugh, to me. A distant look came on to his face. He wondered why on earth I was there. I was sacked. He gave up ostrich feathers too—the final insult.

I left the office frightened by my situation, but also in a temper. I trudged glumly a good deal of the way to the Boulevard Saint-Germain where the lights were brighter, and suddenly I realized I was free. I had a month's money in my pocket. I felt the abandon of the workless. My sexual instincts, distracted by the anxieties of having to earn my living, came undeniably alive. I made a reckless decision, and the sight of Sacré-Coeur on its hill had a curious part in it. I have told how, when I first arrived in Paris, it seemed like some evil and exotic bird regarding the city with cynical eye, and frightening. Now it frightened me no longer: I felt it connived with me. The erection symbolized one thing only and blatantly. I found myself looking into the windows of pharmacies. I was working up courage to buy a packet of contraceptives.

The bother was that I knew only the slang words for these objects. My first attempt was at a small shop of the shabby kind. The assistant came to the counter, but I was unable to speak to him because of his face. He had a red nose with white pimples on it; he looked sly and horrible; his condition (I imagined) being the result of some sexual disease. I quickly changed my mind and asked for a headache cachet, and when I got outside I threw it into the street. I walked on looking for a larger, less unpleasantly intimate shop. The next shop had several women in it. I moved on. At last, after passing and repassing the door and making a cautious study of the assistants in a larger shop, I went in. They wore white coats and looked like an impersonal priesthood. But when one of the men asked me what I wanted, my aggressiveness turned to nervousness. The French language became jumbled up in my head and vanished. I stammered out "French letters." The young assistant was puzzled. I tried one or two more slang names in a voice that was scarcely a murmur. The assistant was mystified. Another and older assistant came up and said: "What is it for?" In the state I was in I could not tell him, except in a way that was meaningless. He listened and then suddenly he said: "In the second drawer." A package was brought out and carefully wrapped up. I rushed out of the shop.

The experience exhausted me and indeed my sexual desires. I took the packet home and put it in my wardrobe. Slowly a strange feeling of power, of being at last at one with the world came over me; indeed it was so strong that I forgot the packet itself and never thought of taking it out with me. It was a sort of hidden capital. Its immediate effect was to make me start writing again and to think of living by writing only.

3

From the beginning my efforts succeeded. I wrote an account of the walk to Orléans; also a portrait of one of the *bouquinistes* on the quays. I went to see the old man and his wife in their attic in the Rue de Seine. These articles were accepted, soon published and paid for. I went on to an article about Chartres. This also was accepted. Although I wrote each one three or four times, I found them easy to write and, for a while, was proud of them.

When I read in memoirs about the Paris of the Steins, Sylvia Beach, Joyce, Hemingway and Scott Fitzgerald, I am cast down. I was there. I may have passed them in the street; I had simply never heard of them. Nor had I any notion of what they were trying to do. I had really carried my isolation in England with me. One evening I did see a number of young people walking up the Boulevard Montparnasse with a thick, blue-covered book, like a telephone directory. They went to the Dome, the Coupole or the Rotonde and sat there reading. I asked a young Irishman whom I sat next to at the Dome what the book was. He was dressed in green and wore a cowboy hat. He was surprised to be asked such a question. The book, he said, was *Ulysses;* for years "everyone" had been waiting this great moment. He allowed me to read the first page; its adjectives and images annoyed and flustered me. (In fact it was a good five years before I could bring myself to read the book.) I did not know that I was living at the center of a literary revolution. I was an outsider, and younger than the writers and painters who were becoming important; and if I *had* known, I would still have been under the delusion that before I could know anything about modern literature I must catch up with the old. When I did hear of Tristan Tzara, I was angry because he was smashing up a culture just as I was becoming acquainted with it. The only artist of importance I talked to was the Russian sculptor Zadkine. He took me to his studio for half an hour, and I stood there in a crowd of primitive African totem poles, twelve feet high. I was speechless and came away lost.

There was a great difference between the American crowd who swamped the Left Bank at this time and the handful of Europeans; the French avoided this international circus. The Americans belonged to the generation who, for the first time in their history, had made a mass exodus from the United States. Always alert for the new thing, they arrived in gangs, dressed up in gaudy shirts, and played the Bohemian part. They had a lot of money and took over cafés and restaurants and hotels. They drank heavily and brawled, which shocked the French. They boasted they had bought Europe. But one or two of them were sensitive and seriously encouraging. If I said I was "trying to write," they enthusiastically announced to their friends that I was "the writer."

I became friends with an American painter and his wife. He was a frowning, slow-thinking man of forty, whose face was sullen with inner struggles that he could not get out except in sentences like: "What a painter wants is a place near a good whore-shop—like Van Go or Says-Ann," or in blasts of boasting. His hair stuck up in spikes and his blue eyes seemed to be bursting with tears he could not shed: he was of German origin and very sentimental. The sight of me brought out the worst in him. Europe was finished. The Americans had won the war. Europe was shit—a favorite word. America was the largest, the richest, the only country that believed in democracy and peace. The English accent was sissy. We were all homosexuals. What was wrong with us was our servile class system: there were no class differences in America.

He was a living proof of the opposite. He had married a Virginian of superior family. He boasted of this and he resented it at once. The unsure, the ugly, part of American character—I have often found—is very near the surface. But he was decent and had the American virtue of seeing everything as possibility. He was laborious and slow, but when his wife said I was a promising writer that was enough. I was *doing* something. One day, he said with awe and almost affection: "Hold it. You just said an epigram."

His wife was long-nosed, ugly and bony, but very intelligent and attractive. She thought and spoke the things her husband could not get out. He said that my writing needed an illustrator. He would do sketches to illustrate my articles and he'd see if the *Monitor* would run a series. He knew the paper. The editor was coming to Paris. The editor arrived. I met him as he was leaving his hotel. He paused on the steps. He was a gay fellow with a white beard.

"I like your stuff. I'll take ten more with those drawings."

I walked away. Ten. Guaranteed. I was a commissioned writer, not an amateur any longer. No more leather, photography, shellac and glue. The dread that I had no talent at all, a dread that kept me awake at night, left me. The hotel was in the Faubourg Saint Honoré, the scene of my wretched attempt to sell ostrich feathers. I looked into the windows of jewelers, hosiers, tailors, perfumeries; wealth seemed to coat me. I went to an expensive shop that sold luxurious stationery, tooled blotting pads and so on. I went in and ordered a hundred engraved visiting cards, taking care in choosing the print. Afterward I went to the Café Weber and ordered a bock.

Now my life as a professional writer, and the last six months I was to spend in Paris, began. It is true that if I had moved among cleverer and more instructed people I would not have been so late in developing an original imagination. And there is always the danger that people who work hard become blinded by work itself and, by a paradox, lazy-minded.

Since I no longer had to be at shop or office between eight and nine, I lay in bed until eleven o'clock in the morning. I was, I suppose, making up for years of doing work I did not like. I lay in that wide and lumpy bed at Mme. Chapin's until I was woken by the siren at the fire station nearby. Then the life-long panic of the writer's life began. A whole day free, yet eaten by the anxiety of having to write something: the day of false starts, torn-up paper—how I grew to love tearing up paper. And then there was the reaction against the task: to write little sketches of places, how feeble! How could it be important to go to Amiens, to Pontoise, to the stamp market on the Champs Elysées? I was nothing but a hack. And then I had no "adventures"—an old complaint. In trains people talked of little but the price of cheese, the cost of living, or told stories about their illnesses and families. A writer ought, I felt, to know about "low" society, but "low life" is as hard to discover as High Society is. The *Monitor* certainly would not publish anything about the whores prancing about the hotels of Les Halles, with their red dresses, slit up to the thigh, and their hard voices shouting at the draymen below. If I nosed my way up to a *clochard* who had kipped down on one of those iron plates on the pavement where the warmth from the central heating comes through, near the Gare d'Austerlitz, I never got much more than a grunt out of him. The paper would not like that, unless I made him a picturesque character amusing to tourists. And Americans in 1920 loved the picturesque. I began to get the suspicion that I was hired to leave half of life out. Perhaps my discontent was spotted by the editors, who are no fools in matters like this. My first two articles appeared at length: the others were cut to little more than a dozen lines of caption for the pictures.

When I wrote my articles I showed one or two of them to the Danish girl who had been Judy's friend. It had been a joke between Judy and me to call her Hester, for she had a slow, considering manner which (we thought mischievously) went with her height. To our surprise she liked the name. It made her stern and truthful face soften with a yielding pleasure. I used to meet her at a café near the Palais Royal, because she often went shopping on the Right Bank. Her dissertation was done and she was waiting for her parents to take her to the South of France and then home. Hester read and spoke English exactingly well. She was taller than I and this, and her seriousness, made me show off to her; but when we sat down, on the same eye level, we were friends and she stopped snubbing me. In fact, she had the Danish gaiety, with other people, but doubtfully with me. She had a good head, a straight nose and long, narrow lips and big bones. But girls turned into

something else when I looked at them. In Hester's face I saw
libraries and lecture halls and the philosopher Malebranche—
I had never heard of him until then and have only once heard
of him since—on whom she had written her dissertation. I also
saw mountains and fjords, though there are none in Denmark
which, she crossly told me many times, was flat. I could even
see her father, the sea captain, to whom I gave a fair beard;
twice she had been to Canada in his ship. How healthy, free
and confident she was: I was half angry with her for this. I
cannot think why, but I was especially angry because her
father was a sea captain. I felt a strong desire to get her off the
sea. The sea made me sick. Only the pink inside of her long
mouth when she laughed—which was not often—saved her,
in my eyes. It reminded me she was a girl.

I cannot remember our conversations. She told me, of
course, about Malebranche: that has gone too; but I remember
attacking him. She said: "Why do you exaggerate?" or "That
is superficial, isn't it?" or "I read what you wrote. Your writing
is unequal. You will have to learn to say what you think," or
"Be careful. You will lose your integrity," or "I don't understand your attitude." These phrases stick in my mind. She also
quoted Shakespeare to me once: "To thine own self be
true . . ." Suppose, I argued, the self was criminal or amoral?
I was divided between admiration and awe of her. She said I
lacked moral seriousness: I cultivated the lack of it with her.
Look how I had treated Judy! Hester was very moved when she
mentioned Judy and especially about that time at Fontainebleau. Nothing would convince her that Judy and I had not
been lovers and when she said this, there was a change in Hester's face: her eyes became large and greedy.

I gazed at her and thought of the package in my room.

On the Fourteenth of July she agreed, to my surprise, to

come with me to the general dancing and soda-water-squirting along the Boulevard Saint Michel. She squirted soda water at me: that was an advance. A party of us danced in the streets. She had unfortunately brought her professor's son, to whom I recklessly said something about Racine. He snubbed me. I puzzled Hester by dancing with a pretty Hungarian girl who could not speak French, English or German, so we had to make gestures that Hester assumed were intimate; and we were because words were not obstructing us. I still see the sadness of her eyes when, in the end, I took Hester to her lodgings. Hester was silent: she did not believe the story that the girl and I had no language in common. When we got to the professor's house, I made an excited gesture and asked Hester to come to my room. My landlady was away. But, either because I shouted this, or she was too tall, she appeared not to hear me. We shook hands and I left. I trudged back, all the way through Grenelle, and got to bed tired out.

The next day in the streets, people looked pale and ill. In the bar near my room the barman had not shaved and a woman was trying to put her hair to rights by a mirror.

Once more Hester and I met at the Palais Royal. The Hungarian girl was on her mind. Her next remark was baffling: she insisted Judy had told her I had slept with her.

"Tell me the truth," she said.

"But it is the truth," I said. "I haven't."

And then I saw what had happened. I gave a shout of laughter at Judy's fanciful mind. Of course! I had fallen fast asleep under that tree on the hot day of the walk to Triel. Hester was put out.

"Babes in the wood," she said. She did not like being laughed at.

To talk about love is to make love: Hester and I were

81

nervous of each other. I kept tapping the ash off my cigarette into an ashy tray as we talked.

"I wish you'd stop that," she said and put the ashtray out of reach, but I touched her hand as she did this. She took her hand away quickly. The marble-topped table between us seemed to become six-feet wider and to heave like the sea. In the pit of my stomach I could almost hear the voice of a man choking and trying to speak and recasting the same question again and again.

Then Hester said that if what I said about Judy wasn't true, I had slept with the French girl at the shellac office. The voice in the pit of my stomach came blurting to the surface.

"I haven't slept with any girls," I said.

"I don't believe you." I recast my sentence in negative form. I could think of no other.

"If you were not going away, I would have liked to have slept with you."

There, I had got it out at last. I was startled to see Hester's pink face go dead white. I felt I had uttered a sacrilege. A lot of words must have come out of me after that in order to change the subject.

"I have often wondered about you," she said in a satisfied voice. "I don't do that for the asking. I'm engaged to be married."

I got up. "I've got to go," I said coldly because I'd given myself away. I called the waiter and paid him.

"No. You can't go like that," she said. "We must talk."

"Goodbye," I said. She got up too. I went to the door. She called to me. I did not turn round but went blindly out, bumping into some man who was coming in. Once in the street, the strange thing is that I felt hysterically happy. The glass case in which I had been living was smashed. I raced down the street and got into the Métro. I feared she might be following me. When I got home my larynx ached as if my voice had ripped it.

I hoped I would not see Hester again; the more I reflected on what I had said and her reply, the less clearly I remembered it all, and even now, my memory must have made the incident bleaker than it was. I suppose I am drastic because what I am really remembering is the uncouth figure I cut; also, I had fallen back into my defensive habit of expecting disappointment and unconsciously preparing for it. This has some connection with the idealizing of women, picked up from Victorian novels, and punishing myself for it. And then, conceit is all the stronger in a young man who's afraid of love. I was sulking.

For two or three days I tried to work. Then I gave up and went to Montparnasse. There as I walked up the street from the station I heard a sound well-known to me. A man was spitting and hawking a little way ahead of me. I knew him a little. He was a thin middle-aged American and a terrible bore. My desire for punishment must have been strong, for I hurried to catch him up. At other times I had often turned down side streets to avoid him.

Percy was a journalist who wrote fashion articles for American papers. As a bore he belonged to the race of the soft-voiced interminable and insidious who catch you with a note of sympathy and then shoulder you into walls or trap you in doorways.

Like the air, Percy was always moving from one place to another; and, again like the air, he was invisible until you suddenly saw his face looking down into yours, a pale face stamped by pock marks that might have been the off-prints of faded conversations.

He stopped now at once when he saw me. After twenty

minutes he said: "Do you want to come along to the hotel? I'm meeting Fraser there." I did not know who Fraser was, but I was so low that I went.

Percy was distinct from everyone else in this gaudy quarter by his quality of being the Invisible Man, for he wore a dim gray office-going suit, a stained trilby hat, and walked in rapid vanishing little steps. He usually had the remains of a cigar on his lips. He lived in a poor hotel room at the corner of the Rue de la Gaîté. It was a hotel used as a rendezvous for lovers. He was bound to go into a long tale of his running war with the manager about the noises of fornication in the night. Percy had the Calvinist's obsession with the "whorehouse," though he was a pious man who played the organ for the American Methodists on Sundays: an extension of his own monotone. He was an old Radical who hadn't been in the United States for twenty years, and he had been a reporter in one of the Balkan wars. I think of him as one of those lost eighteenth-century Utopians who stray from country to country but who have caught from Longfellow Hiawatha's mania for detail. In Greece he had been imprisoned; and he brought to Paris that fear of foreign police which is so often buried in the guilt that haunts expatriates. Yet Percy was a saint of kinds, a soft touch for all "the boys and girls" of the quarter. Broken painters, girls who couldn't pay the rent, always went to him. He was always doling out small sums of money. If any painter was carried off drunk or starving by the police, Percy was down at the station to rescue him at once. The only work of art he admired was "The Goddam great Cock," which the admirers of Wilde had erected over his grave in Père Lachaise. He was sad because the French police had covered it with a tarpaulin.

We skipped along to Percy's hotel and climbed to the top

floor. Percy spat once or twice into his washbasin in his small room. He was reminiscing about Trotsky. Shortly Fraser turned up, a red-faced and suspicious little Cockney mechanic.

"Aren't we going to do anything?" said the Cockney, uneasy about my being there.

"He'll watch us," said Percy.

"We do it most Saturdays," the Cockney said. They got out a light round table and a pile of manuscript in single-spaced typing for me to study while they got going. Table turning was their bond. They were chasing spirits on the other side. They were secret agents between the living and the dead.

"We've had Hamlet three weeks running. You couldn't stop him," said Percy. "There it is." He handed me a bundle of manuscript.

They put their hands on the table. They waited and waited. It was a gray day and rain came on.

"Nothing there," said the Cockney.

"Ah, there's something," said Percy. "He's trying. Maybe it's Hamlet again. Perhaps he didn't finish. Is that you, Hamlet?"

No answering knocks came.

"Hostile presence," said the Cockney, indicating me.

"Perhaps I'd better go," I said.

"No," said Percy. "They're about." He got up, made another spit into the washbasin and picked up the papers. "We've had Julius Caesar. We had Bismarck. George Washington." One or two Greeks had poured out their monologues.

"Perhaps they want you to join in," Percy said to me. So we all sat with our fingers on the table. Occasionally there was a slight move, but nothing happened. I thought of my great-uncle Arthur, the cabinetmaker, in York, who had upset the Bible-reading branch of my Yorkshire family by getting through to Burton, the author of his secret Bible, *The Anatomy of Melancholy,* with a signalman who was a friend of his in that city.

"They get like that," said Percy. "They get sulky or something." We had to give up the séance. We passed the rest of the afternoon listening to Percy, who read us pages and pages of literary material from the other world. Occasionally a fretful woman would turn up in the complaining notes of all the speakers, who seemed to live in another version of Montparnasse. I think this woman was his mother. We were listening to a minced-up installment of Percy's autobiography.

When I got back to my room there was a note under my door. It said: "Where have you been? I called this afternoon. I am terribly worried. I have some news I want to tell you. Hes."

Victory, of course. I do not propose to tell in all its detail what happened between Hester and myself in my room when she came to it. Our encounter was helped because I had only one chair, in which she sat for a short time and dabbed a few softening and attractive tears from her eyes. The thought thundered in my head that I was on the point of holding in my arms the serene author of a dissertation on Malebranche, a philosopher (she had told me), who had written a work entitled *De la recherche de la Vérité.* There was a bit of rational protest when we had got to the hooks and buttons. I excused myself and took my package into Mme. Chapin's kitchen. I opened it and made a terrible discovery. The priests of the pharmacy, either out of cynicism or malice, had sold me a box containing twenty pills for the liver. I searched for hope in the directions in four languages. I read the list of chemical content. I had not taken a pill of any kind for years, and had no notion of what any medicine outside of a cough mixture was designed to do. I knew little about contraception. It occurred to me that these pills must be the things the French used, perhaps having esoteric knowledge of the action of the liver upon the sexual organs, and in a sudden fit of faith and superstition I swallowed one, indeed, to make sure, swallowed two. Recklessly I went back to Hester, but the sight of her pulling a garment over her head, and the long white back of a living woman who was an image no longer, brought me to my senses and made me tell her of the disaster. She did not understand and, half-undressed and sitting on the bed, asked to see the package. She read the directions carefully.

"Is there something the matter with your liver?" she said.

"No, it's not that," I said and had to explain again. She said, in her advisory voice, that she never trusted things like that.

She said: "You must take it back to the shop. You must get your money back."

"I couldn't. I've taken two."

"Well, it's their mistake," she said, and pulled the garment back over her head. The Sorbonne, the lecture halls, the libraries, the imaginery fjords of Denmark vanished as I looked at her and all I can say is that, after some grapplings and false rammings, during which she talked fractiously, nineteen to the dozen, down went Malebranche and the captain of the ship. I looked down at her and saw two tears on her smiling face.

We went out and walked tenderly by the river, where the lights were going down like spears into the water. Hester suddenly stopped. For the first time I heard her laugh out loud. She stood there laughing her head off, she was nearly doubled up with laughter and clung tottering to my arm. She could not stop.

"And you took two of them!" she said. "I've just seen what you were trying to tell me." And off she went again. Passing people were astonished by her. She recovered.

"I am sorry. Why are you looking so sad?" I wasn't sad. To make up for her laughter she said very seriously: "You may not realize it, but your ideas have influenced me a lot."

My ideas! What ideas? I had only one: terror that she would be pregnant. The philosopher Malebranche returned to reassure me. She had one or two young men, it seemed, in Denmark who were interested in him and her; and she said she knew how to look after herself. We sat closely in a restaurant and twice during the meal she put down her knife and fork and laughed like a Viking. People said: "Americans!"

In the next five days, which were all we had, I said she must break her engagement. She frowned at me tenderly. Her parents arrived: the captain had come to the surface. They were taking her for a spree. The captain had a tuft of fair hair on his chin (I saw, when we all met at the professor's), and it made me gaze at Hester. Her small tuft had been fair, too. But the Captain, who did not speak French, cottoned on to me and said roguishly that if only they had had time, he would have asked me to show him Paris.

"I will write," said Hester in the dark hall of the professor's flat. We shook hands. Her hands were long. It was awful leaving her. But I noticed as I went away how every man, woman or child I saw seemed more real to me. The whole of Paris ceased to be a dream and became alive. I had so often heard or read of the disgust and guilt of sexual love; I realized I had never believed these tales and now never believed them again. But often as I walked about I would look at the faces of women, hoping I would see something of hers, and at every corner for a long time I had the illusion that only a minute before she might have turned down there.

. . .

I went on a wet day to Amiens and wrote about it, but slowly luck turned against me. My money was running out. Mrs. Lang's promise to pay me back came to nothing, and I could not get payment for my articles. There was—I heard—a lawsuit going on in the holy city of Boston: I knew nothing of the delicacies of the religion, but it seemed that the Divine Mind had split in two and—in the general phrase—someone had let Error in. Both parties were accusing each other of witchcraft, a common accusation among the congregations, as I was soon to find out. In practical terms, the *Monitor*'s funds were frozen. Fortunately Mme. Chapin stayed on in Tours, and I could skip paying the rent.

I was back in my fear that I should have to leave Paris and go home. I was saved by one more check from a London review, but after that things went very wrong. A time came when I had to sell back my books, first one at a time, then two at a time: for two volumes I could get a cheap meal. So two by two, the row on my mantelpiece got shorter and shorter.

I wrote to Hester, but the letters became fewer. At last one came from Cape Town. She was going to be married. She had emigrated. And then I heard no more. Geography, that I loved so much, had swallowed her up.

I went on selling my books: off went Balzac and Boileau, Maupassant, Vigny and Hugo, to be converted into soup, *noix d'agneau*, a *cassoulet*, ham sandwiches. I was soon down to an anthology of comic verse and Rabelais. I stuck to that; it was expensive.

Poverty makes one morose, envious and lethargic. I had a special hatred for small vans delivering food. I grazed off the menus outside restaurants. People eating there struck me as sordid and dogs as unnecessary. I developed lingering habits, if I met an acquaintance, of seeing if I could cadge a meal. I was far too proud to borrow from some of the Christian Scientists I knew, but from whom I had drifted away; and my father's habits, as I have said, had given me a fear of debt.

Mme. Chapin came back. I evaded her. The good woman said nothing but, noticing that I did not go out in the evenings and sat eating a sandwich only, she got into the habit of bringing me a bowl of soup and invented a tale that she had brought back some pâtés of Touraine. The thing that reassured her was to hear me typing; but I had nothing to type, and if I heard her coming from her kitchen to my room I would start typing anything that came into my head to deceive her.

I sold one of my suits, a gray one. At last I ate my last book. The injustice of being forced to this sacrifice made me give up my principles. I would have to borrow for my next meal. The enterprise made me brash, and I began to feel contempt—contempt for my victim, whoever he should be. I arrived outside the Dome and there he was—Percy, of course. I hadn't seen him since the séance.

"Where have you been?" he said. "I haven't seen you since the Fourteenth of July. Fraser and I have been worrying about you." My grin was ravenous.

"Could you lend me two francs?" I said. I explained my dilemma. I joined the long list of his charities in the quarter. The saintly bore paid for my dinner and gave me two francs more.

When the benefits of this feed had passed off in the next two days, I was tempted to become one of Percy's regular following of beggars. After all, the tradition of debt for writers was an honorable one. I could not humiliate myself to rich friends: only to Percy whom, in my heart, I despised. The old puritan pride which had stiffened me had become shady and hypocritical.

Soon I had only a few centimes left. Perhaps Mrs. Lang or the paper would pay? Perhaps there would be a letter? I searched all my clothes and my room, even under the bed, looking for one more dropped coin, but there was none. In the next six days I ate half a small roll per day. Hunger excited my imagination. What would it be like to starve? I got interested in my sensations, in the rumblings in the empty cave inside me, in my giddiness and my dashing indifference to traffic—for I seemed to be flying when I crossed the street. I talked to myself loudly as I walked. To go out by day was tormenting, for one saw people who had eaten; it was better to go out late at night when no one much was about my neighborhood. One night I went out to look in at the door of the nearest café bar. Rain had set in heavily. I had no coat and the cold rain thrilled me. More suffering! I just stood, letting myself get soaked. I had once been in this bar with a young pianist who used to play Coleridge Taylor to the sharp daughters of a French Protestant clergyman in Asnières—a scene from André Gide, I recognized later in life—he puffed like a steam engine as he thumped out the piece: he had gone back to England but, in a mad way, I half-expected to see him come puffing out. Instead, a ludicrous thing happened: a tipsy young student went into the bar, casually picked up three hard-boiled eggs from the counter, dropped them one by one on the floor and marched out shouting: *"Ils sont tous morts les amoureux."*

The world had simply come to a grotesque end: I walked home down the Rue Raynouard, past Balzac's house. I thought of him scrambling through the trap door when his creditors came after him. I stopped outside two closed warehouse doors where I had once seen a procession of five rats run out and disappear into a hole further down. One could eat rats. I was fascinated by this idea. It was nearly midnight when I pushed the button of the outside door, shouted, "Chapin" as I passed the lodge of the concierge, whom I could see in bed, through his little window, and splashed across the courtyard to my room.

Mme. Chapin had not gone to bed. She was waiting up for me: she had never done this before. There was enough light in the little dark passage for me to see there was a change in her, or perhaps in my exhausted state every thing and every person looked unreal and half-dreamed. I could see her white nightgown under a black overcoat—it was a cold time of the year—and her hair was drawn back from her forehead, which looked broader and paler, showing two fine lines across it, and the hair was let down in two long plaits at the back. She looked severe instead of placid; the plaits made her look like a fierce schoolgirl, and her voice had changed. We always addressed each other as Monsieur and Madame.

"Monsieur, I must speak to you."

Then she saw I was soaked with rain; it was squelching out of my boots and onto the floor she so often polished.

"Look at my floor. Get your shoes off," she said sharply.

She pushed into my room ahead of me and lit my lamp.

"And look at you! Your jacket! Your trousers!"

Sharp fingers gave a pull at my shirt.

"And your shirt! Get them off." She opened the wardrobe. "Where is your other suit?" she turned and accused.

I had, of course, sold it. "At the cleaners," I said.

"Get your pajamas," she said, and picking up my boots, as I took my jacket off and my belt, she left the room with a prim and huffy look I had never seen before. It was strange (I thought afterward) that Mme. Chapin, who came into my room every Sunday when I had nothing on and had to grab for a towel, seemed to think now there was something unspeakable about seeing me undress. A new, threatening formality had come between us. I was afraid of her and got into my pajamas and dressing gown—the one my mother had given me on my twenty-first birthday. Now Mme. Chapin came back.

"Where are your books?" she said, looking at the empty mantelpiece. "And your typewriter?"

"There!" I pointed to the side of the wardrobe. I had hung on to that.

"Ah!" she said. If that had gone I think she would have screamed. The sight of it calmed her. She said, as I stood there dazed, "You have always been frank with me. You are not like my Pole. I have a right to know—are you leaving me?"

Oh, dear, the rent! But she did not mention it.

"If you are leaving me, I have the right to a month's notice."

When she said "the right" her eyes became bright with anxiety and I, in my weakness, could not stop grimacing as if I had St. Vitus's Dance; instead of a sentence a noise that was like a yawn came out of me. "No," I tried to say.

Well, what was it? Had I been drinking? Drinking? My voice squealed when I said I hadn't.

"Get into bed," she said. "You are ill. Oh, my God."

And out of the room she went again. I heard her groaning in the kitchen; it was a relief to hear her return to her familiar lamenting voice. Presently she came back into the room with a bowl of soup.

"Sit up and eat that. You can't deceive me," she said. "I've seen it for a long time. What has been happening to you? I've seen you've not been eating. God, if your poor mother knew."

She watched every spoonful go into my mouth. I was slowly able to stop grimacing. She went to get a glass of wine.

"I'm not afraid to give you this. It is good wine from my village."

I drank it, and when she stood questioning me in the next

half-hour I was liable either to mumble or shout. It was a struggle, for her eyes didn't stop staring. The rent, I thought, was in her eyes.

"I'm waiting for my money to pay the rent," I said. "There has been a delay." I had to stop my tears when I said this, but she was evidently lost in suspicion.

"Where is that beautiful suit?" she said again.

In wine out came the truth.

"I sold it," I said.

"You sold it! And the money for that beautiful story?" She was terrifying.

"Which one?" I was confused.

"The one I showed to the father."

"I lent it to a friend." I managed to get that out.

Mme. Chapin looked suddenly older.

"Oh, no, you didn't," she said. "I know young men. You are like my Pole. Oh, God, you threw it away to sleep with some *fille*."

"I didn't," I said. I didn't realize I had shouted the words. The shout made Mme. Chapin straighten and step back.

"I've seen the sheets," she said, and the beginnings of mockery ran along her lips.

"You poor young man," she said. "I suppose you gave it to your pretty cousin."

"No. I lent money to her mother!" Then, thinking this would be an advantage, I told her the whole story. Out came the Mexican Revolution, the wild rides on the hacienda, the pistol, the dreadful husband. Mme. Chapin was caught and carried away by it. As I got to the end she was turning to the mirror over the mantelpiece and looking at herself; then she remembered me and said: "The rich! That's what those rich women are like. They are worse than kept women. At least *they* give something for their money!" And added: "Her mother!" I thought I made it better by confessing that Mrs. Lang was not my aunt.

"That," said Mme. Chapin drily, "I knew well, young man."

There was no more to say, and she came to the bedside to ask me if I wanted more soup and took the bowl, and that would have been the end of it. But the bugle went off at the barracks, clearer and harder, as if it were in the room itself, because of the wet night. You could picture the man with his chest out and his cheeks swelling. Mme. Chapin gave a jump and dropped the soup bowl on the floor.

"Oh, my God!" she cried out, and put her hand to her breast. She stood there trembling. She leaned against the wall. "My heart!" she said weakly and panting. Suddenly she snatched my hand and pulled it under her coat to her breast.

"Feel my heart. I am choking. Can you feel it?"

Her heart was indeed thumping, but I could feel her breast. Her hand was holding mine hard there. Her breast was not, like Hester's, the small breast of a young woman.

Mme. Chapin hesitated and took a long breath.

"Soldiers. That filthy war," she said sadly, pushing my hand away. And then, sighing, she picked up the bowl from the floor. She considered me.

"In the morning I will lend you five francs," she said in a tender voice. "Get something to eat before I come back from work," she said.

She came in in the morning and put five francs on my table and left.

All day I could feel the roundness of Mme. Chapin's breast, but I forgot it in the afternoon because a miracle happened. I had eaten, and then I went along the Boulevard des Italiens looking into the cafés where Mr. Shaves often sat after lunch with his friends. He knew many people in business and in the theater and he had said once or twice he'd keep his ears open for news of a job I could do. He was there, bumptious and pleased, his cigarette holder sticking up in the air under a lilac halo of smoke. His socks, which were in blue-and-yellow stripes, showed at the ankles and joined in his joy of life. When he saw me his smiles went.

"Where have you been?" he said. "People have been asking at the church."

I didn't tell him much. He didn't appear to listen. One of his friends said to me: "You've lost weight. I wish I could."

I joined them nervously and I saw in Mr. Shaves the mean, shrewd look of his that usually followed his loud laughs. He said that when his wife came back in a week's time they'd ask me to a meal. He kept staring at those boots of mine that had belonged to Pierre; they were worn down and shabby beside his and when I left I felt he was watching me. I did not realize that Mr. Shaves was regarding me in a daydream of envy; that, in a sense, he wanted worn-out boots like mine. I took the Métro back to Auteuil; with food inside me I was wondering if I could write an article on starvation.

Mme. Chapin was out, but there was a letter on the floor. It contained francs to the amount of £15, a large sum in those days. They came from the young Christian Science Reader— the one who was no longer an abstract painter—who said he and his wife were concerned that I had not been paid for my writing and I needn't hurry about repaying the money. It came out eventually that Mme. Chapin had been up the street to talk to the old lady with whom I sometimes had my excruciating French conversations on Sundays; that this woman knew the painter; and that Mr. Shaves had telephoned the painter also and said I looked in a bad way. I went up to

Montparnasse, ate an expensive meal, including the largest plate of *cêpes provençales* I have ever seen; nowadays, they would kill me. I paid Percy back the money I had borrowed. He was so astonished that he lost his power of monologue and went off with a shade of disappointment in his face, discerning perhaps that I showed signs of ceasing to be one of his clientèle. He had the Bohemian's scorn.

I went back to Mme. Chapin's. She was in her long black overall once more. She looked older than she had the night before when she had held my hand against her breast. I paid her the rent and we resumed our formal conversations, I thanking her for her kindness, and she saying that she had always had confidence in me. This experience must have exhausted me, because I tired of Paris. The enchantment had gone.

Basil Shaves's play came on at last after three postponements. I went to see it with Mrs. Shaves and her children. There was a large audience in one of the Paris *salles*. From the moment the rigged-up curtain rose and Basil came bounding on and shouted at Mrs. Gilbey: "Here's a nice thing. This is a b——" Basil Shaves was a success. All his vulgar mannerisms were there: his habit of boring his finger into his ear, his scratching of his armpit, the wagging of his shoes when he sat admiring the shape of his leg; the looks of hurt, meanness, absurdity jumped into his face; he looked outraged yet cunning, virtuous yet dubious. The casting was perfect. Basil Shaves was there to the life and yet was morally and physically Gilbey. He was so pleased with himself in the part that, like all amateurs, he could not help glancing at the audience halfway through his longer speeches; but that look was one of wonder at himself.

There were good notices in the English papers and one in

a French paper. He and the woman who played Doris—I had met her once with some of his friends in the Café de la Paix; a thin, dark woman with intense worried eyes—were the stars. "A tragedy," he had said to me at the time. "Married a French actor who left her with two children." This scandal of the theater made him regard her as a very superior woman. "Can you imagine her in an office like ours? The men round her like flies. Why not another slice off a cut loaf?" Mr. Shaves could be very crude.

It was not long after this that Mr. Shaves sent me a note saying there was a job for me if I would take it. An English company he had mentioned at least six months before was coming to play Shakespeare. Hébertot had taken them on. The great Hébertot! I went to see him. He received me as if I had come from an embassy. He was nervous of not getting an audience. The job was to canvas the English and American colony and sell blocks of tickets. The good thing about it was the high pay, which could be collected every evening at the box office. I took on the job.

My last efforts as a salesman were as poor in their results as my earlier ones had been. Happily Hébertot did not notice this for a long time. I bought books again and a green velour hat with a wide brim. It was in a shopwindow and I used to visit it every day dreading it would be sold, until I could risk the expense. The hat was my religion. I decided that I would go to London and see if I could get the money I was owed by the *Monitor* or if I could get a job from a London paper as a Paris correspondent; otherwise I knew that it would be stupid to stay in Paris. I had met too many Frenchified Englishmen. For two years I had lived thoughtlessly from day to day. I could not go on like this. Still—clinging to a last hope that I still might see more of the world—I left my luggage behind with Mme. Chapin and went back to London.

. . .

Before I left I heard bad news of Mr. Shaves. It came from a man who worked with him at the bank. The husband of the woman who played Doris, and who had been acting in America, had come back with some large scheme for starting a new show in Paris. Mr. Shaves had always been fascinated by this man whom he had never met: he had "ruined" his family. The sight of a ruiner, coming at the time when Shaves himself had shown that he could act, must have turned his head. As easily, as dreamily, as he had cashed my first check, he cashed a couple of large ones for this man. They bounced. American banks do not forgive the wandering mind. Shaves was sacked. I saw him at his café.

"I have ruined them," he said. "The bank has fired me."

"I heard," I said. I can only describe his appearance as haggard but ecstatic.

"I've got my chance," he said. "We're going to London, too."

What did I get out of my two years in Paris? Freedom above all and love of it has never left me. Self-confidence, too. I had rebelled successfully. I could stand on my own feet. I had another language, so I could now become two persons. I had had a large amount of time for reading; it was a small capital. I had learned to be absurd, was willing to see what happened to me. Above all, I had had feckless pleasure, a thing suspected by the calculating, constrained and anxious lower-middle-class from which I came; to whom, all the same, I owed the habit of working hard. I was in the simplest way happy. My only dread was that I would be forced back into the world I had come from.

And what did I get from France itself? I have known French people far better—their character, their literature, their arts—since that time, and have even written about them. It has been hard not to smuggle in some of this later knowledge here. What I gained, lastingly, was a sense of the importance of the *way* in which things are done, a thrift of the mind. I also began to see my own country—a very powerful one at that time—from abroad; and I felt the beginning of a passion, hopeless in the long run, but very nourishing, for identifying myself with people who were not my own and whose lives were governed by ideas alien to mine.

4

On the train out of Paris I did myself well in the restaurant car, sitting opposite a middle-aged man who dropped his food down his waistcoat. Bunches of hair grew out of his nostrils and ears, and when he spoke he did so with puffs of kindly importance. When he told me his name I knew he was a celebrated political writer; long articles of his appeared in the *Times* and even longer ones in the heavy monthly reviews that still survived from the nineteenth century. He bathed in opinions, telling me that certain remarks of his had upset Clemenceau, affected the Treaty of Versailles and caused trouble in Poland. The belief that they have redirected the course of history and agitated Cabinets is (I found in due time) chronic among political journalists. He congratulated me on writing for the *Monitor*. He gave me his card. I pulled out my French one. Something about him made me feel I was a man of the world, yet he disappointed me. Young men are snobs. He talked loudly and effusively, and everyone in earshot became aware of his importance. With growing malice, I watched him splash more sauces on his jacket. Not to be thought less a man of the world than he, I unwisely drank a glass of Benedictine, which I didn't really like. I have not done so since; for at Dieppe a strong wind was chopping up the water in the harbor and once we were out on a very rough sea, I was sick down the side of the boat. The oily odor of that liqueur hung about me for weeks afterward. (For years I used to be seasick in the Channel, the Irish Sea and the Bay of Biscay, and sometimes thought of Hester's father.)

A last, with patriotic English joy, I saw the white cliffs through the storm and, with disgust, smelled English cigarettes and beer at Newhaven. I saw the pink, masked faces of my humbugging countrymen. I felt the prison growing round me as the quiet English train passed through Bromley to Victoria. It would have been more sensible to go from there directly home, but there was an unwritten law in our family that his sons must show themselves to their father first in Middle Street, off Bartholomew Close, and travel down with him. He was still the master mind. I went up the stone stairs of his small factory, which was a building of fear to me, into his spotless and lavender-scented showroom. He stood in his white dustcoat at the other end. For years all of us were anxious about the set and mood of his face when we met him.

"You are late," he said. It was his usual greeting: the unfortunate man, so feminine—or was he such a Yorkshireman in disposition?—could not resist putting himself in a position of advantage. He fed on the creation of guilt.

"Where is your luggage?" he said.

I explained I was going back to Paris. He stepped back.

His face took on at once his look of incredulity and insult, though I know he was glad to see me and I proud to see him. His affront turned to annoyance. I thought he was going to be sick. My clothes were shabby—I was wearing the awful green velour hat with the wide brim, the Montmartre boy's worn-out black-and-tan high-heeled boots. How sons appall their fathers! When I spoke he looked puzzled and then angry. I easily pick up accents, and I had a marked French accent, which I exaggerated. Inevitably we took a cab—one of the few surviving growlers—from Bromley Station. By the time we got home my father's struggle with nausea and affection broke down.

"I wish you'd stop gesticulating and shrugging your shoulders and raising your eyebrows all the time like a French-man. You've got lines on your forehead already. You look like an old man. And I can't understand a word you say, your voice going up and down like that."

Mother was gay and reckless: "He always raised his eye-brows, Walt. He takes after Gran's brother Gill."

This was an unhappy remark. That long-dead relation's only skill lay in the dashing way he drove a fish cart. Mother's connections were vividly low.

(I forgot to say that over my French boots I wore spats: they were too large but they covered the holes in my socks.)

When I said that I had left all my things in Paris be-cause I had only come over for a week or two on "journalistic business," my father could not speak. My mother anxiously defended me, but she was as worried as I. And then she said: "Give him his letter." Father went out of the room for it, and brought back a letter that he had, of course, opened and read.

"It's to you from a girl," he said. "A girl called Judy. Have you been writing to a girl? Have you been seeing this girl?"

My father could put a criminal emphasis on words like

"this" and "girl" and "letter" and the word "seeing"; an emphasis so sexual that it made one grow hot.

Judy had written one of her large theatrical scrawls in purple ink, and after wishing me a happy birthday, she had added one of her silly lines: "Dearest Puck. I hope you haven't forgotten our children."

"What is this about children?" said my father.

"Yes?" said Mother, "You haven't . . ."

Those children were the snails at Saint-Cloud. There was nothing from Hester.

There were, I soon heard from my mother's frightened whispers—she was secretively changing the subject—the usual difficulties in the "business," but these were glossed over. "Let's be happy," she said. For, eventually, after a very un-French meal of mutton chops burned black and mashed potatoes, my father expanded. He had fallen in love again—with a new house. Sometimes he called it a "shooting box" or "a hunting box," words that evoked the life of a country gentleman for him, dreams of field sports and air. The child of the Yorkshire moors still longed for air. He would be buying tweeds, knickerbockers, perhaps guns. Mother said drily: "We go there every Sunday. Oh, yes!" And so they did. They picnicked in the garden of the abandoned place while Father talked of the woods, the songs of the birds and the moorlands of the north. He missed the heather.

On Sunday, we all went to the "shooting box" for me to give my opinion. Mother sat in the back of the car, a Sunbeam, with her hands over her eyes, moaning "Are we there yet?" just as in thunderstorms with her head under a cushion, she whimpered, "Is it getting lighter?" There were the usual remarks about the Divine Mind driving from my youngest brother who was about twelve or thirteen, as we grazed a bank or two. When we got there, Mother groaned to me that being a London girl, she would be driven "out of her natural" by the loneliness, and was upset by the amount of the fare to London, the "shooting box" being another twenty-five miles "out." The place was less eccentric than stark. It was nothing but a kind of superior bungalow built of brick. The owner had built in a bathroom a couple of yards from the main building. You had to make a dash for it, sheltered only by a glass roof. The thought of Father making a short skip in his pajamas in the open to the place in the mornings made us laugh; but to Mother, the whole thing seemed dissolute. Her mind quickly ran to the indecent.

"I mean, Vic, if you wanted to . . ." One of her characteristic unfinished sentences.

The affair had been going on for the best part of a year, as these things did with Father; but the crux of the matter was waved away. He hadn't the money. And Mother, in her dishonest manner, pretended to be upset. Miss H. would not let him take money out of the business. We were on the edge of one of our great family quarrels.

My father, who had been so opposed to my becoming a writer, was impressed by my one or two successes in the English weekly reviews, but most of all by my getting two or three things published in our sacred paper, the *Monitor*. (I ought to have said that he had paid for my typewriter). His opposition, from the beginning, had everything to do with his wish to be in command of what all his children did. He was enraged when my brother, the following year, bought a third-hand motorcar and then sold it for another; powerless, he made a subtle effort to get hold of the check, saying it would be "better if it passed through my bank" (one knew, once passed in, it would never pass out) on the excuse that my brother should not become extravagant.

Father was distressed by the quarrel in Boston—it had ended in the death of the American editor who, to use the jargon of our sect, had been "handled" by "Animal Magnetism"—for Boston was a holy city to him. He wanted to go and have a row with the London editor in his office. I said I would deal with him. I went to the office in the old Adelphi Terrace.

The odd thing about the *Monitor*'s London editor was that he was not a journalist. Mr. Bassellthorpe—as I will call him—was a tall, brotherly Englishman. He was masterful, shy and forgiving in manner. I was in awe of him. He was the first famous Christian Science lecturer I had seen, a top figure in the movement and well-off. Background: Quaker family, Charterhouse and Cambridge. His voice was kind and suggested some warm beverage. His accent notoriously puzzled American audiences when he spoke to them of the "pah of prah." He was embarrassed by his present difficulty, but said he could only ask me to be patient. My work was good and I would soon be paid. He put me on to H. M. Tomlinson, who wrote about books for the paper and who also worked with Leonard Woolf on the most distinguished of the weekly reviews, *The Nation*. Their offices were a few doors down the street.

I had never met a well-known writer before. I had read Tomlinson's book on a voyage to South America, *The Sea and the Jungle*, which many critics thought equal to any of Conrad's writing about the sea; also his books on the Pacific islands and the Thames. He was an adventurous traveler. His prose was elaborate; he used strange adjectives, words like "obsidian," strenuous metaphors, and dilated and pessimistic generalizations about human fate. He was pertinacious with *le mot juste*. His manner of writing was admired in English journalism of the distinguished kind. Here is a passage from the powerful description of a small ship in an Atlantic storm:

The ship would roll to that side, and your face was
brought close to the surface of the bare mobile hill
swirling past in a vitreous flux, with tortured lines of
green buried far but plain its translucent deeps . . .
The hills were so dark, swift and great, moving barely
inferior to the clouds which travelled with them, that
collapsing roof which fell over the seas, flying with the
same impulse as the waters . . .

One reads of:

The foundered heavens, a low ceiling that would have
been night itself but that it was thinned in patches by
some solvent day.

For longer than I ought to have done—for it was not *my*
style—I tried to write like that. *The Sea and the Jungle* is a
mixture of rhetorical and plain narrative and a minor classic
in the genre of bad voyages; he knew sea life. One can explain
Tomlinson's manner, especially his pessimism and afflatus,
from his own life. He saw experience as a stoic's punishment.
A wharfinger's clerk, beginning in the humblest newspaper
work, he projected himself as a sort of defeated but irrepres-
sible Napoleon against "the powers and presences." His prose
might be traced back to Carlyle, to Browning's verses; certainly to Meredith and Stevenson. At the end of the century,
writers like Henley and Belloc, took it up and it entered journalism through C. E. Montague and *The Manchester Guardian*. Leonard Woolf scarcely mentions Tomlinson in his
autobiography, though he worked with him every day: there
was scorn for images among the lucid Bloomsbury rationalist,
though not in Virginia Woolf.

My interview with Tomlinson took no more than a minute or two, and on the stairs outside his office. He was a stocky,

dogged man with a flattened nose and very big ears, and he wore the wharfinger's bowler hat; and he was quick with the overworked journalist's bitter phrase.

"I'll tell you what to do. Go back to Paris. Who the hell wants to work in this damn country, in the state it is in. Hang around the Chambre des Députés and the political cafés. Pick up what is behind the political gossip. Hardly anyone knows how to do this. Get under the French skin."

"I'm not interested in politics."

In Tomlinson one was up against the 1914 war in person. Too old to be a soldier, he had been a courageous war-correspondent, embittered by the horror of trench warfare. *The Nation* had supported the "conchies" and had published the indignant protests of Siegfried Sassoon and Robert Graves after the losses on the Somme. And Tomlinson was willing to serve on a poorly paying review like *The Nation* in order to keep the public conscience alive. To him, I was one of the soft pups of the new decade; and it is true that those of us who were too young to be in the 1914 war felt at a loss with the men who had been in it. We were far less grown-up; and they rarely had anything to say to us for the next few years. They clung to-gether; in any case, the distance between a young man of twenty-one and one in his late forties is enormous. It takes years for the distance to shorten. Not until the war novels came out in the late twenties—one of them by Tomlinson himself—was much said about the realities of that war. The *other* war in-terested us more: the war of what was called "the new moral-ity" against the old, and the Russian revolution.

I moved on to the editor of *The Observer*: J. L. Garvin. Fleet Street used to produce histrionic editors. I found Mr. Garvin with his head in his hands, as if writhing in a prophet's agony, conjuring up thought, and it was a long time before he could raise his head to look at the anxious youth before him.

He uttered at last: "I do not believe in the present. I live in the future, months, years ahead."

I sympathized as best I could. At last, the moment he had been conjuring came out: "Go to South America," he pointed to the window. "That is the continent of the future. No one knows anything about it. Go there."

Not, however, for *The Observer*. He had glanced at two of my articles!

Presently Mr. Bassellthorpe paid up and asked to see me. What, he said, did I know about Ireland? Almost nothing, I said. All I knew was that the Irish Treaty had been signed and that, as was foreseen, the Irish were fighting one another. The Four Courts had been besieged, several of the leaders of De Valera's revolt had been shot. Griffiths had died, Michael Collins had been killed. Sickening. The war was dragging on. Why, I did not know.

Mr. Bessellthorpe smiled with relief at my ignorance. The readers of the *Monitor* in Boston and Ireland, being mostly Protestant, were in a state of civil war themselves. Wasn't the Roman Catholic Church one of the manifestations of Animal Magnetism? I might be just the young man (Mr. Bassellthorpe thought) to describe how people in Ireland lived their ordinary daily lives, despite the civil war. He pondered. At last he risked it. Six articles, he said: £25 the lot, to include expenses. If I succeeded I might become the paper's correspondent in Dublin for a year. The existing one, a woman, was causing the paper trouble.

Mother groaned when I got back to Bromley and told her the news, for that day another murderous Irish ambush was reported in black headlines in the evening paper.

Only the *Monitor* (which was really more of a daily magazine than a daily newspaper in those days, and had great prestige among liberals in the United States), and only Mr. Bassellthorpe—who, as I say, was not a journalist—could have sent a young man as untrained and innocent as I was to Ireland. And only an American paper, with the American impulse to ask no questions and give anyone a chance. I had never been in a newspaper office. I did not know how one gathered news. I did not know that one could actually call on a government office or a politician. I thought it wasn't allowed. I knew no one in Ireland. My only interest was in describing scenery, and I considered myself very bold if I introduced a human being into it. Countries existed for me only for their literature, and now I found myself faced with the life H. M. Tomlinson had suggested to me, and which I had rejected.

I went back to Paris for my belongings. I wrote to Hester boastfully: there was no reply. I walked with confidence through the ever-growing crowds of artists in Montparnasse, keeping my ears open for Percy's hawking. Sure enough, I heard it. *I* stopped *him*—the reversal of our old relationship. He gaped at me. I could see he could not believe I was there.

"Where have you been?" he said. "We've all been worrying about you. How did you get out of Germany? We tried to get through to you. We heard you'd been beaten up by the police."

They had got out the table.

"You came through. You said you were in Coblenz, in danger, appealing for help. We kept on trying and you came through clearly. You said they had shot you dead."

He was puzzled but not upset by my death nor was he elated by my survival.

"It must have been someone else," I said.

"No," he said. "It was you. I've got the script."

There is no arguing with a man's religion. It is tempting to an old man to play with the idea that there was something symbolic in Percy's words and to say, "Yes, he was right. My youth had gone." What had really passed was careless happiness. I had crossed a line and henceforth I would know happiness, but I would also know pain.

I went to my room and looked at it for the last time. I shook hands with Mme. Chapin. She had, to my eyes, become suddenly much older as she said goodbye.

5

On a misleading sunny day on the first of February, I took the train from London to Holyhead. In a heavy leather suitcase I carried a volume of Yeats's poems, an anthology of Irish poetry, Boyd's *Irish Literary Renaissance,* Synge's plays and a fanatical book called *Priests and the People in Ireland* by McCabe, lent to me by a malign Irish stationer in Streatham, who told me I would get on all right in Ireland so long as I did not talk religion or politics to anyone and kept the book out of sight. Unknown to myself I was headed for the seventeenth century.

The Irish Sea was calm—thank God—and I saw at last that unearthly sight of the Dublin mountains rising with beautiful false innocence in their violets, greens and golden rust of grasses and bracken from the water, with heavy rain clouds leaning like a huge umbrella over the northern end of them. My breath went thin: I was feeling again the first symptoms of my liability to spells. I remember wondering, as young men do, whether somewhere in this city was walking a girl with whom I would fall in love: the harbors of Denmark gave way to Dublin Bay and the Wicklow Hills. The French had planted a little of their sense of limits and reason in me, but already I could feel these vanishing.

Once through the customs, I was frisked for guns by a Free State soldier with pink face and mackerel-colored eyes. I got out of the local train at Westland Row, into that smell of horse manure and stout which were the ruling Dublin odors, and was driven on an outside car with a smart little pony to (of all things, in Ireland!) a temperance hotel in Harcourt Street. It was on this first trot across the city that I had my first experience of things in Ireland not being what they seem. I have described this in a book on Dublin which I wrote a few years ago. The jarvey whipped along, talking his head off about the state of the "unfortunate country," in a cloud of Bedads, Begobs, God-help-us-es, but turned out to be a Cockney. The Cockney and Dublin accents are united by adenoids. Cab drivers are, perhaps, the same everywhere.

It was now dark and I went out into the wet streets. Troops were patrolling them, and I was soon stopped by a patrol and frisked once more. More friskings followed as I got to the Liffey. It was enjoyable. I didn't realize that my green velour hat from the Boulevard des Italiens, with its wide, turned-down brim, was an item of the uniform of the I.R.A. I went straight to the Abbey Theatre. In the shabby foyer, a small middle-aged woman with gray hair, and looking like a cottage loaf, was talking to a very tall man. He was unbelievably thin. He seemed to be more elongated by having a very long nose with a cherry red tip to it. The woman's voice was quiet and decided. *His* fell from his height as waveringly as a snowflake. The pair were Lady Gregory and Lennox Robinson. He took me to his office for an hour and then we went into the theater. To an audience of a dozen or so people (for the civil war kept people away), the company were going through the last act of *The Countess Cathleen,* in sorrowing voices. They went on to the horseplay of *The Shewing-Up of Blanco Posnet.* Both plays had caused riots years before when they were first put on. Now the little audience was apathetic.

Soot came down the chimney in my room at the hotel when a bomb or two went off that night.

The spell got a decisive hold of me in the next two days as I walked about the comfortable little Georgian and early Victorian city, where the red brick and the brown were fresher and less circumspect than the brick of London. The place seemed to be inhabited only by lawyers and doctors. The mists of the bog on which it is built softened the air. Complexions were delicate, eyes were alive with questions. As you passed people in the street they seemed to pause with expectation, hoping for company, and with the passing gaiety of hail and farewell, with the emphasis particularly on the latter. There was a longing for passing acquaintance; and an even stronger longing for your back to be turned, to give a bit of malice a chance.

The civil war was moving to the southwest; now De Valera's men—called with beautiful verbal logic the "Irregulars"—had been driven out of Dublin. I had seen the sandbags and barbed wire round the government offices, and the ruins of O'Connell Street; now I took a morning train in cold wet weather to Cork from Kingsbridge, the best of Dublin's monumental railway stations, a station that indeed looked like a fantastic chateau. A journey that normally takes two or three hours took close on fourteen, for at Maryborough (now called Port Laoise), we stopped for the middle of the day, while they got an armored engine and troops to escort us. I had seen pictures of these extraordinary engines in books about the Boer War: I suppose the British had dumped a lot of them in Ireland. One of the exquisite pleasures of the Irish (I was soon to find out) is pedantry: a few of us, including a priest, left the train and went into the town for a drink, sure of finding the train still there after a couple of hours. It was. It gave a jolt. "Are we starting?" someone asked. "Sure, we haven't started starting yet," the porter said.

The afternoon faded as we went across the bogland; at Mallow it was dark, and there we got into cars to join another train across the valley. The viaduct had been blown up. We eventually arrived in Cork in a racket of machine-gun fire. I hesitated. But the passengers took it for granted and a barefooted urchin who took my case said: " 'Tis only the boys from the hills." The firing went on, from time to time, into the small hours, and patrol lorries drove up and down. One stopped at the hotel and after a lot of shouting and banging of doors, a posse of soldiers came into my room, got me out of bed and searched the bedding and my luggage. They looked respectfully at my books, and one of them started reading a poem of Yeats and said if I kept to that I would be all right.

Cork is a pretty city, particularly in the dappled buildings of its riverside quays and estuaries. By this time my mind was singing with Irish poetry. I went out into the countryside to see how Blarney was surviving the revolution. It was surviving in the best of its tradition. I plodded round with a farmer whose chief ejaculation was a shout of "Blood and hounds," when his narrative needed it. It often did. Back in Cork, I went to the theater, where Doran's well-known touring company were playing a different Shakespeare tragedy every night:

my earliest experience of *Macbeth*, *Othello* and *Hamlet*. Doran's company had been slogging away in England and Ireland for years. He himself was a studied ham with a huge voice. He hogged the plays, of course, and put such a stamp on his roles that it was pretty well impossible to distinguish Hamlet from Macbeth, or Macbeth from Othello. The theater was always packed. When Hamlet said his line about everyone being mad in England, the house cheered. I had gone with a commercial traveler from Kerry who came back to the hotel, and then he and one or two other commercials recited Shakespeare to one another for the rest of the evening. I couldn't understand a word the torrential Kerryman said, but Shakespeare was tempestuously Elizabethan in a Kerry accent.

I traveled across Tipperary to Limerick, arriving there in one of those long, soft brown and yellow sunsets of the West, with the white mists rising from the Shannon. The Celtic twilight was working on me. I sat up drinking with a satanic engineer; and, thinking it was about time, I tried that night to write one of my articles. I found that after two or three whiskies my pen swept across the paper. When I read the thing in the morning, I saw it was chaotic and I tore it up. That is the last time I ever wrote on alcohol.

Limerick was in an edgy state. It had just been relieved of a siege and there was still a crack or two of sniping at night. There was a strike on at the bacon factories; and there was an attempt to start a soviet. I went to see the committee and politely took my hat off and made a small French bow when I went into their room. The leader told me to put my hat on: they had finished, he said, with bourgeois manners. We had a wrangle about this because, although I am shy, I am touchy, and argued back. We had a rapid duel of sarcasms. He was one of those "black" Irishmen one occasionally comes across; there was another, a waiter at the hotel in Limerick who threw a plate of bacon and eggs at a customer. He was a big fellow who looked murderous every time he came into the dining room with a plate.

There occurred in Limerick one of those encounters which—looking back on it—I see as a portent. I found there a very serious young Englishman—in fact, a Quaker—who took me to a house outside the town. As we climbed up on an outside car, he whispered to me not to talk on the long ride out because, he said, his situation was delicate. He had caught the Irish love of conspiracy, even the whisper. When we got to his house he told me he had been in the fighting against the Sinn Feiners, but had lately married an Irish girl. I think he had been in the Auxiliary Police. Except for having his tennis court shot up now and then, he said, when he and his wife were playing in the afternoons, there was not much trouble now. The English have stubborn natures but, I saw, could get light-headed in Ireland. Into the sitting room, which was furnished in faded Victorian style, with pictures of lakes and vegetation on the walls and the general Irish smell of rising damp, came an elderly woman wearing a wig of black curls and with a sharp, painted face; and with her a pale little girl of twelve—I thought—one of those fey, unreal Irish children with empty blue eyes and untidy russet hair. She looked as if she had been blown down from the sky as, in her tiny skirt, she sat barelegged on the floor in front of the fire. She was *not* a child of twelve; she was the Quaker's wife, and very excitable. The shooting, she said, livened up the tennis, but they were afraid for the strings of their rackets, because in these times you might have to send them to Dublin to be restrung. A brother-in-law came in, a man who sat in silence, breathing sociably, as Guinness after Guinness went down. I gazed from the old lady to the girl, from the brother-in-law to the ascetic-looking young Quaker soldier, and could not see how they could be together in the same house. In how many Irish families was it to seem to me that the people had all appeared accidentally from the wheel of fortune, rather than in the course of nature. The old lady chattered about balls and parties, about Lord this and Lady that, about the stage—was she an actress? In her wig, paint and her rings, bracelets and necklace, and her old-fashioned dress of twenty years before, she was nimble and witchlike. Indeed, she got out a pack of cards and told my fortune. I dropped the Queen of Spades. She sprang on it with glee: "You will be surrounded by women who intend to harm you." I walked back to Limerick late, feeling, as I was so often to do in Ireland, that I had stepped into a chapter of a Russian novel. The smell of turf smoke curled among the river fogs and I was not sure of the way in the dark. I waited for a shot or two, for the Irregulars liked to loose off at night to keep the feeling of war alive, from behind a friendly hedge. There were no shots that night. It was an eerie and pleasant walk, like a ghost story told in the dark.

I went on to Enniskillen, the border town, all drapers, hardware stores and useful shops, brisker in trade than the towns of the south, a place half-Orange, half-Catholic. The town clerk, a twentieth-century man, was the kind who enjoyed the comedies of fanaticism, but the jokes rippled over the surface of the incurable seventeeth-century bitterness. It is often said that Irish laughter is without mirth, but rather a guerrilla activity of the mind. I was stuck in Enniskillen for another cold wet Sunday, when the only other guest in the hotel was a glum commercial traveler from the English Midlands, a man with one of the flattest minds I had met up to then. Careful with his money, too; his father was an undertaker and the son used the motor hearse at the weekends to give his girl a ride. He was to be—from my point of view as a writer—the most important man I met in Ireland, but it took me ten years to realize this. I wrote down every word of his I could remember.

I look back upon this Irish expedition with an embarrassed but forgiving eye. I see the empty mountains, the bog and the succulent marshy valleys, the thin, awkward roads, through a steam of strong tea. The sun came and went, the rain dripped and dried on my hat. I stuffed with fried cod, potatoes, potato cakes, scones and butter as I read my Yeats and Synge; the air, even when cold, was lazy and I couldn't get up until eleven in the morning. I was thick in the head, with no idea of what to write about until, in despair, I was driven to write flatly everything I saw and heard. The "everything" was a torture, for I discovered that places overwhelmed me. Every movement of light, every turn of leaf, every person, seemed to occupy me physically, so that I had no self left. But perhaps this means I was all self. It was with a conviction of failure that I sent my first four articles to the paper and sat staring into a "jar" of Guinness. I was dumbfounded to get a telegram from London saying my articles were excellent.

Alas, I have seen them since. They are very small beer. They are thin and sentimental; but here and there is a sentence that shows I was moved and had an eye. They were signed by my initials and that is why from then on people dropped my Christian name—to my relief—and I was called VSP or RSVP. My literary name developed from this. I preferred the impersonal, and to have added the "t" of Victor to a name that already had three, and was made more fidgety by a crush of consonants and two short vowels, seemed ridiculous.

In this short trip I had easily rid myself of the common English idea that Ireland was a piece of England that for some reason or other would not settle down and had run to seed. I had heard at school of "the curse of Cromwell." I ardently identified Irish freedom with my own personal freedom, which had been hard to come by. A revolutionary break? I was for it. Until you are free you do not know who you are. It was a basic belief of the twenties, it permeated all young minds, and though we became puritanically drastic, gauche and insensitive in our rebellions against everything we called Victorianism, we were elated.

I became the Irish correspondent. It was momentous. I had a career. This was no time for living the dilapidated day-to-day life I had lived in Paris. And there was the religious question: I had lapsed in Paris, where I had been the average sensual young man. Now I found myself employed by the paper from whose religion I had lapsed. It seemed to be my duty to reform. The shadiness of puritans! I threw my last cigarette into the Liffey, gave up drinking wine, beer and whiskey, though my tastes there were youthfully moderate. I was really more austerely the Romantic idealist than puritan, for I soon found the Calvinism of Ireland—scarcely buried under Irish high spirits—distasteful and indeed dull; my nature rebelled against it.

I lived in Dublin in two periods, and I write now mostly of my first year there when, far more than in Paris, I lived in my imagination. When I reread nowadays the German court episode in Meredith's *Harry Richmond* and of the ordeal through which Meredith's young romantic passes, I recognize something close to my Irish experience and indeed to other experience in my youth; like Stendhal, Meredith is outstanding in his observation of easily inflamed young men.

If Ireland moved me, it also instructed me. As a political education, the experience was excellent. One was observing a revolution: a country set free, a new young state, the first modern defeat of colonialism. Sitting in the press gallery of the Dail, day after day, listening to the laughing, fighting voice of

Cosgrave, the irony of Kevin O'Higgins or the tirades of the old defeated Redmond was like being at school taking a course in the foundation of states. I realized what a social revolution was, although I was (inevitably as an Englishman and Protestant) much more in the old Anglo-Irish society, the majority of whom reluctantly accepted the new regime, than among the rising Catholic middle class. I did not really know them until many years later. I was carried away by Irish sociability and nervous scorn of England into thinking I was in the contemporary European world. I was not, but there was the beguiling insinuation that Ireland was in temperamental contact with Paris and Italy and had by-passed the complex social preoccupations of industrial England. (Joyce's flight from Dublin to the Continent was an example of the Irish tradition.) The snobberies of the Ascendancy were very Colonial—as I now see—though not as loud as the Anglo-Indian, not as prim as the Bostonian: they came closer to those of the American Southern states. (There is a bond between Anglo-Irish writing and the literature of the American South.) In Ireland, shortage of capital and decaying estates had given these snobberies a lazy but acid quality; in many people there was a suggestion of concealed and bloodless spiritual superiority. English snobbery was based firmly on vulgar wealth and a class system energized by contention, and very mobile; the Irish was based on kinship, without wealth. The subject is perfectly displayed—though in an earlier generation—in *The Real Charlotte* by Somerville and Ross. Noses were kept raised by boisterous and tenuous claims to cousinage.

Ireland is really a collection of secret societies; for a rootless young man like myself, this had a strong allure. I was slow to see that I was meeting an upper class in decay and at the point when it was disappearing in boatloads, from Dún Laoghaire every day; and that I was really living in a world far more like that of Mrs. Gaskell's novels in the prim and genteel England of, say, 1840 to 1860 (except that old ladies had been using the word "bloody" in company freely for a couple of hundred years). Genealogy, as one could tell from the libraries and the number of societies given to it, was the national passion.

The easygoing life in this Victorian lagoon was delightful to me. It is often said that in Ireland there is an excess of genius unsustained by talent; but there is talent in the tongues, and Irish manners are engaging. I sat in my office in St. Stephen's Green, a cheerful outsider in Irish quarrels, turning myself into the idlest of newspaper correspondents. I lodged with two Protestant spinsters in a sedate early Victorian terrace house in Waterloo Road, where they left me cold meat and pickles and a pot of strong tea for my supper; they popped up every quarter of an hour if I had a young woman to visit me, to see that nothing was "going on." Dublin was a city so gregariously domestic that the sexes did not care to meet without other company. The English were deplored as coarse sensualists who ate too much, were sex-mad and conventional.

The pleasant, wide eighteenth-century streets of Georgian Dublin were easing to the mind, and the wild mountains over which the weather changed every hour excited the fancy. And there was Dublin Bay, so often enameled and Italianate. More and more, I was idling at Blackrock or Dalkey, with a crowd of young men and girls, watching the sea or walking across the mountains as far as Glendalough or the Vale of Avoca, and scooping a kettle of water out of a stream in the heather, for a picnic.

My mind fed on scenery. The sight of lakes, slatey in the rain, or like blue eyes looking out of the earth in the changing Irish light; the Atlantic wind always silvering the leaves of beech and oak and elm on the road to Galway, empty except for a turf cart or a long funeral; the Twelve Pins in Connemara, now gleaming like glass in the drizzle, now bald, green and dazzling; the long sea inlets that on hot days burn their way deeply inland beyond Clifden, where the sands are white and the kelp burns on them; the Atlantic coming in stormily below the high cliffs of Moher; and the curious tropic of Kerry.

My brother came over from England, and with two girls we borrowed a horse and cart and went slowly across to the West and back; and in Clare, which was still in a disorganized state, we attracted the "boys from the hills," who kept us up dancing half-sets, singing all the rebel songs and finishing up with "Nancy Hogan's Goose." Two young Englishmen with two unmarried girls! The scandal of it! There was a lot of talk in Dublin. I do not think only of landscape but of the wide disheartening streets of the long villages and the ruined farms of the West; and the elaborately disguised curiosity of the impulsively kind but guarded people, looking into your eyes for a chance of capping your fantasy with one of theirs, in long ceremonies of well-mannered evasion, craving for the guesswork of acquaintance and diversion.

The darker side of this was blurred and muddied and stinking: the dramatic character of the misery. In Dublin, the tenements were shocking; the women still wore the long black shawl, the children were often barefooted. You picked up lice and fleas in the warm weather in the Dublin trams as you went to the North Side to the wrecked mansions of the eighteenth century. The poor looked not simply poor, but savagely poor, though they were rich in speech and temperament. They were always ragged processions of protesters, on the general Irish ground that one must keep on screaming against life itself. There were nasty sights: a man led by a couple of soldiers down a mountain road with his wrists tied behind his back.

I think of the story of the house close to a lonely cottage

I had in my second Irish period, at the sea's edge near Clifden. It was no more than a two-roomed cabin with a loft and, with the Irish love of grand names, was called Mount Freer and had once belonged to an English painter. (A pensioned-off sailor owned it.) Near it was the manor, or farm, a ruinous place of rusty gates and scarcely habitable, occupied by a bank manager from some inland town. He was very ill and was still suffering from the shock of having been badly beaten up in a raid on his bank in the civil war. He was not alone at this time. His brother, a cropped Australian ex-soldier, had come over to look after him for a while. I used to go shooting rabbits with the Australian in a deserted graveyard. It had belonged, the Australian said, to the ferocious O'Flahertys, from whom the people in Galway had in the far past called on God to protect them. He was trying to persuade his dim, sick brother to go back with him. If the sick man saw anyone in the road he would climb gingerly over the stone wall and dodge away in a wide, lonely circle across the rocky fields to the house. I knew the Australian well. He was a good fisherman. We used to go out and spear plaice in the sands and catch mackerel. Many a fry we had. Often I walked, as night fell, to look at the wink of light on Slyne Head—America the next parish. He told me the brother refused to go near anyone.

"The poor bloody brother, he has the idea he stinks. He thinks he's got a bloody smell on him. He'll never come near you." His house had almost no furniture—simply a couple of beds, a table and two chairs—and if I went there, the sick man slipped away and hid in another room. Eventually the Australian had to leave, and when he did the "mad feller," as he was called, cut his throat or hanged himself. Thank God I'd left before that happened.

It has been said that the Irish live in a state of perplexity. The poet Patrick Kavanagh has written that the newborn child screams because it cannot bear the light of the real world. Yet, from Shaw onward one finds the Irish saying they are not dreamers but are realists. Not in the literary sense of the word "realism," but in the sense of seeing with cold detachment where exact practical advantage lies. I would have said their instincts are tribal. They evade the moral worries of settled societies and there is a strain of anarchy in them: they can be charitable and cruel at the same time. It is self-indulgent to generalize like this and, anyway, the Irish do that more coolly then we English do. But one has to make something of the way they turn tragedy to farce and farce back into tragedy; and when in the thirties I wrote a story called *Sense of Humour,* a piece of premature black comedy, which was set going by the meeting with that glum commercial traveler I had met in Enniskillen, it expressed something of the effect of an Irish experience on myself.

One of my acquaintances among the gentry class—how naturally one associates the word "gentry" with the same class in old Russian rather than with an English equivalent—took me down to a mansion he had inherited together with a title he detested. He was not one of the raffish, shooting kind, and he was too simple and plain a fellow to care much about the brilliant group of Anglo-Irish intellectuals who still dominated Irish life. He was a bit deaf and was thought dull—"I hear he's a decent kind of feller." He was by way of being a gentleman socialist, and the "good society," in that sense, interested few Irishmen. The decent fellow had a social conscience and had to bear the curse of landowning. It had fallen on him by accident. As a poor boy he had been sent off to Canada, where he became a Mountie; in the war he had been one of the early flying men. Suddenly he came into "the place"; he married a beauty whom he bickered with, because he refused to have anything to do with fashionable life in Ireland, London or Italy. His real taste—but as a social reformer—was for low life on the Dublin quays. After I left Ireland I heard he had sold his mansion to the nuns, as many Irish landlords did in the end (the Irish Church having a shrewd eye for property) and cleared off, at a moment's notice, without telling a soul, to America. He is now dead.

This weekend was my only experience of Irish country-house life in the civil war. The war was still sputtering away when we drove off in a little French racing car with planks strapped to the side of it. This was to outwit "the clowns" on his estate who had burned down the mill he had built—part of his practical socialism—and had dug trenches across the key roads to prevent him getting home. A true Irishman, he was more than half on their side. At each new trench we got out, put down the planks and drove across. He loved the comedy.

We drove into a large demesne. The mansion stood empty above its lake; he had built himself an efficient little villa near it. When we got in, we found the house had been invaded by "Irregulars," who had come searching for guns and ammunition. The servants were hysterical and a parrot imitated them, calling out "Glory be to God." He went up to his bedroom, slid back a panel in the wardrobe: there was a good supply of untouched weapons, but girls among the raiders had gone off with his wife's riding clothes, and one of the men had emptied a gallon jar of ink over the drawing-room carpet. The raiders had found a safe in the estate office, but could not open it. So they dumped it in the middle of the lake. My host rang up the local military who put on an offensive.

"We'll send down the Terrorizer," the officer said. The Terrorizer and his men rowed about the large lake very happily. It was a lovely afternoon. Her ladyship came down in the evening. She was a slender and handsome dark-haired woman with fine features and an amused sparkle in her eyes, and a despairing voice. She treated me very kindly, but firmly, as the social peculiarity I was, because I had not changed into a dinner jacket. (I didn't have one.) Still, despite her high-class groans, she was an amusing and witty woman. The more snobbish she became, the rougher her husband.

"She's talking a lot of rot," he'd say down the table, jerking his thumb at his wife. I felt, like another Pip, one of my moods of Miss Haversham worship coming on, for a caustic, mocking tongue and beauty combined were irresistible. I put on dog and burst out with a long speech about a new book of D. H. Lawrence's.

"What extraordinary things are going on," she said. "How very unpleasant."

The next two days I was put through a short course in Irish country-house life. We went out fox-cubbing in the rain with a lot of wind-reddened country neighbors. We got very muddy. I was never one for the sporting life. We went for a drink to a large dark house, where the family portraits looked like kippers. A man was dumbstruck when I told him I didn't hunt, shoot or fish. "What do you do?" he asked coldly. I naturally supposed this was directed at my employment. I told him I was a journalist. He looked shocked and had never heard of the paper. Trying to think of a comparable English paper, I said, "It's like *The Manchester Guardian*." He stepped away, making a few short sarcasms about that traitorous "Sinn Fein rag." (In Ireland, I've nowadays heard it called "The Niggers' Gazette.")

The following afternoon we went riding. I had never been on a horse before. To me the animal smelled of the leather trade. I was surprised to find that horses are warm. I gripped the reins as if they were a life line; I was jellied and bumped by its extraordinary movement. The party began to canter and I was tossed in the air and I got a fixed smile on my face. We arrived in a field to try some jumps. A wicked old trainer shouted bits of advice. I went over one or two gaps and arrived—surprised and askew, but still up. So they tried some more difficult jumps. The party hung about waiting for the slaughter. The animal rose, I fell on its neck, but I did not come off. The stakes were raised; at the next jump the horse and I went to different parts of the sky. I was in the mud. I got up and apologized to the horse, which turned its head away. Afterward we walked and trotted home; it seemed to take hours. Back in the house, I felt someone had put planks on my legs and turned my buttocks into wooden boxes. So my life as an Irish sportsman and country gentleman came to an end. Still, I had stayed with a baronet. I was snobbish enough to be pleased by that.

I like curious clothes. Back in Dublin I stayed in my riding breeches, bought at a cheap shop in Dublin, and wore them for weeks after, as an enjoyable symbol of the Irish habit of life, until someone tactfully suggested I looked like a stable boy.

There was one seminal and lasting gain in my time in Dublin. The Irish revel in words and phrases. Their talk is vivid and inventive. They live for the story. I had no idea of what kind of writer I wanted to be, but there were many, in the flesh, to offer me a new example, and who woke something in me.

In their twilight, the Anglo-Irish—the descendants of Normans, Elizabethans, and Cromwellian soldiers—especially, had discovered their genius. Yeats was in Merrion Square, AE (George Russell) was editing *The Irish Statesman* next door but one; James Stephens, Lennox Robinson, Lady Gregory were there. And so was the young Liam O'Flaherty—not

Anglo-Irish—and Sean O'Casey was working in his slum room on the North Side. There were other good dramatists, and there were the gifted actors and actresses of the Abbey Theatre, where I went every week. There one could see not only the plays of Synge and writers of the Revival, but masters of tragic form like the unjustly forgotten T. C. Murray—who was "native Irish"—and Shaw, Ibsen and Strindberg. Literature was not to be studied or something to be caught up with, but to be practiced and at once. In writing, the stories of Liam O'Flaherty excited me, for he had the Irish gift of writing close to the skin of life. The best Irish writers have always had a fine surface. They have always had élan. The writing is clear and sensuous and catches every tremor of movement in the skin of the human animal and of landscape. The prose is athletic and flies along untroubled as if language were their life. Then, the Dublin bookshops were excellent. It was in Dublin that I read Katherine Mansfield, Chekhov and D. H. Lawrence, and Joyce's *Dubliners,* hoping to catch his sense of epiphany. In 1923 the short story, like the one-act play, had a prestige. I wrote my first stories in Ireland and Spain.

Living among writers who were still at their good moment added to my desire to emulate them. I had the—to me—incredible sight of the beautiful Mrs. W. B. Yeats riding a bicycle at St. Stephen's Green; and of AE, also riding a bicycle and carrying a bunch of flowers. I had tea with James Stephens one Sunday at that hotel at Dún Laoghaire, where people go to daydream at the sight of the mailboat coming in from England, that flashing messenger to and from the modern world. This gnomelike talker sparkled so recklessly that one half-dreaded he might fall into his teacup and drown. One afternoon I took tea with Yeats himself in his house in Merrion Square.

It was a Georgian house, as unlike a hut of wattle in a

bee-loud glade as one could imagine. To begin with, the door opened on a chain and the muzzle of a rifle stuck through the gap. A pink-faced Free State soldier asked me if I had an "app'ntment." I was shown in to what must have been a dining room, but now it was a guardroom with soldiers smoking among the Blake drawings on the wall. (Yeats was a Senator and he had already been shot at by gunmen. Upstairs I was to see the bullet hole in the drawing-room window.) Presently the poet came down the stairs to meet me.

It is a choking and confusing experience to meet one's first great man when one is young. These beings come from another world, and Yeats heightened that effect. Tall, with gray hair finely rumpled, a dandy with negligence in collar and tie and with the black ribbon dangling from the glasses on a short, pale and prescient nose—not long enough to be Roman yet not sharp enough to be a beak—Yeats came down the stairs toward me, and the nearer he came the further away he seemed. His air was birdlike, suggesting one of the milder swans of Coole and an exalted sort of blindness. I had been warned that he would not shake hands. I have heard it said —but mainly by the snobbish Anglo-Irish—that Yeats was a snob. I would have said that he was a man who was translated into a loftier world the moment his soft voice throbbed. He was the only man I have known whose natural speech sounded like verse.

He sat me in the fine first floor of his house. After the years all that remains with me is a memory of candles, books, woodcuts, the feeling that here was Art. And conversation. But what about? I cannot remember. The exalted voice flowed over me. The tall figure, in uncommonly delicate tweed, walked up and down, the voice becoming more resonant, as if he were on a stage. At the climax of some point about the Gaelic revival, he suddenly remembered he must make tea, in fact a new pot, because he had already been drinking some. The problem was one of emptying out the old teapot. It was a beautiful pot and he walked the room with the short steps of the aesthete, carrying it in his hand. He came toward me. He receded to the bookcase. He swung round the sofa. Suddenly, with Irish practicality, he went straight to one of the two splendid Georgian windows of the room, opened it, and out went those barren leaves with a swoosh, into Merrion Square —for all I know onto the heads of Lady Gregory, Oliver St. John Gogarty and AE. They were leaves of Lapsang tea.

I can remember only one thing he said. We had got on to Shaw, whom he disliked. I murmured—showing off—something about Shaw's socialist principles. The effect on Yeats was fine. He stood now, with a teapot full of tea in his hands, saying that Shaw had no principles. Shaw was a destroyer. Like lightning, Shaw flashed in hilarious indifference, and what the lightning briefly revealed was interesting but meaningless. This has always stuck in my mind, but of the rest I remember nothing except that with solemnity he pointed to the inner door of the room and said that, sitting in this room, he had experimented in thought transference with Mrs. Yeats, who sat in her room next door. As I say, I had seen her out on her bicycle and I have often wondered, as the eloquent mind expelled its thoughts to the wall, whether Mrs. Yeats was always next door at the time. He was kind enough to walk with me to the Irish Senate nearby, and I was overcome when he leaned on my shoulder while he lifted a foot, took off his shoe and shook out a stone. I noticed he had a pretty blue ring on one of his fingers.

I went to see AE in the office of *The Irish Statesman,* the weekly review that preached cooperative farming. He was a large tweedy bunch of a man with a beard, a talker who drowned me in beautiful phrases of a mystical, theosophical kind. The walls of his office were an extension of his mind, for they were covered with golden murals of ethereal beings. He must have been the kindest and most innocent man in Ireland, for he was a slave to the encouragement of young writers. When I wrote my first story, he took it at once, kept it for two years, and almost with tears of apology sent it back saying it was crowded out. This was inevitable. AE's talking overflowed into print and occupied nearly the whole paper. I sat again with both Yeats and AE at Yeats's house, while Yeats praised D'Annunzio and AE tried to argue him out of the admiration. I watched the soot on Yeats's fireplace, for AE distracted himself during Yeats's long utterances by making designs in the soot with Yeats's poker.

The only playwright I knew a little was Sean O'Casey. He was still living in his tenement on the North Side, a smashed fanlight over the door. His room was bare and contained only an iron bed, a table and a couple of poor chairs. He always wore a cloth cap in the house. A fire of cheap coal dust was smoldering where a kettle was singing—a true sign of the old Ireland. On the shabby wall was a notice he had printed:

GET ON WITH THE BLOODY PLAY

He was writing *The Plough and the Stars* at this time. Again, only one thing remains of his conversation: he was angry because he said that the "authorities" were trying to keep the poor from using the public libraries, on the grounds that they would spread their diseases through the books. I'd been angered myself by that argument when I was ten and had read it in a book by Marie Corelli.

. . .

It was my duty to go to Ulster now and then, and there, after crossing the Boyne, beyond Dundalk, the political grafitti were violent: "To hell with the Pope" or "Ulster will fight and Ulster will be right" or "Remember Derry and no surrender." I walked round the gray and dismal walls of Londonderry; odd to think of the most sorrowful and lilting of Irish ballads bearing the name of that ugly and raging city. I looked beyond the drizzle to the empty hills of Donegal. I went again to Enniskillen, where I met the only Orange man I really enjoyed. He was a solicitor and a fantatic who boiled at the thought of the I.R.A. just a mile away. They tried to kidnap him. He had one chink in his armor: he had married an amusing woman from the South. The bond in Irish marriages, it struck me often, was a common interest in battle; and in the course of their frisky warfare, the wife succeeded in getting her husband to laugh at himself after one of his rages. He was telling me about the night raid on his house and how his wife, as a foolish woman would, had run to the window and beat on a tin tray to call for help, while he got out the gun he always kept under the bed.

"I always keep one up the spout. That's the lesson you don't forget in the British Army."

But his wife joined in: "And it went off just as he got it from under the bed." There was a crash of china. He had shot the chamber pot.

Belfast was detestable. The only "decent" hotel at that time was grubby. The city is the most dreadful in Ireland. The Ulster accent, a bastard lowland Scots, is harsh, and is given a sort of comic bluster by the glottal stop imported from Glasgow. (It is strange to think that Henry James's Ulster ancestors may have spoken in this manner.) The humor is boisterous; the fanaticism is brutal and the relations between the Ulster employers and workers were rough; it was a simple matter to rouse national passions so that social reforms were checked. The minority of the liberally minded were the merchants and middlemen; the manufacturers were more obdurate. Still, I have known genial Ulstermen. It is no good trying the Southern Irish game of evasion, indirection and covert conspiracy with them, at least not with the Protestants; one has to stand firm and hit back hard. They understand that and, like plain-speakers in northern England, they grin.

I speak, of course, generally; one can always find the gentler and more reasonable spirits. One of these, whom I always went to see, was a very distinguished writer—now forgotten and lost because he buried himself in Belfast—called Forrest Reid. He was a friend of Yeats and E. M. Forster and his few novels have an element of pagan symbolism that is present also in Forster's early short stories, and reflect something of Yeats's mysticism. The idea of the ghost or revenant, some shade of a lost culture or a guilt appearing out of the past is often found in Irish literature. Reid's autobiography, *Apostate,* describes his upbringing in Belfast. It is a minor classic, and it will stand beside Gosse's *Father and Son.* He was indeed an apostate in that awful, rainy and smoky Presbyterian city: he was a genuine pagan. He stayed there as if in hiding, I used to think. He lived alone on the top floor of a sour house, shaken by industrial traffic, and opposite a linen mill. The smoke hung low and blew into his windows, so that he had been obliged to bind his thousands of books in white paper covers: not very practical in that place for the smuts stood out on them. One passed old bicycles in the hall, then climbed stairs of torn linoleum to his bare room, on the table of which there was usually a pile of novels for review from *The Manchester Guardian* and a bone of cold mutton pushed to the other side of it. He was the first book reviewer I ever saw. He was a thin fellow and he had a strange nose, very long and thin, that tipped up suddenly like a small hook at the end. He had AE's habit of poking the soot off the back of his little fireplace as if looking for secret intimations. After sniffing out politics in mills and newspaper offices, or coming back from some Orange beano at which an English politician would be trying to beat the Orangemen down before they all started singing (of all songs) "Oft in the Stilly Night" by Tom Moore—I would make for Forrest Reid's room to hear softer and more civilized accents. It was a relief after a day with a shipyard owner. There was one to whom I spoke about Forrest Reid.

"Wratin' poetry don't drave no rivets, yoong man," he said.

I may exaggerate Reid's isolation, for there is a decent university in Belfast, and the Belfast playwright who wrote that biting farce *Thompson of Tir-na-Nog* must have been worth knowing; but it was odd to find a mystic, deep in Blake and Yeats, among the linen mills. Why didn't he go South? Perhaps because of some core of Ulster obstinacy or of family chains that are so powerful in all Ireland.

Naturally, by pleasing the pro-Free State faction in Dublin I had angered the others. The Divine Mind instructed them to complain to the paper. They even sent anonymous letters: I had thought my upper-class coreligionaries would be above that. It was rumored that I had gone off to the country with the girl who worked with me. I had, and very chastely —the "open road" was a chaste movement. I was called back to London; I supposed I was to be sacked.

The situation, I found, was different. By the end of 1923 Ireland, which had attracted the newspapers of the world since 1916, had ceased to be interesting. No one wanted to read about Ireland any more. And Mr. Bassellthorpe—very

English in this—had grown sick to death of his Irish troubles. I sat in Mr. Bassellthorpe's office. He praised my work, saying however, that I must beware of getting swollen-headed. It would have been truer if he had said I had a brain but no head at all. He came nearer the truth when he suggested I had become youthfully addled. He had elected to become a father to me.

He took me to the Bath Club for lunch. I carelessly said I admired Yeats. I was surprised to find he had read Yeats thoroughly, and he politely but abruptly told me of my error. The poet had the fatal Celtic tendency to sensuous mysticism, to abominations like the Wisdom of the East; he was obsessed by sex. So was Mr. Bassellthorpe; his face fattened into blushes when he used this word. When we got to coffee he came out with what had really disturbed him. The Irish had never been distinguished in the visual arts, he said: I had written the notice of an art exhibition and sent a photograph of one of the pictures. He brought out the picture from his pocket. I forget who had painted it. It had been inspired by a line of Synge's: "And he, rising up in the red dawn." It was the back view of a savage-looking and naked middle-aged tinker, with hairy legs, standing in a patch of bog, against a riotous sunrise. How could I like it? "He's not even a young man," said Mr. Bassellthorpe. There was no suggestion of the Ideal. I did my best to defend it in a stammering way. He said, unforgivingly: "That is what Ireland does to the mind."

He said he had read a line in a Gaelic poem which ran: "What does the salmon dream?"

"A salmon does not dream," he said firmly.

After this he became more lenient. He had talked to an Irish peer who had complained about my political writing, and Mr. Bassellthorpe had defended me. At the mention of peers, my ears pricked up and, in a worldly way, possibly due to the influence of the Bath Club, I dropped the names of one or two with titles whom I had seen in the Irish Senate. Mr. Bassellthorpe was not going to let me get away with that. They were only Irish peers, he said, and they ranked lower even than the Scots. His thoroughly English satisfaction in placing peers socially relieved our luncheon. He changed the subject. There had been a coup d'état in Spain: the paper's correspondent there had retired. Would I go there? He would pay me £400 a year, and the paper would pay the fare.

The suggestion of Mr. Bassellthorpe was tormenting. In Ireland I had wanted to be an artist of some sort, like the Irish writers I read or knew. I had daydreamed of settling there. I remember sitting on a rock in the summer on the little island called Ireland's Eye near Howth and thinking how tragic it would be to leave this beautiful place. I was living—if my Irish friends were not—in an unreal world.

The torment had a private aspect. Naturally, I had fallen in love again—this time with the young woman journalist who worked with me, a troublesome business because the Major, her father, detested me. He would get up from his daylong game of patience and leave the room muttering about "the nasty little clerk" his daughter brought to the house. I was clearly not a gentleman. And certainly had "no money"—i.e., no private means. I had, in fact, £14 in cash. Mr. Bassellthorpe's move put everyone in a panic for I had to leave Ireland almost at once. The young woman and I had been nosing our way out of friendship toward marriage; now, in a rush, it was upon us and to the indignation of our fathers we were married.

6

At the beginning of January in 1924, shortly after my twenty-third birthday, we set off for Madrid. We spent two days in Paris on the way and went up to Montparnasse. I saw no recognizable face. Had everyone been "passing through" like myself? The Rotonde had become very expensive and vulgar. Smart night clubs were springing up. The quarter had become a tourist spot. The one or two restaurants that had seemed so pleasant to me now looked cramped. The gleam of my Bohemian days had gone, my own Bohemian gleam with it. Even my shoes were clean. That silly notion of "becoming French"! I was as English as I could possibly make myself. The lines of Henri Murger came back to me:

*Je veux bien consenter à regarder le passé, mais ce sera
au travers d'une bouteille de vrai vin, et assis dans un
bon fauteuil. Qu'est-ce-que tu veux?—je suis un cor-
rompu. Je n'aime plus que ce qui est bon.*

Basil Shaves had gone to London. I knew that, because
he had stayed for a while near my parents in Bromley and had
made their hymn-playing piano ring with "Cutts of the Cruiser
What-Not" and Albert Chevalier songs which so cheered my
mother, bringing back the old days, that she talked and
laughed about it for the rest of her life. My brother, now successful in the artificial silk trade, had got the expert in ruin a
job selling stockings and ladies' underwear.

I would have liked to have heard Percy hawking up the
boulevard to show him that I had gone up in the world; but
Percy was not there. Mme. Chapin had moved too. The bugle
went off at the barracks opposite my old hotel, and its note did
not cheer me.

We took the night train, second class, in low spirits. Marriage had stunned us. I spoke no Spanish. The only thing I
knew about Spain was that it had had the Inquisition and that
the Armada had been defeated. And I also had garbled memories of pictures of Granada, the scene of the novel I had written a hundred pages of when I was twelve. I have written two
books about Spain since that day in 1924: the first in the
twenties, *Marching Spain*—long out of print—and, in my
fifties, *The Spanish Temper*. I shall do my best not to repeat
myself, but it will be difficult because Spain was to bring about
a fundamental change in my life. Until now I had picked up
my education as I went along. In Spain the matter became
more serious. Irish sociability had made me a careless amateur;
in Spain I was to get one of those moral shocks that make one
question everything one has taken for granted.

At Hendaye rain was driving out of a cold sky; across the choppy bay I saw one of those big cheese-colored baroque churches that seem to bully the town like some shabby and portentous old bishop. The old Protestant scorn and rancor rose in me. The grass growing over the railways tracks at Irun, the battered goods wagons, rotted by use, sun and rain, the liverish faces of the silent officials, who seemed so thin that the yellow straps of their green or blue uniforms were holding them together, and their exhausted laconic manner suggested people who were waiting for death with the little that was left to them: their dignity. Through France, people were as rosy as lawyers and almost buttered. Here they looked corpse-like. In the train the passengers were heavily wrapped up, glum and silent; well, it was early in the morning. One looked out of the carriage window at the driving clouds and the smear of drizzle low over the Pyrenees and the sodden Basque mountains. The rain spouted off the heavy, wide eaves of the little towns. (Years later I was to see people dancing in the town squares there under umbrellas.) Swollen and rocky rivers flooded through ravines. Although the train was a *Rapido,* it trundled along on the wide gauge that had been built to prevent another Napoleon dashing straight in from France (the French use narrower tracks), and stopped at every small station. Wet and silent Basques got in. Only after fashionable San Sebastian, where *Madrileños* entered, was there the dramatic parrotlike chatter which the Basques, like the Portuguese, silently despise. A youth got in playing a guitar for money between stations for a while. Another youth slid back the door of the compartment, opened his jacket wide and shouted, with a look of desperation: "Knives?" He had six rows of knives of all sizes slotted into the inside of his jacket. No one answered.

The journey from the French frontier nowadays takes

about eight hours. In 1924 it took thirteen, and in our case, nineteen, for one of the two engines broke down as it failed to get up the steep gradient from Ávila into the snow of the Guadarrama mountains. But long before this, about two in the afternoon, we got out of the rain of the Basque provinces into the daylong sunlight of the tableland of Castile, here some two thousand feet above the level of the sea.

I have described the effect of this sudden sight in *The Spanish Temper*: the slow journey through a landscape unlike any other in Western Europe, the monotonous yet bizarre moon landscape of flat-topped mesas that proceeded like a geometry under a clear cold sky and dry winter sun. I had never seen anything like this before. I was magnetized. The bleached yellow of the soil, sometimes changing to metallic pinks and cindery grays; the curious associations of desert harshness and serenity, especially of desertlike space and of distances that ended in wildernesses of rock; and then of sierras that seemed to be cut out of the sky as if saw-blades had sliced them, and toward which some mule team straggled along the rare roads; all alerted me. I daydreamed of getting out of the train and crossing Old Castile on foot or by mule. I recognized, though there were no windmills here, the country of Don Quixote's adventures. We slumped into towns as if the train had suddenly come upon them by accident, so cunningly were they hidden in the creases of the plateau: Burgos, Vallodolid, Medina del Campo, Ávila, Escorial—those names burned into my mind. On the crowded platforms families of peasants camped; it seemed that a population was patiently migrating. There is a line in one of the notebooks of Albert Camus which was made for me: "One of our contemporaries is cured of his torments simply by contemplating a landscape for a long time."

Landscape, the sight of nature, has always had an exciting yet appeasing effect on me. This landscape of Castile caught me at the right time. The landscape of Andalusia is voluptuous. Italy is richer. But here in Castile, far from the sea, one could see the bare flesh and bone of the earth.

The sight of wide stretches of country and sky liberates the mind and lifts some of the load from it. When I was young, especially in adolescence, and aided often by some poem I had read, distant scenes were an extension of my mood and myself, when I saw the lineament of the horizon changing to colors that became impossible to distinguish, until they became frail and transparent as they touched and broke against the sky. There, distance seemed about to speak. But, now in the Castilian scene distance was hard and taciturn. The colors themselves were harsher in the foreground and there was, above all, an exact sight of shape and line. The earth did not fade into the transcendental; rock was rock, trees were trees, mountains were mountains and wilderness was wilderness. There was nothing of the "deeply interfused"; there was something that could be known and which it was necessary to know. There was a sense of the immediate and finite, so much more satisfying than the infinite, which had really starved me; a scene of the physical not of the spiritual. I felt I was human.

I felt also that I was being watched and critically regarded; not so much looking as being looked at. The transcendentalist dream in which I had lived up till then came to an end—or so I believe. I was being cured. It is true that the clarity of the Castilian air which, in summer or winter, flutters against the skin of one's face, was a novelty to a northerner in whose countries mistiness and uncertainty blur the edges of objects and feelings. Here one began to see exactly. I have few recollections—though I must be wrong in this—of seeing the clouds move fast over Castile in the winter or the autumn. I remember only clouds that were still, as if embossed on the sky. I was no more than a mortal jot.

The Spanish language, which is clearly pronounced in all its syllables and all its masculine emphasis in Castile, had its effect on me, and indeed intimately, before I knew a word of it, even on this journey. George Borrow calls it "the lordly language of Castile." I mentioned this in one of my books on Spain, but not the rather absurd personal consequence. The train stopped at Medina del Campo and one of the porters there—who, I afterward heard, was noted for the power and beauty of his voice—called out the name in the measured and resonant manner of the region. Voice and man stuck in my mind. The name was a sentence. I was liable, in the next few years, to nightmares of physical violence in which I was attacked and defeated by terrifying enemies. Then, one night, when I was in France, I dreamed that the porter at Medina del Campo had annoyed me, telling me the train had gone when I knew it had not. I fought and grappled with him and flung him victoriously on to the line before the oncoming train. After this I had no more dreams of violence. I have heard many interpretations of this dream, especially from amateurs of Freud; but, only last year, did the likely fancy occur to me that it had some connection with a childish battle with my grandfather, a very alarming man. I once shouted at him—when I was a child of five and in a temper—that I hoped he would be killed by a train at the level-crossing near Sedbergh in Yorkshire. I got a spanking. I still feel the sting of his hand. Was the station at Medina del Campo the dream scene of a revenge twenty years late, and not one of congested sexual passion?

One of the curious sights of the journey, when darkness came, was the blackness of the dark, the nearness and size of the stars, and the yellow lights, scattered and individual, of distant towns. There was no glow of the motoring age above them. Each light in a window, though it might be miles away, was distinct and itself, as if it were the signal of a person or a family.

In those days you did not make reservations at hotels—or at least I didn't. It seemed to me a loss of freedom to know where one was going to stay. Inconvenience was worth the gamble. Outside the station in Madrid, as in other Spanish towns, small hotel buses waited in charge of drivers who had hurriedly put on their hotel caps and came shouting at one. A small man, one of those Spaniards who look like little monkeys, got us; we ground and rattled over the cobbles out of the North Station near midnight to a rather expensive hotel where the central heating seemed to be puffing out thick waves of hot olive oil. I had caught a bad cold in Paris and my temperature boiled up in the night. In the morning sleet came down. A heavy Spanish meal gave me diarrhea within an hour or two—one of the very few experiences of Beethoven's disease that I ever had in Spain, though I always ate recklessly, especially of the strong dishes. The prices at the hotel were more than we could afford. I had the name of a Spanish lady in the Plaza Isabel Segunda who turned out to be not Spanish but a German who had married a lawyer. He had died a year or so before, leaving her with three young children. Our meeting was eager and mournful. She found us rooms with another widow, an Andalusian from Puerto Santa Maria, who took us in at a small dark flat on the ground floor of a street off the Castellana and there, sleepless because of the all-night banging of the bells of a church opposite and the shouts of the night watchman who trudged the street with his lantern and javelin, I settled down to influenza and days of heavy snow.

. . .

The altitude of Madrid is about 2300 feet, and in the winter the cold is biting and the incessant wind from the Guadarramas is dangerous. My first impressions of the city were gloomy. I had expected another Paris, but here the brisk and gay Latinity were missing. The people in the street, all in black, walked about with a look of long mourning about their persons: the place seemed shut in some pinched and backward period of the nineteenth century, the "modern" itself being long out of date and sad. The cafés were feebly lit, the shops were small and dim. There was the sour smell of charcoal in the doorways, for most people cooked on charcoal, and sat in their houses with their feet on pans of charcoal or ground olive stones; and, even so, in their shawls or coats and with their knees tucked under heavy tablecloths for warmth. In 1924 the Puerta del Sol was still the center of Victorian cafés. Barefooted children ran coughing their lungs out and poor women screamed out the names of newspapers and sold lottery tickets in the wet. One passed enormous cold churches, their huge jawlike doors open, and inside lit only by the altar candles: they seemed to me like warehouses of melancholy and death. In the mornings dozens of plumed hearses went up the Castellana; a large number contained the tiny white coffins of children. At night, many of the men wore long black capes with red velvet linings, and walked muffled up to the eyes with scarves against the wicked wind. The men's faces looked anxious, as if concealing a personal agony; but if a woman was walking with them, it was strange to see that she was large, strong, calm and unmuffled. The women felt no terror of the cold. At this time—in 1924—women were not welcome in cafés. In one or two, a few blowsy-looking ladies might be seen together at the back, but the Madrid streets and cafés were emphatically for men only. They sat for hours, their feet shuffling in the litter of shrimp shells and sugar papers, staring into a glass of water, drinking poor coffee or chocolate and very rarely wine or beer.

My impression was of morose silence; yet this was only half true. The silence of a café was broken from time to time by a sharp clap of the hands: a waiter was being called. If people did talk, they shouted. The city was noisy in the pleasureless way of New York. The ruling noises, apart from clapping and shouting, were the slashing and croaking row of mule teams that straggled across the city; and the scores of small yellow tramcars that inched along in grinding processions. It was common to see twenty or thirty of these traveling boxes jammed up in the center and to be bumped by them as they went clanging up the narrow streets. The ostentatious Gran Via, built out of the enormous profits made during Spain's neutrality in 1914, was far from finished and soon ended in that typical Spanish sight: the vacant lot of baked or frozen soil according to the season.

A man's wealth could be pretty accurately guessed by his size: if he was well off he had a great belly on him; if he was poor he was skinny. There was a large number of fat priests about—I had not seen as many, not even in Ireland—sitting about smoking cigars or playing cards. Madrid had little industry: the place was packed with government employees, most of them obliged to do two or three jobs to keep alive. Delay was the only serious labor. The first two words one heard in Spain were, of course, *mañana* and the shrugging *nada*—the nearest to the Russian *nichevo* in Europe, uttered in all shades of meaning, but rooted in indifference to all egos except the speaker's own.

As I say, these were my earliest impressions in January 1924. I was soon to change them entirely, but I record them because the tens of thousands of French, German, British and American tourists who pour into Spain nowadays—and even those who came to Spain in the thirties at the time of the Republic and the Civil War—can have no idea of what Spain was like in 1924. Only two roads, the Carreterra de Francia and one diverted by way of Extremadura from Madrid to Seville were completely passable. There were not many modern hotels outside of Madrid, Barcelona, Seville and at the Alhambra. The only foreigners who came were a few businessmen, a handful of students from England and Germany and a few tourists who went to Seville and Granada. There were scarcely any motorcars because of the state of the roads. The trains (many of them mixed goods and passenger trains) waited while goods were unloaded and crawled for hours from village to village: and the provinces were so cut off from one another by the mountains of the country (for, after Switzerland, Spain is the most mountainous country in Western Europe) that they lived, felt and spoke almost as separate nations. Madrid was a small city, with only one building thirteen storeys high, and the population was about eight hundred thousand.

I had brought with me the only English books worth reading: Havelock Ellis's *The Soul of Spain,* Borrow's *Bible in Spain* and Ford's *Gatherings,* written in 1840. But in Paris I had picked up a new English book at Brentano's: *A Picture of Modern Spain* by J. B. Trend, who was later professor of Spanish at Cambridge. (I met him months later in Madrid. He was a rosy, precise little man, a sweet-tempered and curate-like figure who concealed a black Protestant fanatic inside him, though that rarely came out.) His book eagerly demolished the Romantic legend of Spain, created by the French, especially by Bizet's (not Mérimée's) *Carmen* and Théophile

Gautier; he also reconsidered the "black legend" in the light of what had been written by the new Spanish scholars, polemical writers and novelists of the "generation of '98." They had reacted violently against the incompetence and illusions that had led to the loss of Cuba in that year.

The late husband of the German lady had grown up among these people; she had lived a long time in Spain and worshiped them—there is no other word. She was young in middle age, with stedfast face and big earnest blue eyes that easily moistened with tears. She particularly worshiped the new educationalists who had sprung up, among them the disciples of Trend's hero: Francisco Giner de los Ríos, the lay saint now dead. They had founded a free school in Madrid; that is to say one in which there was no religious instruction: also the Residencia, a modern attempt to provide a collegiate life, inspired by Oxford and Cambridge. It was run by Alberto Gimenez, the son-in-law of Manuel Cossio, the great El Greco scholar, and had associations with the historians, scientists, novelists, critics and poets—Antonio Machado and the young Lorca, still a student; with great figures like Menedez Pidal and Altamira in history; Ramon y Cajal, the surgeon; Ortega y Gasset, Azorín the exquisite essayist, Unamuno (then in exile), Pío Baroja, Perez de Ayala, and many brilliant journalists such as Luis de Araquistain, who was to become a figure in the Civil War of the thirties. The Duke of Alba was their patron. They were hated by the Church and the new military dictatorship and were the most interesting intellectual group in the country.

The widow was planning to emigrate to the United States because she had been left poorly off; but for a few months, since she knew Spanish thoroughly, she gave me Spanish lessons until I moved to another lady, also a widow, who was Spanish. I learned quickly. But mortality hung over the verbs and participles. The German lady was an exacting and melancholy teacher.

There seems to be a link between the Romantic attitude to death one often meets in German literature and the traditional Spanish cult of mortality; and perhaps my lessons and our trips with her family to the Guadarrama thirty miles away, added to my early sense of the gloom of Spain, for we had grieving visits to every house, and in the mountains to every pine tree where she had been with her husband. Her own flat was in the old part of Madrid near the Plaza Mayor on which the severity of the past was imposed. My other teacher, I discovered, came from a fierce Spanish Protestant family, and since under most Spanish governments this sect has been vindictively dealt with—no sign of their cult is permitted on their buildings—she had the fanatic character of the persecuted. Her grandfather had been a priest of the Franciscan mission in Manila, who had become a convert to Protestantism. Still, she was a nimble, gay if aggressive teacher; and her charming daughter had a far more interesting mind than the usual nice Spanish girl of the time. Both these ladies were agnostics now.

So, in a country even more obsessed by religion than Ireland, though with far greater dignity, I found myself among agnostics. After Ireland, it was indeed a relief. I may have been given an austere and one-sided view of Spain by being so close to a minority movement, but it sharpened the mind. I was beginning to have the most valuable experience of my youth, and many of their ideas have remained with me. I became a humanist. Political reaction and civil war defeated these Spanish friends later. Many of the people I knew were murdered, many more went into permanent exile in France, England and Mexico. They were a tragic generation. In matters of education they were powerfully thwarted wherever possible by the Church, especially the Jesuits, and sneered at by the wealthy *bien pensants*. The accusation—that they were diabolical Free Masons and "freethinkers"—was as off the mark as propaganda always is, but also indicates how archaic the ruling Spanish world was. The word "freethinker" had a bad sound in Spain, not so much because of its irreligious connotation as because it smelled at that time of France, the traditional early-nineteeth-century enemy. There is more common ground between Spain and England and Germany than between Spain and France; there is a breach with the Latin which is strange in a country whose language is closest to Latin.

I often had lunch at the Residencia with the students and professors from the Madrid university, one or two of whom were poets. They were men of conscience and sensibility. They tended to be poor, and their domestic lives were somehow shut away. They did not hang about in cafés, but seemed to follow some scrupulous private footpath of the mind between their classes and their homes. I am trying to convey that what the Spaniards respect is, for them, in some way inviolable. Never have I met academics less incessantly pushing. Their dedication was deeply moral. Alberto Gimenez became the most diffident and yet most discreet of my guides. He was a small neat man, under forty, very dark-skinned, with a very shy quiet voice that crumbled his words in the *Malagueño* way; and his skin, especially round the eyes, was meshed in fine lines and seemed to be filled with hundreds of years of Moorish sunlight. He helped me with books and people, in the tortuous personal manner of the Spaniards; there was that long business of finding the right combination of times and persons, so that to go and see Ortega y Gasset (for example), one entered a sensitive web of acquaintance before one reached him at the right moment. There was something of

E. M. Forster's attitude to the sacredness of personal relationships. I tried to find out what Alberto Gimenez believed in—for the disciples of Giner de los Ríos were mysterious believers: he said he would tell me but not before I was leaving Spain. This took almost two years: an example of the retreat into timelessness which is precious to Spaniards.

I knew that the followers of Giner de los Ríos had been greatly influenced by the minor German philosopher Krauss. I never read him, but I have lately looked him up in the *Encyclopaedia Britannica*. He invented a system called Panentheism, a combination of Theism and Pantheism. The world and mankind are an organism. I can see why Krauss appealed to this Spanish group; first for it is natural for the strong Spanish ego to feel that it contains the universe—a mystical notion —and secondly because Krauss believed, as they did, in working from the individual to small groups of men and finally to man as a whole.

When I did leave Spain, Alberto Gimenez kept his promise. I remember how mysterious his manner was. Yes, he said, he was *almost* a Kraussist. His eyes wrinkled; he hesitated and hesitated as he approached the point of "fineness" which tantalizes the Spanish genius. Yes, he said, Kraussism—but with *"algo,"* i.e., something, mystical. What this *"algo"* was I could never discover.

The disciples of Giner de los Ríos were, in a way, puritans of a sunny kind and indeed there is (contrary to popular opinion which has been based on the gaieties of Andalusia), an ascetic and formal strain in the Castilian character. The country of excess is also the country of abstinence. The counterreformation was austere, and the Castilian temper is open but rigorous. The disciples of Giner de los Ríos lived simply; they rarely drank wine; they hated rhetoric; they abominated

Generals—there were nine hundred Generals in the Spanish Army—and refused to go to bullfights. They had some resemblance to the Russian westerners of the nineteenth century, in their wish for a closer contact with Europe and their dislike of "Africanism." They believed in intellectual contacts with Europe, in studying in foreign universities. Such ideas seem harmless today, for many Spanish students now study abroad; but, in 1924, there were violent polemics against the idea in the conservative press, and there were severe political obstructions, particularly by the extreme clerics: the idea of a university residence outside of religious supervision was anathema. But, as Gimenez used to say, "Wait. They will soon copy us." And, in fact, this eventually happened after the Civil War, and with money the disciples could not afford.

Some of Don Alberto Gimenez's reserve was due to a care to keep the Residencia out of the coarse and corrupt rhetoric of Spanish politics. The place existed precariously; there was the fear that Primo de Rivera would close it down as a hotbed of left-wing disaffection—though the General was at heart a liberal-minded man and did not do so. Don Alberto wrote me a long letter twenty-five years later in reply to something I had written about his movement.

> Minority work is exposed to peril because it does not offer action; because of the mistrust of the public, and the dread of stirring hatred and passions which lead inevitably to persecution, the cruelties and monstrous disorder of civil war. The reformer tends to think "Only the elite knows how to work for the perfecting of humanity and can stop the passions of the masses from preventing a wise progress."
>
> Here the error is that the intelligent elite start thinking of themselves as an isolated body. They forget that they are justified in believing they are superior only

when they share their faith with the masses, and that possessing the light of truth is nothing if it is not shared with all the sons of God.

The Giner group, he said, understood this.

Their minds were awake to the "supra-rational" [*sobre racional*], instinctive, historical life of the people, not simply emotionally, but because they knew that once they lost contact with the masses, the masses would plunge over the precipice like animals and blindly follow leaders who encouraged their lowest appetites.

The Spaniards are a mocking race, especially in Madrid. They made a good deal of fun of the puritanism of the Residencia; of the expeditions to the mountains—which no one visited at that time—in the spirit of science or contemplation; and of the attention to Spanish popular traditions and so on. The "disciples" were closer to a real Spain than the rich whose ideal was Paris and the Riviera.

The name of our landlady was Doña Asuncion. She was a pretty little pigeon with a crackling but gaily tripping voice and a glitter to her eyes. I stayed with her all the time I was in Spain. She came of a family of wine importers who had sent her for a while to a convent in Paris, so we stumbled along in French first of all, though her French was almost incomprehensible to me, owing to her Andalusian accent, a form of fast Spanish where the trick is to leave out all the consonants and to turn as many words as possible into diminutives. It is a witty-sounding speech because of the mixture of birdlike notes mixed with joking sounds that seem to come from a mouth full of marbles. The only times she became vehement were when she attacked the priests and the government. She was a simple Andalusian who almost danced with joy at her memories of Puerto Santa Maria, a paradise for her as Alfaqueque was for the typical, provincial Andalusian lady in one of the plays by the Quinteros. We were crowded in her small flat because she had three young shouting sons. Watching us closely, she saw we were cramped and discontented, and she went out to find another flat in which we could spread. In a week or two, she adroitly and with every kind of cry of excitement moved us all into a larger place in Cuatro Caminos, and there we stayed.

The maneuver was a masterpiece of shrewdness and light-heartedness, a conspiracy also made possible by her maid, Fanny, a rough, good-natured girl from Alcalà de Henares with black hair at the corner of her lips. She sang songs about love and death all day long in the kitchen and could not read. She slept on the floor in a sort of cupboard alcove, as it might be the larder, in the kitchen. She and Doña Asuncion sat on little chairs in the wide empty hall of the flat, which had very little furniture—a table to eat off, a dresser, a few cane chairs and beds—and there they gossiped, unless they were sleeping in the afternoons. The only thing that stirred them was the voice of the eldest son. He was the master. He must have been seventeen and did nothing much except to come out of his bedroom at five in the afternoon and shout the word "water" in a voice like the bellow of an indignant animal. At once, in a panic, Doña Asuncion shouted also: "Fanny! Hot water for the *señorito!*" And to her son, in a terror of obedience: "It's coming now." The boy was about to shave, in order to go out "to pass the time" with his "friends"—passing the time being a central Spanish preoccupation and "friend," a general word for anyone. This was the only part of the day in which something approximating to the idea of a "time" was known in the house. Lunch appeared any time between two and three, dinner any time between nine-thirty and eleven. There was a rush to the stove; Fanny dipped a piece of rag in oil and lit the little charcoal fire in it and then fanned the fumes all over the flat with a straw fan. We were privileged: we had a paraffin stove in our sitting room. The need for these meals took the whole family by surprise every day as if they had suddenly woken up from a long daydream into violent action.

Were they dreaming? What were they dreaming about? The answer is, nothing whatever; incuriously and with vacant and passive pleasure the minutes poured through them like sand in an hourglass that had no hours. They were waiting for some passion, some fiesta or some purely formal request, like the son's shout for "water" or Fanny's floor-polishing, to mark the day. The sun shone and they were alive. If there was bad weather, their faces went greenish and stupefied. And all day one heard Doña Asuncion's long drawn-out sigh—an aye-yai-yai of content and Fanny tried another song.

Doña Asuncion and Fanny were polite (once I knew enough Spanish to talk to them) about my interest in Spain, but they looked upon it as a sort of insanity. Spain was something they cursed as if it were a destiny; and, in fact, to them Spain was a myth, perhaps like original sin, uncalled for and unchosen. In their hearts they knew there was no such country. They were living in "the Spains"—as many as there are provinces, towns, villages and finally individual Spaniards. For Doña Asuncion only Puerto Santa Maria had a real existence; for Fanny, Alcalà de Henares.

One Saturday that first winter when sun and ice are in the light and in the air, I walked to that little town of cold white arcades where Cervantes was born; and where the few people about were muffled against the wind. It was only sixteen miles from Madrid, and this was my first attempt to get closer to that yellowing, sharp-edged landscape. Fanny was stupefied, then she shouted in ecstasy about the fiestas of the town, the young man whom she would marry in a few years, the families there, the superb food, the beautiful drinking water; and in the end called down from the balcony to the maid below, the news that I had seen "her" town.

In the next two years we would often talk about it. At the back of her mind there may have been a doubt, for there is an undying idea that foreigners who come to Spain are "spies" (usually French spies) "making plans," a tradition dating from the Napoleonic invasion. Fanny was a level-headed girl and with a free tongue and without a touch of servility or of malapropism in her. Like all Castilians she spoke her language decently and knew her proverbs. She lived by custom and knew who she was: I do not mean that she was stolid. I am sure that whatever happened to her (and appalling tragedy may have, in the Civil War, or she may have committed savageries as both the rich and the poor did), her identity, as we call it, would have remained with her. It appears to have been built into the race. She carried herself well, with innate pride, but not of the vulgar flamenco sort. And so did Doña Asuncion. In this there was nothing to choose between mistress and maid, and that—outside the *petit-maître* class— was general in all classes. Doña Asuncion was not a practicing Catholic.

There was little in the way of news for a newspaper correspondent to cable from Spain. And if there was anything urgent—the resignation of one of Primo de Rivera's military and naval team, for example—I was certain to miss it, through incompetence. I did try to learn this part of my trade, but I had never been under a brisk editor's hand. I wrote background pieces. I was, I confess, vain of being an amateur. I never visited the embassies and avoided the English and Americans. This was a mistake, for the British Embassy, particularly, had lifelong Spanish experts. Luckily for a journalist, Primo de Rivera was a lazy dictator, bent on seeing that nothing happened in the country. His chief efforts were practical: snubbing the old politicians, seeing about roads, badly needed— and crushing Basque and Catalan nationalism, a permanent obsession of governments in Madrid. I read the newspapers, hung about with South American journalists who, in one or two cases, were novelists and had been Cabinet Minister in their own countries. I went to the international telephone office, which was then scarcely more than a corridor squeezed between a barber shop and a café in the Puerta del Sol. The parliament was closed: I sought out the deposed politicians to see if anything was going on there. Nothing was going on. I became the "stringer" for *The Manchester Guardian* and wrote an obituary notice of the dictator for their morgue. In the evenings I heard the day's rumors from a reporter at the Café Gijon. The story was always the same: jokes about the Generals; soon the King would abdicate because he was directly responsible for the heavy Spanish defeat in Morocco; a coup, even a revolution would occur and there would be a Republic. These events did not occur for seven years, long after I had left. The only foreign correspondent who had a true finger on the Spanish pulse was De Caux, a gentle, skeptical, lazy-voiced Hispanophile who wrote for the London *Times*. He seemed to know every village in Spain and the political bosses of every province with quiet intimacy. He wrote very well. It was a pity that he was too idle and shy to write a book about Spain. It would have been as good and wise as Richard Ford's if he had. He was partly French, but perhaps it was because he was a fatalist that he was so close to the Spanish temper. How terrible the life of the wise is: the Spanish Civil

War broke his heart, and his Irish wife, a very severe and very Catholic lady, went mad.

"How terrible," I said when I met him again in his old age. Tears were briefly in his eyes.

"One learns that life is a tragedy," he said. "One can do nothing against Fate." He considered me gently—I was then in my fifties—and said: "You were inclined to be a little severe when I first met you. You have changed. Everything changes. That is the only meaning of life."

He was right. I *had* become a severe young man. I was alone for long stretches of time in Spain, for my wife was homesick for Ireland. Spanish life repelled foreign women; the lives of Spanish women were strictly enclosed. And I, too, was enclosed in my intense Spanish interests. I would spend the days and nights sitting over an oil stove in the early freezing weather, reading Iberian history, in Oliveira Martins and Altamira. I was deep in the Moors, the re-Conquest, the Council of Trent, the counter-reformation, gripped by a view of Europe and life itself so dramatically opposed to the one I had been brought up in.

One of my earliest efforts in reading Spanish was an autodidact's aberration. Croce was all the go at the Residencia. I got a book of his essays on essences: it is, I think, the first book in Spanish that I ground my way through. I had scarcely heard of aesthetics, unless Roger Fry's theory of "significant form" counts as that. As fast as I had mastered one sentence of Croce, the next one drove it out of my mind. Little notion of his argument remains with me, for I am no thinker or philosopher. But Croce seemed—and this was what kept me going —to convey that it was necessary for the artist to get to the core of his experience. I am sure now that Croce meant something far more intricate than this and probably something very different too. But I made him say what *I* thought, because to strain after the essence of things had become a mania with me. I connected it with the laconic. I have noticed since how often writers totally misread when they admire. I was cheered on because I discovered Unamuno learned English by translating Carlyle—of all people—into Spanish, because he was captivated by his manner.

I come now to two decisive experiences. I have a skeptical temperament, and it was a relief to me that there was no Christian Science Church in Madrid. I had grown sick of Christian Scientists in Ireland. Church services bored me. Alone at this time in Madrid, I started to read Unamuno's *Del Sentimento Tragico de la Vida.* The opening sentences were a violent shock to one brought up on the diluted transcendentalism of Mrs. Eddy:

> *Homo sum; nihil humani a me alienum puto,* wrote the Latin playwright. And I would go further and say, *Nullum hominem a me alienum puto;* I am a man and I regard no other man as a stranger. Because the adjective *humanus* is as suspect to me as the abstract noun *humanitas,* humanity. No more of "human" or "humanity"; no more of the simple adjective or the adjectival noun; only the concrete noun: man. The man of flesh and bone, who is born, suffers, dies—above all, who dies— the man who eats, drinks, plays his part, sleeps, thinks and loves, the man one sees standing before one's eyes and who one hears, the brother, in very truth a brother.

And the agony of this man is that he knows he will die and yet passionately desires immortality. Unamuno's book contains the Spanish paradox: life intensely felt in the flesh and made whole by the contemplation of death.

This is not the place to expound or discuss Unamuno's book. From Spaniards one gets the sense of the whole, not of the divided man. It irked his fellow liberals who were rationalists. He was dangerously personal, irrational, paradoxical, a mixture of Quixote with the mischief of Sancho Panza. His vigor enlivened. He was a Catholic, but of the independent almost Protestant Basque kind, and he even had the nerve to defend Philip II. There was a touch of Chesterton in him, a touch of the Welsh preacher too. He was an excellent essayist. From now on, after my Irish aberration, I was the man of flesh and bone.

Another writer who affected me strongly was the novelist Pío Baroja. I went up to the Guadarrama mountains to Cercedilla and started reading his novel of the Madrid slums, *La Busca*, in the train that crawled hour after hour in the rising heat of June. I had a toothache. I spent the day scrambling up a dry torrent-bed and then walked for miles in the pine woods there and came down at some small *posada* to eat a poor thin garlic soup and two "pairs of eggs," as the Spaniards say. The light in the rough inn was too feeble for reading by; I had to share a room with three laborers and their wives, who kept the windows closed; and in the night my toothache was agony. I walked off the next day with a face blown up like a football. The heat was violent. The only diversion of the walk was half a mile of processional caterpillars as fat as my fingers, who were traveling up the road, head to tail. I killed a few; they joined up again and went on. I sat for hours in a small railway station until the *mixto* came along. It took something like six hours to get to Madrid, shunting and unloading at every station.

So I read *La Busca* with desperate concentration to conquer the pain of the abscess. At last there was an explosion in my head. I spat out a foul liquid; the abscess had burst. I don't think I have ever read a novel with such care, looking up every strange word in the dictionary. And what I discovered was that Baroja was a kind of "essence" man. He wrote in short, accurate, dismissive sentences. His feeling was dry. His attitude to life showed an emotional indifference. He put down with a bleak pungency what he saw. His pessimism, his disbelief and his pity, burned. He was an anarchist.

Baroja had written dozens of novels and was to write dozens more. They were curt reports enlivened by contemptuous opinions. I saw him several times in Madrid, at first in an old house run by his sister. He had pale blue eyes, a flour-colored face, a short beard and wore a beret in the house. He and his brother had run a bakery when he started writing. He had a Wellsian twinkle in his eye.

I went to Pío Baroja's *tertulia*. All Spaniards like to hold *tertulias* in cafés or at home, a meeting of strictly chosen friends (and an occasional stranger), always the same ones, who sit, rarely drinking anything except a cup of coffee, and often not that. Many of these were gatherings of eight or nine distinguished persons whose talk was familiar and also fantastic, but Baroja was fond of surrounding himself with very ordinary people of curious character; a doorman, a minor clerk, were among them. At five in the evening the cafés were full of such groups. There was one café of the Calle Alcalà where one could see a *tertulia* of Generals, another of journalists, another of politicians and so on. The *Madrileños* love to live publicly in small "courts," and it was common at the hour of the *paseo*, between five o'clock and the late dinner, to see these groups walking up and down the street together, slowly, for hours, pausing for a long time when the subject got interesting, before settling into some café. An official would be surrounded by his friends and hangers-on. And there were always spies. The women held their *tertulias* in their houses; the men in the streets. One could see this not only in the capital, but in every town in Spain.

It was impossible to make sudden arrangements in this timeless world in which a person's daily habits were his unchangeable law. You could not say, "Let us do this or that tomorrow or next week," for although there might be enthusiasm for the idea, it would soon turn out that the right "combination" had to be found, a combination depending on waiting for the moment, not of convenience, but of mysterious collective impulse. In the meantime, one waited passively, "passing the time" until, like a sudden fire, the impulse was ignited. It might take weeks and weeks to ignite. The instantaneous habits of Europeans struck Spaniards as an impoverished restlessness of mind.

There is a theory that the mind of the Spaniard is one where the image of an intention and the will to act on it come rarely together; but when they do, then the action is sudden and often violent. The central point of Ganivet, the writer, who first raised the question of the Spanish lack of will after the defeat in Cuba, was really the failure of the image and act to merge. One heard the word *"gana"* every hour; unless the *gana* or wish-will to do something visited one irresistibly, one did not do it. The famous *nada,* or nothing, is related to this. There is a line in one of Baroja's novels that exactly describes this state. It refers to a bird:

> *Parece que busco algo; pero no busco nada.*
> [It may look as if I am seeking something; but I am seeking nothing.]

When in the thirties I came to write a story called *The Evils of Spain,* it was based on a dinner party in which we all tried, and failed, to come to a conclusion about visiting Belmonte, the bullfighter, at his estate, in Seville. Belmonte was with us. The initial difficulty was in choosing our food: after that the matter dissolved into fantastic anecdote. The story is a very accurate rendering of a real Spanish conversation, one of those things that fall occasionally into a writer's lap; but it leaves out the problem of the visit which the collective will found unseizable. The subject matter vanished to the backs of my friends' minds, although they were all for going "the day after tomorrow." The strange thing was that the expedition *did* eventually come off a year later, when I had long given up taking it seriously, indeed I went off alone. The intention was genuine, but it was the sudden arrival of a master-personality, a sort of dictator, that took the group off on their romp. In Spain one is always waiting for a Godot or personality of this kind. Belmonte, the master-technician of the bull-ring, the thin, scarred gypsy with sharp eyes, had earnest intellectual aspirations. He listened with detachment to his future guests and, in a silence, politely asked me what I thought of T. S. Eliot, of whom he had heard. He liked to keep in with "the intellectuals."

7

I n the spring I went off alone by train to Seville to see the Holy Week processions. It was the first time I had been in the south. The white city smelled of roses, jasmine and orange blossom, of olive oil, anis and shrimps. I stayed in the pretty Barrio Santa Cruz listening, after the long silences of the afternoon, to the bugles of the military bands accompany the processions of the *cofradías* to the continual whisper of feet, the trit-trot of the carriage horses. The heat was heavy. In Sierpes, streaked as all the streets were, with the candle-drippings of the *cofradías*, one saw the fat owners of the olive groves or their relatives, their trousers high on their enormous bellies, sitting stupefied by sun in the clubs. It was a wealthy city of bull breeders and olive growers, and a very gay one, given heavily to sherry drinking. In the countryside the peasants lived wretchedly on their eternal gazpacho, dipping their bread into it, a poor meal, but Spanish bread is the best and most nourishing in the world. They lived in huts where the rush walls were beginning to be replaced by the flattened petrol can. There had been savage peasant risings in Andalusia—hence the hatred of the Civil Guard, who really ruled the peasants. I had read and heard about it from Fernando de los Ríos, one of the "disciples." The Anarchists were strong in Andalusia. There was a theory, which had something in it, that the Andalusian ideal was to see how little one could live on, how few one could make one's material wants, an inheritance perhaps of Arab or desert culture: happiness was in the little and the less. The wealthier Andalusians are famous for their parsimony, and if their possessions are great, their way of living is usually simple. A rich man like Belmonte was certainly very frugal.

I stayed with a widowed relation—yet another in my long list of Spanish widows—of Doña Asuncion. The house was pretty and white, its balconies were hung with flowers, and I was given a simple room on the ground floor, with an alcove at the far end in which the maid slept, a fat little girl who snored all night. The daughter of the house was a great beauty, the son was a doctor, busy in his surgery next to my room. (Seville is a bad place for rheumatism.) The mother was a dumpy, shrewd woman who charged me an enormous price for my board and lodging, telling me how lucky I was to find a place at all. I was indeed lucky. She was a real *Sevillana*, placid and proper to look at, but with shrewd, mischievous eyes. She was determined that I should do everything according to formality and custom. I must get up late, drink my coffee, and not shave until five o'clock, for the *paseo*. Before that I would have eaten a heavy lunch and slept.

Afterward, the young doctor and I were out most of the

night. He was a young spark, but a conscientious guide. I wasn't let off a single procession or the singing of a *saeta*. He explained all the time that Seville was the most beautiful and richest place in the world, packed with the wittiest people in Spain. Mockery and tricks play a strong part in the *Sevillano's* character and, of course, Don Juan's love of the boastful phrase. The doctor scored off me continually. His nerve was remarkable. Determined to get me into the *Miserere* Mass at the huge cathedral, to hear the Miserere sung by Tito Schipa, without having to buy a ticket, he pushed me through a back door, with hurried whispers to figures in the darkness, until I found myself planted in the choir, only four places from the archbishop. I felt I had been captured by the Inquisition or had got on the throne in Buckingham Palace. Between two very old priests who were going through their chants from parchment books two feet across, I stood without knowing when to stand up, sit down, pray or go through a pretense of chanting too. Thank God, I had a jacket and tie on, though dressed as I was among all the gold and purple I was a glaring mistake, with the air of a burglar or some creature who would be arrested if caught. Worse, the young doctor had withdrawn and left me to it. I gazed as apologetically as I could at the archbishop, wondering if I should signal excuses, or run. If he saw me he did not show it; after all there must have been a hundred priests in the choir. Presently I was distracted by the old man next to me. He must have been in his eighties and nearly blind. He mumbled, got up and sat down in the wrong places, and was so unsteady that I thought he would fall on me. To the other side of me was another of these saints of second childhood, staggering too. The heat of the candles was strong. The encrusted gold of the choir was heavy and seemed heated too. I sweated and at last the Miserere burst out. It was a full theatrical performance and drove off my panic.

The young doctor and I went off to the Kursaal, the night club with a shocking reputation, and I saw from my *palco* the fat young bloods of Seville, cuddling their mistresses and everyone talking regardless of the singer or dancer—until he came to the crucial technical difficulty of *cante hondo,* when everyone falls silent to see if he does the thing well, for at errors in song or dance the Spaniards shout in anger.

I have often been to Seville since that time. It is a deeply provincial place. The comic spirit of the city is crude. I have seen a respectable elderly man solemnly empty a castor of sugar onto the head of his friend in a café, with careful, expressionless dignity. The *piropos* are notorious. An extremely tall woman scholar, an American, working in the Archives of the Indies in my day, was told by some road workers as she passed to "Come back tomorrow and let us see the other half." In the foreign colony there was an English doctor who interested me, when I met him in his old age. He was an interesting example of what I call the Maugham fallacy in sentimental travel. Maugham has a typical story of meeting a young doctor in England who is tempted to go to Seville as a doctor, but who will be obliged, if he does so, to break his engagement to an English girl and risk giving up a safe medical career in England. Romantically, he decides to go to Seville. There he blossoms as a Silenus and has a string of superb gypsy mistresses: his gamble is a romantic success.

The doctor in Seville was the original—or so he complained—in Maugham's story. I guessed the real story might have other aspects and I went to see him. He had a very pretty house. Now in his seventies, he was irritable.

"Stomach all right?" he said. "Chest? No bowel trouble? You haven't been—er—a naughty boy?"

He was disappointed to hear I was in good health and

looked coldly and defensively at me when I told him I was a
writer.

"We've had them all down here—Hemingway, Maugham
. . ." He ran off a list of popular English and American novelists, riffraff, he said, not a gentleman among them. "I'm the
doctor in Maugham's story. I don't mind the lies—we've all got
to live—but I should like to have what Maugham made out of
me. All of them, for that matter."

Every foreign writer, he said, had put him in their books.
He'd been portrayed as an English spy, as an agent in the Civil
War, a gun runner, above all the scandalous lover of Carmens
by the dozen.

He was a pleasant bald man and there was a look of dog-
gish contempt on him as he swelled with his importance: the
fact that he was a simple doctor and yet had other selves that
roamed the world.

"I don't mind what they said. But where's the economics?
They made a packet out of me. What did I get?"

While we talked—we had gone to a bar—we were being
pestered by a barefooted little girl who knew him well and who
was trying to sell us lottery tickets.

"She knows me, the little nuisance. She knows I won a
damn big prize in the lottery two years ago. When I hadn't a
bean in the world. I tell you frankly, I've been ruined three
times in this country. Sunny Spain! Spanish women! Here,"
he called to the child. "What is the most important thing in
Spain?"

"The peseta!" said the child, quick as a rat.

The doctor smiled for the first time and put his hand in
his pocket, but the hand stayed there.

"I've been here forty years. In the thirties the tourist traffic went in a night. If I hadn't won that prize I'd have been on
the streets."

I bought a ticket off the child and she at once ran off bawling at people getting off a trolley bus. The doctor went on:

"And remember this: when I came here forty years ago I wouldn't have touched the tourist side. We had a very exclusive colony. It was unpleasant for a man in my position, but I was forced to do the hotels—but this last knock was the worst. Not what you expect in old age. I'm down," he said with shame, "to treating Spaniards—the aristocracy. They're the meanest of the lot. It's like getting blood out of a stone."

He had ceased to be a "character" now. He was denuded of his fiction. Presently he said, with malice: "What would you say if I told you who that kid was who sold you the ticket? Suppose I told you that kid is one of So-and-so's?" The writer he named was, at that time, one of the most celebrated of English popular novelists.

"You'd say I wasn't a gentleman. You'd say I was a liar. Anyway, what would I get out of it?"

I realized when I left him that a great revenge on literature was in his docile and offended head. Marked down, watched and stalked by writers, the doctor was turning rogue. Even I might be his next candidate; indeed he was becoming a writer himself.

Usually I traveled second or third class on the Spanish trains, for there the Spanish crowd came in and were good company. Often the women traveled with a pet bird in a cage: everyone took their shoes off, and when they unpacked their large thick cold omelettes, they were careful to offer them first to everyone in the carriage. At the stations, which were often a couple of miles from the towns they served, water sellers calling out *agua fresca* walked up and down in the red dust of the south and the pale dust of Castile. But in 1924 I traveled back from Seville first class, for it was a fifteen-hour journey.

In the next compartment was extraordinary company. There was the stout red-faced figure of Arnold Bennett, wearing a wide-brimmed Spanish hat tipped back on his head, leaning out of the window at every station and taking notes. Stretched out full length covered by a rug, despite the heat, was Lord Beaverbrook, his little monkeyish face glued to a book called *How to Understand the Drama:* and opposite, sitting in the middle of the seat with his hands hanging down between his knees in dismal boredom, was Tim Healy, the old Governor General of the Irish Free State and destroyer of Parnell, a man with the wickedest tongue in Ireland.

My Spanish journeys were many. I often went walking in the Guadarrama Mountains, to Avila and Segovia, staying in the rough inns, sometimes sleeping in the common bed-room on a sack of straw. In the summer three of us walked over the Picos de Europa from Santander, eventually coming down through the terrifying gorge of Cangas de Onis to the fishing town of Llanes, where the local youths stoned us as we walked in. Stoning strangers was not uncommon. In this expedition I did, by accident, the longest walk of my life: nearly forty miles over two high ranges of mountains. There were no real roads, but simply wagon tracks, riverbeds and shepherds' paths which vanished when we got to the top of the pass, and we had to guess our way down. Luckily it was moonlight when we scrambled down the last eight miles and got to a poor inn and slept in a room with a raw goatskin, stinking, drying in the only window. We lived on river trout in the inns. We were not at the bottom of the range and were so exhausted that we traveled by a rattling little diligence with a calf roped to the roof and its groaning head hanging over the side looking in at us. It was the most frightening bus journey of my life: our bones were shaken to bits and we were sick after it.

It was a pleasure to miss an English Christmas and to go off through Extremadura to Cordova, Seville and Ronda and Granada, and then round the coast to Barcelona and back through Aragon. It was a rough journey, especially in Granada where we had to ford rivers and in Valencia where the high wheels of the orange carts had cut ruts a foot deep in the dust of the unpaved roads. They were notoriously the worst in Spain. This journey was done by car, and crowds would gather round us in the towns. We left all our belongings lying in it and no one touched a thing. Unlike the Italians, the Spaniards are sternly honest people. A lot of excitement was caused by the fact that my wife was driving. People shouted: "A woman driving!" and rushed after us. In one large *fonda* where a crowd was having luncheon the proprietress rushed forward, accusing: "Is it true that your wife is driving?"

"Yes. I can't drive."

"Let me see your hands."

The woman took my hands, held them up to the guests. My hands are small. She said: "A man with hands like that could never drive a car."

Spain was too stern to be picturesque though I suppose certain places in Andalusia and the Mediterranean coast might have met the Victorian prescription. That coast is ruined now.

The spring rains drove in to Granada as we left and the dirt or unpaved roads were washed away in waves of red mud; torrents rose to the bridges and flooded the ravines and valleys; the rain drove with a Spanish ferocity. It was usual for rivers to be simply wide beds of stones with only a pool or two of water in them, but now they were rushing floods that washed away the roads. At one likely spot for crossing where the water seemed calmer, we were hailed by a group of wild-looking gypsies a hundred yards away. They had posted themselves there with ropes, hoping for rescue money. They hauled us across, putting up the price high when we got to the middle. It ended in a rowdy haggle, but we got out of it. I had never seen rain so wild and so solid, rain that in fact set the soil in motion, as if the earth were pouring too. It excited me—I was not the driver! And so excited me that a few months later when I was alone again in Madrid and was glad to be off the empty streets where the August heat burns through the soles of your shoes, I sat down at Doña Asuncion's to write my first short story. I had up till then thought of writing mainly as description of landscape. My narratives were packed with mountains, hills and foliage and I ransacked my mind for nouns and adjectives and metaphors to describe them. It is true that I had put an occasional human being in, but the emphasis was on physical description; now I began to put in words of talk. But since I was an attentive listener to peoples' words, the only talk that got into my writing was the simple, commonplace remarks they made to me. Now I had to advance to the very different task of making people talk not to me but to each other.

My trouble was that I had no story to write. I was full of stories without knowing it. The difficulty of the young writer is that he does not recognize what is inside him. My mind really evaded any story I knew. Life—how curious is that habit that makes us think it—is not here, but elsewhere. But I sat down to try because I was tiring of my life as a newspaper correspondent; it seemed superficial and I was not good at it. In my heart I despised news and was confused by opinion. But I remembered all that rain and those gypsies in Granada. I found in the newspaper some account of a gypsy quarrel. Somewhere in this I suspected there lay the most alarming thing in the world: a subject. I called the story *Rain in the Sierra.* It was very short, but it took weeks to get it into shape. A good three years passed before it was published in *The New*

Statesman. I have not read it since for I dread the prose I shall find there and I am rather ashamed of having written on the Spanish gypsy, the corniest of subjects. Still, I had begun.

Halfway through my last year in Madrid I found a Civil Guard on horseback outside the building where I lived. He handed me an official document. It was a summons to appear before a military court: the charge: cabling an attack on King Alfonso to America. I had not done so, but I had written articles in which the strong antimonarchic feeling was reported. I asked Alberto Gimenez what I should do. The important thing was, he said, to pretend not to understand Spanish and to take with me an interpreter, a man I already knew, who was a professor of medicine. He had to pass himself off as an official interpreter.

We went to an untidy back room in a side street off the Gran Via and found a collection of grumbling colonels who were saying the whole thing was a farce. My role was to look stupid and speak French, for my professor did not know any English. The professor adroitly sympathized with the colonels for having dug out a person as ignorant as I was. There was a long wrangle about whether a professor could legally be an interpreter, but the colonels gave in and questions began. I understood the colonel's questions, but I could not understand my professor's terrible French, and the colonel in charge gave me a hard look when he caught me almost answering the question before the professor had translated it. In the end the case was dismissed, owing to the confusion of the professor and myself. Afterward, the professor was very hurt because I could not understand his French, but he saved his honor by saying I had obviously never been in France because he could not understand a word of mine.

·　·　·

My time was coming to an end. General Berenguer who was thought to be plotting against Primo de Rivera was being sent to exile in France. It was the only piece of real news to occur during my stay and, for once, I raced off to see the riot that was expected at the North Station, when the General went off on the night train. It was easy to find him. He was a large smiling man with two deep belts of chin. He leaned out of his carriage window and was waving to a court of admirers. The train moved off. There were shouts of *viva la libertad* from young supporters, who were easily arrested after a scrimmage with plain-clothes men. The moment of violence was heady: I dreaded I would myself shout, and slunk away glad not to be arrested. I have a terror of the rage that might spring up in me if I got into an excited crowd.

This was the end of Spanish news. Primo de Rivera seemed to be there for ever. The only flutter was a revival of the Riff war and I was sent to Spanish Morocco. A gale was blowing at Algeciras and we had a horrible crossing. All the tables and chairs got loose in the saloon and piled up against the portholes, and then swept back. An army officer and a priest kneeled among the debris praying loudly for most of the journey; and the first sight I saw in Africa was the bodies of dozens of drowned mules, swollen with water, washed up on the shore. We arrived in Tetuán by a little train at sunset to the sound of rifle shots from the Riff and Spanish outposts in the hills overlooking the town.

My incompetence and laziness as a newspaper correspondent was demonstrated here. A born newspaperman would have gone in search of Abd el Krim or have pestered the Spanish military for secret information. Or he would have invented. I did find one or two Moroccans and got something out of them, and I did find myself spending a morning in one of those

Moorish houses—so like Victorian tearooms inside—that are in the white-walled alleys. I remember the ballooning pantaloons of my host, his fez, his teeth. An enormous naked Negro lying drunk, dead or asleep was in the gutter outside when I left. I remember too my first ghetto, if that is the proper description of the Jewish quarter, for the narrow streets were squared off like a chess board in order that the district could easily be controlled. The old Jews stood, long-bearded and wretched-looking, at their doorways, among the flies and stenches of the street. I was horrified. I supposed these must have been the descendants of those who had been expelled from Spain in the fifteenth century. I had seen the battlefields of Anual, where the Spaniards had run into disastrous defeat a few years before. Everyone in Spain, especially the poor whose sons were conscripted without chance of evasion, hated the miserable colonial campaign. It was the efficient French who conquered Abd el Krim in the end. I was too soaked in Spain to find this part of Morocco understandable and when, afterward, I was sent to Algiers, Constantine and Tunis, I felt uneasy in the first colonial state I had seen outside of Ireland. Also in Algeria I felt the guilt of being a tourist who is passing through and who is a mere voyeur. I still feel that. Yet there are rewards. In 1946, when I first read Camus I found that something more than a superficial knowledge of his scene had seeped into me when I was twenty-four. And when I look at a Matisse odalesque sitting on one of those ugly Moroccan leather cushions, thick-browed and sullen, small images from the distasteful journey come back to me. I recall the insipid couscous; the French bourgeois lady in the tram in Algiers calling out about the Arab woman sitting near her: "How she stinks, that Arab!"; the cold stoniness of the "bled," the steppe that lies between the hot coast and the cloudy Atlas mountains;

the misery and rapacity of the Kabyles in their villages. And the occasional scenes, when one is incredulous; down the mountain path comes a chieftain-like figure out of a film, riding a pony, with a rifle across his saddle and behind him a veiled lady clinging.

My *Wanderjahre,* though not my travels, were coming to an end: they had only a year to go. The paper was getting tired of my Spanish articles and invited me for a short stay in the United States. I went reluctantly, for I too was getting tired of the writing I was doing. I had been fortunate in being able to travel; but, looking back upon myself at twenty-five, I can see I was a prickly and difficult young man. I was glib and quick to see, but slow to grow; however enlivening it is, travel has the serious defect of taking one away from the stimulus and criticism of contemporaries in one's own country. One is too much alone, too much the passing stranger. And then, my marriage had not gone well for either my wife or myself.

After France and Spain, Boston seemed dead and dreary, except for its spectacular thunderstorms. I hated the Holy City. The American boom was on, and one could not exaggerate the complacency of a people who had been so cut off from the rest of the world by self-congratulation. The faculty of self-criticism was not yet born. I have heard since that Boston was not the place for seeing the Jazz Age and, in any case, I was shut in by my own frustrations. Only two journeys interested me: a short trip when, getting lost in the forest trails north of Quebec, I spent a week or so in a lumber camp among the French-Canadian lumberjacks, bitten to death by the myriad of black flies of the forest primeval, and a long walking journey among the poor whites of the Appalachians.

I went there because I heard one could find traces of Elizabethan English. It was peculiar, but not Elizabethan. The experience became an exercise in writing dialogue: I filled my notebooks with pages of it, covertly written down in the shacks where these poor people then lived. They were docile, half-starved, long-nosed, hospitable Baptists. The men shambled about in jeans and always carried a gun and spoke in a drawl difficult to understand. You simply knocked on a door and they took you in instantly, fed you on what they had—which was salt pork, pastry, apple butter, molasses and black coffee. There was nothing else. The women married at about fourteen, had families of up to twenty children. They were inbred and, certainly, backward. I met a whole creek full of feeble and bony Pritchetts: the patriarch of the tribe said he had "fit" in the Civil War—on the side of the North, of course. Few had ever seen a Negro; I heard no folk songs, but if there was nothing Elizabethan in the language, there were grandiose names. There were Apollo and Leander Bacchus, a Beaumont Starr and Gash Alison who claimed to be a Turk. He was a legend —I never met him:

> Thar haint no one the like of Gash Alison. He's the travellingest man I ever seed. Seemed like as though he jes' went sportin' and broguin' aroun' peddlin'. I haint seed the like of thata one. He jes' went snoopin' aroun' like you uns, peddlin', totin' things on his back and gettin' folk to take him in o'nights. He sure was the talkingest man I ever seed. He used to tell us about Canady and Jerusalem. He uster say thar haint no better water nor the mountain water in the worl'. Hits plumb pure. Thar haint nowhaur Alison haint been.

I wrote it down. The tradition of the American monologue was alive:

Nat'rally thars a sight o'things bin writ that haint never occurred. Like ol' Uncle Durham uster say that every time a story crossed water it doubled itself. Did you ever hear of Phil Morris's defeat? That's a true un. Phil, like the rest of us, was in a kind o mixed-up business. Hit'd be hard to say what kinda business, it'd be with one thing and another and nothin' reg'lar. Waal, we was up in the woods and thar was snow on the ground and the country was mos' friz up. We lit a fire and Phil sits him down offs with his boots to kinda rest up his feet. Waal, during the night, one of them boots get pushed into the fire and burned up. And in the mornin' Phil sent up a great hollerin' and had to take him mocassins out of his leggins and walk back sixteen mile in 'em. An' ever since they have called that place Phil Morris's defeat.

We spent a night in the shack of a family who had left the mountains to work in a cotton mill in South Carolina, but had been thrown out of work. I arrived on the very day they had returned to the shack they had left. It was hidden behind corn grown tall and was almost roofless. There was a husband and wife, their son and daughter and an old woman. We all slept in one room, partly under the stars, and were bitten all night by fleas. The house was ten miles from the nearest store, five miles off the wagon trail, with two rivers to ford, and the little holding was on a very steep hillside. It was in sight of one of the highest peaks in this part, with the fine name of Clingmans Dome. The mountaineers were poorer than European peasants. One saw many deserted shacks. The topsoil had gone. I find a note:

> Beaumont Starr's farm. He left las' spring. Hit was too hard. Siles gone an' wore out an' nothin'll grow in that thar.

We climbed hour after hour through steep woods of pine, balsam and hickory, through maple and walnut, and sometimes huge chestnuts shot like isolated gray columns out of the thickets. We climbed, as I say, from creek to creek, sometimes through woods and thin fields of sumac, michaelmas daisies and goldenrod; the creeks smelled of fallen apples and once we saw a wild girl dressed only in a sack with holes for her head and arms in it, stirring an iron pot of the apple butter with a stick. The walls of the shacks were rarely papered, but when they were, it was with tailors' catalogues and newspapers: and there was usually an iron stove with a pipe going up through the roof in the middle of the room, round which the men would sit on cool evenings, spitting gobs of tobacco that hit the stove with a hiss. We all jawed away contentedly. They knew we had "come over the Waters," but geography was myth to them. Some thought France and England were in the "next state."

When I look at the prose I wrote at that time, I am shocked. What can be the origin and meaning of those bizarre lyrical outbursts, those classy metaphors and finicking adjectives? Here, for example, I am at the top of a mountain in Tennessee:

> From our "necket" we could see our ridge slung like a firm hammock of green from knob to knob, a blue green causeway crossing the water of sky, or broad and churned with green and chopping light like the wake of a steamer. Distantly was Clingmans Dome, with the other gray hosts, while a wide surf of cloud lay fixedly, mazedly upon them. From their highest elevation bannered a stilly chrome wash of startled light.

One must grant the passion for words in themselves: I am not ashamed of that. But what a bombardment! What is the cause of all this show of strength and affectation? Well, youth is the period of assumed personalities and disguises. It is the time of the sincerely insincere. Some of that writing was, perhaps, the expression of unsatisfied or diverted sexual energy; some of it was due to a mistaken notion that one could write as a painter painted: the visual world made a violent impact on me. But I think now that the key reason is that I was beginning to suspect the tameness of my matter, and in a rather shady way was trying to make it more important than it was. I was "covering up." The result is a strange mixture of the diffused, the strenuous and the coy—but why? Because I had arrived at no settled view of life. There was a desire for hardness in the twenties; no bad thing, but even hardness has to be coherent. I had a long struggle with this kind of writing. Naturally, editors were puzzled and bored. I had come out in a rash. They had had enough. Readers felt no need to watch a young writer so patently teaching himself to write at their expense. I went back to Ireland.

In my second time in Ireland, the Romance had gone. The city itself had changed. The Anglo-Irish Revival was thinning out. Yeats had left for England. Soon Sean O'Casey went. One could smell the coming reaction and the dullness of growing religious domination. I became aware of Irish self-destructiveness. I am not much of a roistering man, and long hours in Dublin pubs, where the same stories—getting better and better, of course—go round, did not attract me much.

But I had some time to myself, and Ireland did revive in me the desire to be a writer of stories. I sat down and wrote my second short story: *Tragedy in a Greek Theatre*. It was published at once in *The Cornhill*. I wrote three more: *The White Rabbit, Night in a Corsican Inn* and *The Mad Feller,* about the sick man in Connemara. These had to be rewritten many times, but a year or so later I did find publishers for them. The *Monitor* gave me this leisure, but their saintly patience was running out: my prose was at last too much for them. I was sacked.

This was a disaster, but one of those disasters to which a writer owes so much. It was a liberation.

8

━━━◆━━━

I left Dublin and, after the singsong of Welsh voices at Holyhead, got into the night train for London. The love affair with foreign places was not quite over, but the heart had gone out of it. I was back in England. After the chancy sky of Ireland the English sky looked smoky and glum, and the huge black Greek arch at Euston was a symbol of defeat. I was back where I had started nearly seven years before, with very little money, no job and no prospect of one. I knew scarcely anyone in London. An Irish student at the Slade had lent me his back room in Charlotte Street and when I got to it the excitement I had felt in those two happy years in Paris came back to me. I was alone. My wife joined me later. Now I could make a real beginning.

The room was separated by double doors from another

used by two girls who were painters, and was large and dirty. The floorboards were bare. The place stank of mice which scampered out of a safe where stale food had been left; the sour smell of old tea leaves came out of a sink in the corner; there was a gas ring on the floor by the cracked marble fireplace and there was a cane-seated folding bed. On the first night, when I got into it the two ends folded over me and trapped me: I was still caught by the leg when I struggled out. There was a small table against a wall and a chair, and a big gray-lined box with doors to it at the side, with the name Colonel Guise painted on it—part of the traveling equipment, I suppose, of some officer in the Indian army. The only elegance was a towel rail in mahogany. It was later claimed from me by an earlier occupant who had left it behind a few years before. I did not know that I had come to live in the quarter of London occupied by many well-known artists. I was to hear the names of the Bells, the Woolfs, Duncan Grant: I did not know anything about them.

One looked out of the back window at the low roofs of small workshops where lathes whined all day, and on a dogs' home. The dogs barked at the howling London cats half the night, and women came to windows and shouted down at them. Some threw things. In the next year or two I moved about among such rooms in Fitzroy Street and Charlotte Street, but never reached the distinction of Fitzroy Square at the top.

Most of the cement-colored Victorian houses were let off into rooms for tailors, cabinetmakers, picture-framers, small craftsmen, and as studios. Italian grocers kept stores of wine and food in the basements. The population was a mixture of French, Italian and Swiss and Cockney. These houses usually had only one lavatory and there was competition among workers and tenants to get into it. The situation at a framer's called Drowns was made indelicate by young apprentices who sat kicking the pedestal, smoking or whistling half the morning. At night it was not uncommon to see a policeman struggling on the pavement with a man he was arresting while the small hostile London crowd stood by watching fair play. The only time I saw a crowd moved to action was when two women were fighting. One knocked the other down and made to stamp on her face, at which the men advanced and roared out "No" and pulled the woman off. London has a deep regard for the rules. There were several cases of D.T.'s. I remember a man racing along demented driving off imaginary rats from his throat.

The houses had their special smells; one of my rooms was over a flat and cellar which seemed to be full of cheese. The Italian owner hired a Rolls-Royce and chauffeur every weekend and went off with his huge, high-tempered English wife to Southend. Returning on Sundays they had drunken rows. He was a timid old man who begged me to pay him in the cellar, where he worked among his cheeses and his wine, in case his wife should get at it. Many of these houses were infested with fleas and some of them with bugs. One Saturday I caught thirty fleas on my leg and, going out to the chemist's to buy sulphur candles to kill the plague off, I was told that every chemist in the neighborhood had sold out. It was a street of very cheap Italian and French restaurants—lunch at Vaiani's cost 1s. 10d. I used to see Prince Mirsky there, reading for his *History of Russian Literature*. At Losseneggers lunch was 11d. Most are Cypriot-owned now and are very expensive and fashionable. Bertorelli's alone retains the old Charlotte Street character; it was reckoned cheap then, but was a few pence beyond my means.

My wife had had a success at the Abbey Theatre, acting in a play by Martinez Sierra; when she eventually came over to London she got a small part in a repertory company. Our money was running out. I applied for every journalistic job advertised, never failing to give the useless information that I was good at French and Spanish. I tried the weekly reviews that had published one or two things of mine; nothing came of it for a long time. I wrote to the editors of all the other weekly reviews—there were about eight—sending them samples of my writing. I had been reading *The New Statesman* for two or three years, and I picked out a sketch of two Dublin tailors. After six months the literary editor, Desmond Mac-Carthy, wrote to say he could not publish it, but would consider anything else of the kind I liked to send. I was down to my last few pounds before my luck changed.

A school of languages in Oxford Street advertised for a translator. I went down Charlotte Street to the offices. A number of shabby men—teachers and translators—were hanging about on the stairs. I found a girl sitting at a typewriter and chewing gum. An elderly Greek was shouting at her. My arrival stopped the row. The Greek considered me, hissed questions and gave me a Spanish business letter to translate. It was simple. I was taken on. I went back to my room to translate a dozen business letters from French and Spanish at the rate of ¼*d.* per English word.

Excellent English language! It takes at least seven English words to render four from the Latin tongues, and one could add a few polite forensic phrases. I made the sentences long. Back in Charlotte Street, my landlord was on the doorstep waiting for the rent. He was at war with many of his Bohemian tenants: there was a tale that one could palm oneself off as one of the distinguished painters if one put on the right manner. He let me off this time; the next time he was rude; the third time I was able to pay him. I had graduated: the Greek gave me a pile of foolscap documents each thirty pages long, which were specifications for the laying-out of airfields in

France, Switzerland and Spain. For a few weeks I made anything from £1 10s. to £4 a week. Then it all came to an end: I have bad handwriting and, impressionistic as usual, I had failed to consult a technical dictionary.

I went to see Leonard Huxley, who had published my *Tragedy in a Greek Theatre* in *The Cornhill* magazine. I had been paid the decent price of twelve guineas for it, and I had got another two guineas when it was published in E. J. O'Brien's *Best Short Stories of the Year*. Leonard Huxley was then in his fifties, a tall, talkative figure, a Greek scholar and Alpine climber, with fanciful gray whiskers. Like all the Huxleys he was mellifluously well-educated. For an hour or so he poured out charm, quotations and classical references very fast, and I see now that what attracted him to my story was that it was set in the Greek theater at Taormina: he assumed I was a Greek scholar too. The subject of the story was close to me: a painter is made to turn out commercial muck by the hotelkeeper to whom he owes money. Huxley turned down my next story, indeed it was never published. It was about the seduction of a housemaid in Cheshire. (*Vieux jeu*, he said. His published letters show that he was very shocked by his son's novel, *Antic Hay*. I enjoyed its blasphemies and ribaldry.)

The disquisitions of Leonard Huxley were followed by the languid and studied aesthetic manner of Edward O'Brien. English short-story writers owed a lot to his interest. He was an American expatriate and a mixture of the dilettante and the man of business. His fine pale blue eyes were like stones. I had up to now got on better as a writer with Americans than with the English people I knew: the English seemed always to have been at Westminster or Eton or Bedales and Oxford or Cambridge. They had acquired a standard precocity. They offered me that sociable, ironic discouragement on which they had been brought up and on which English intellectual society had tested its wits for generations. O'Brien's advice was American and practical. He told me it was indispensable to meet the "Bloomsbury Group." I had never heard of it. I didn't even know *The New Statesman* had a connection with it. He said I must live in Bloomsbury. I was not sure where Bloomsbury was, but was too proud to say so. He also said I should live if not in Bloomsbury then in Cliffords Inn, where very cheap rooms—once occupied by Samuel Butler—could be had. I was put off by these strategic suggestions. I know it is the habit of many young writers to attach themselves to distinguished elders, but I was too proud to do so. I left him, got a map of London and found that I lived in Bloomsbury without knowing it, or rather just across Tottenham Court Road from it. Cliffords Inn, I discovered, was fully occupied by well-off lawyers.

I did manage to write one or two very short stories for *The Manchester Guardian* on Irish and Spanish subjects and I was lucky with a weekly review called *The Outlook*. The literary editor was another American expatriate, Otto Theis. He got me to write one or two short sketches and he went carefully through my prose, weeding out my wildest metaphors. He and his wife, Louise Morgan, were a great help to me. I was allowed to write a review of *The Notebooks of Nathaniel Hawthorne*.

And then there was the benevolent Mr. Bassellthorpe. He was worried about me and was distressed by my tastes: did my admiration for Aldous Huxley, D. H. Lawrence mean that I was obsessed with sex? I did not care to say so, but I thought sexual frustration poisoned mind and body. Mr. Bassellthorpe had noticed a strain of satirical pessimism in my writing: that, he said, was natural to youth. But my pessimism was not of that kind: it was the expression of the dislike of the bland, meaningless optimism in which I had been brought up in a quarrelsome home, and if my bitterness was a defect there was energy in its comic form. He forgave me, but with discomfort. I thought I might collect some of my sketches of travel and publish them in a book, and he said he would help me there; in the meantime, it occurred to him there was a minor job I could do. The pay was scarcely £1 a week, but the duties were light and a writer ought to have a steady job to fall back on. Perhaps, eventually, I might review books. After one of his well-chosen lunches, washed down by a glass of tonic water, I was given the job of the Hon. Librarian to the Bath Club.

The first difficulty at this exclusive London club was that the members expected to find there a dozen or more new books every week and were always exasperated by the librarian's choice. The second was that the club's library catalogue was years out of date and that members took out the books and didn't return them. I would have to "chase up" the members: from their point of view—many of them hunting men—this would be like the fox chasing the hounds. There was a committee meeting once a month under the chairmanship of Lord Desborough. I had to attend.

The Bath Club was a grand place. A number of its members were racing men or the sporting rich. They were keen on erotica, so keen that a French novel called *La Garçonne,* popular because it contained a page or two on sexual penetration, had to be kept, with several others, locked in the secretary's drawer. I was not allowed to lunch at the club, except by invitation of a member. One, who was a member of the library committee, saw hope in me; he was an expert on porcelain and a man keen on getting the members off books on hunting, shooting, fishing, murder and sex and on to ceramics and cultural subjects. At committee meetings I was expected to put in a word of support. This made me suspect to Lord Desborough, a distinguished and wily gentleman of the "old school" and a great friend of King George V. My ceramist had only to say that some antiquarian work ought to be bought for the library, for Lord Desborough to damn the proposal shortly by saying the King had just shown him, for example, an "awful nice" little book about wild duck, with color plates, or something of the kind. The ceramist tried once to outflank Lord Desborough by saying: "It's a scandal. There isn't a decent atlas in this club." And, considering the extent of the British Empire at that time, it was.

"What do you mean, not a 'decent' atlas?" said Lord Desborough.

"I mean a really good one, where you can see the detail." What detail did the ceramic expert want to see? The ceramist wanted to see, for example, a decent map of Arabia, the exact position of the archaeological sites, wadis and oases. That, Lord Desborough said, sounded like a damned big atlas. The ceramist said, Not enormously big. How big? said Lord Desborough, bringing out his guns. One you could put on a table and look things up in, said the ceramist shakily. What did he mean by a table? What size table? Like the one we were sitting at? Lord Desborough asked. It was a large table. The ceramist hesitated. "Well . . ." he began.

"Take four footmen to lift it," said Lord Desborough. We slid off the interest in atlases and it was here that Lord Desborough played the trump card I have mentioned: that "awful nice" book about wild duck the King was so keen on.

I had collected my sketches. Mr. Bassellthorpe had a publishing friend who would like to see them—a Mr. Hicks-Flannell. I went to see this sad and intelligent man briefly one foggy evening, when I found him poking a low fire in his lodgings. He was skeptical. One thing about his appearance discouraged me: like Mr. Bassellthorpe he wore button boots. But, unlike Mr. Bassellthorpe, Mr. Hicks-Flannell was lean and melancholy. He had the fated look of a bookish man resigned to the disappearance of the remains of a small private inheritance. God would never fail—would never dare to fail—to answer the prayers of Mr. Bassellthorpe. He would just nod His head, acquiescing in the unassuming regularity of his views; perhaps even flattered. In an evangelical way, God was just a bit of a snob. Mr. Hicks-Flannell's prayers would be treated parsimoniously, simply because they were anxious. He talked of the hopeless prospects of a collection of essays. My manuscript came back in a week. He had shown it to his partner, a Mr. Eddie, who had instantly turned it down.

I was not surprised. The stuff, I saw, was thin and scrappy. Twenty years later I met Mr. Eddie for the first time in a night club. He was elderly and had given up publishing. He had retired to the seaside. He said if he had only known! "Frankly," he said, "if you had only not come through Hicks-Flannell."

This was news to me. Frankness in Mr. Eddie made him look shady. He was a pale, round, obsequious man with a psalmy voice, combined with the manner of the racing tipster, a man free with unction and binoculars. He dropped, from time to time, a confiding aitch—Icks-Flannell, for example. He chattered on. It seemed that Mr. Eddie could not forgive Christian Science for being issued under the imprint of a name so close to his own. He made his partner responsible for the irritation. If Mr. Hicks-Flannell brought in the ms. of a book on Greece he suspected that he was pushing it for religious reasons, so he would say (he giggled at this) that he'd just got a much better book on, say, Turkey, by an atheist or a Buddhist. The partners were engaged in religious warfare.

How did writers and painters manage to live and yet keep their independence? How did my elders, D. H. Lawrence, Katherine Mansfield, Aldous Huxley, live? My crisis was becoming desperate. I could not go on drifting. But I had another stroke of luck: I managed to sell a secondhand car I had had in Dublin for £60. My wife and I split the sum in two. It was capital.

The thing to do was to write an original book of travel. I had just read D. H. Lawrence's *Sea and Sardinia* with despairing admiration—despairing because why was he so "inside" his subject and I so brittle, cold and "outside" what I was writing about? Through what defect of character, and especially of feeling, was I so shut in upon myself? But there was a lesson I could follow: the short, compact subject, made personal. I got maps and decided to walk from some spot in the south of Spain to the north, and to write of nothing but the walk. Because I had little money—and had to save some for my return—I had to shorten the journey. I decided to take a ship to Lisbon for economy's sake and walk from Badajoz to Vigo, through a part of Spain that was little known and, in patches, was notorious for poverty. It was also the route of Wellington's armies, though that historical interest was incidental to me. So, taking *Tristram Shandy* with me, and fortified on the way by thrillers by E. Phillips Oppenheim, which I found in Catholic bookshops, I walked across Spain.

I have described it all in *Marching Spain*—note the deliberately ungrammatical, protesting, affected title. Though I have a tenderness for the book and think some pages rather good, I am glad it has been out of print for forty years. The few people who have read it give me a knowing grin now. I don't blame them. It has a touching but shocking first chapter of exhibitionist prose; but despite the baroque writing of the rest, the mistakes of fact, and the declamations, it is original and has vigor. It is the work of a young man worried almost to illness by lack of money and by the future for a lot of the time. As he tramped along he was doing accounts and stamping out his anxieties with his heavy boots. I posed as a photographer working in the picture post-card trade. In the book I was purposely silent about knowing Spain already because I wanted to preserve an instantaneous impression; and indeed in the stories and criticism I was to write later on in my life, the instantaneous and "first sight" of the object has been my infatuation. Critics have noted a preoccupation with religious cranks, thinking that because of my upbringing I must have sought them out. This is not so. I had little religion left. I am always eager to listen to anyone. My first encounter, simply as I walked down a street in Badajoz, was with a group of Spanish evangelicals.

The weather was good. The sun burned. The nights were cold. I was strong. I did my twenty miles a day, slept in simple *ventas* on the stone floor—after I had sat round a stick fire with the family and ate what the women fried there. The poor were more interesting than the well-off, and the Spanish poor did not whine. They were whole in their manliness and womanliness. I once shared a pigsty with very clean piglets. Food was very scarce. I lived on "pairs of eggs" and bread, except in the towns, where I made up for it. I found a dirty inn only once. It was in a large village, used by commercial travelers—who peddle from village to village—where the pillows were soaked in years of their old hair-oil and the sheets sour with sweat. I got to the Tagus, deep and golden in its gorge, one evening and there I was badly poisoned after eating a powerful garlic stew with some railway workers at a hut on the line. I recovered after a terrible time in Palencia where, in the middle of the night, I saw the cook asleep in his cotton "combinations" snoring on the kitchen table. I crossed the Gredos mountains and sat on the roadside talking to the traveling shepherds of the *mesta* and listening to the sheep bells; then further north the weather broke, the rain washed the road away, and I got one of my spectacular bronchial attacks. I gave up at the last stretch to Vigo, for I had grown weak; and in Vigo I had just enough money left to get a comfortable bed for a few days. The guests in the dining room were startled by the graveyard cough which has been my pride since I was a child, and I sat all day staring at the superb bay of the seaport, waiting for the boat home, counting my money over and over again and down to one glass of beer a day. A South American on the boat went the round of the ladies lifting up his shirt to show them the scars of his operations. He had a success.

Back in London I moved from one furnished flat or room in Bloomsbury to another, taking places because people were away for few weeks. I wrote chapters of my book, now here, now there, and managed to get bits of it published as I went along in the *Guardian* and weeklies and finished it in a room above the Italian grocer's in Fitzroy Street. (A good deal of this neighborhood was destroyed by bombs in 1940: this house went too.) This room was unfurnished. I got my books out of Ireland—there were six hundred by now—and a carpenter made a bookcase and also a table, to a Spanish design. I bought a birchwood chair with a high back. I still work in this chair; this furniture made me feel I really was an author. I clipped my papers to an old atlas—I moved to a pastry board when the atlas wore out. Stability at last. Here I finished the book, and a new young literary agent, A. D. Peters, found me a publisher at once: Victor Gollancz at Ernest Benn's. I was to be one of his notably unsaleable young authors, impervious to all his enormous advertising could do for me. He advanced me £25. That paid for the furniture.

I was writing the book one steaming afternoon when in came a figure from my past: my remote past, for when one is young three or four years seem like thirty. This was Basil Shaves, no longer the rolling *boulevardier*, but fitfully playing the part of the brisk businessman and member of a Bohemian club. His state was still trance-like. My poverty jogged him into nostalgia for a minute or two. I was eating an apple and threw the core out into the street; he admired this gesture of a carefree life. After his bad luck at the bank in Paris, as I have said earlier, he was selling women's wear to small shops in the suburbs of London. He had hung around theatrical agencies first of all, showing them his notices of *Fanny's First Play* but, as he apologized to me: "I'm too old." His hair was curly gray now, he was stouter and suetty; but he still broke out into a line or two of his Italian arias. When he heard I was writing a book, his well-known phrase came out: "Well, what d'ya know!" He liked being a salesman. He loved his little house in the suburbs. He adored England. He was home! My brother told me that customers rang up and asked who this opera singer was. He sang orders out at them.

I promised to visit him, but put it off from week to week until one day I had a message that he was ill. I found his villa —"my little English home"—on a new building estate where the roads were still stretches of rutted wet clay. There he was, in his pajamas and dressing gown, and he showed me around. But, presently, when we sat down, he got up again and switched on the light, though it was daytime. He left the room and went round switching on the lights all over the house, came back and said irritably: "The lights are on," and went off again and switched them all off. After that he went upstairs. His wife said he'd gone to bed; he had a temperature. But down he came, switching on and off, and said "hullo" to me as if he'd never seen me before. I reminded him of "Cutts of the Cruiser What-Not." He was puzzled. He'd never heard of it. I recited it to him.

> *When homeward bound*
> *My old ship runs aground*
> *I love it, I shriek with glee.*

Mr. Shaves did not smile. He was dying. He had had a stroke a week or two before and had been found wandering lost in the streets. In two days he was dead.

Marching Spain appeared in 1928 and was briefly parodied by two painter friends, under the title *Reaching Slade*. The first review was in G. K. Chesterton's paper, *G. K.'s Weekly*. A whole page was given to it. The reviewer picked up his merry knife and plunged into one of his funniest feats of satirical butchery. He portrayed me as a lunatic juvenile prig, dressed in Shaw's jaeger suiting, a teetotaller, probably belonging to the Ethical Church, given to vegetarianism, eugenics, birth control, an ignoramus in religion and a wrecker of the English language. I had upset him by an aside on Spanish pictures of the Crucifixion which, he said, I made to seem like a bloody morning at Smithfield Meat Market. The last was a fairish comment, for even now the cult of pictures of the Crucifixion—especially the Spanish—horrify me. The sadism, so marked in Christian history and especially in Spanish history, shocks me. But I took the point: that taste and sensibility were not as strong in me as I thought they were. I know I had blustered—though not in order to attract public attention but, naturally enough, to attract my own attention to myself. It was myself I was addressing privately as if I were looking at some lost stranger.

I was not upset by the review. It was long and witty and as full of exaggerations as indeed my own book was. I have always suspected that it was written by that very original English humorist, Beachcomber; himself a stout Bellocian walker in the Pyrenees. The next review was in Leonard Woolf's *The Nation* and had all Bloomsbury's acid scorn. Crude; small beer, they said. True enough. It was the kind of review that makes a writer wince; but I had the vulgar instinct for survival. Another reviewer reproached me for ignoring the upper-class Spaniards and concentrating on the poor. Desmond MacCarthy's *Life and Letters* praised the book. My excesses were passed over as youthful follies and the writer ended by saying I knew the Spanish people well and that Belloc and Borrow would gladly "find a chair for [me] at their table in the inn." The reviewer of the evangelical *British Weekly* liked the Protestant tone and announced that I was "a genius with a brain packed in ice." I have talent, but no genius, yet the phrase was a near-miss. I *had* intended my images to have a hard, icy and brainy flash. I had always liked Meredith's "brain-stuff" and I was growing up in a period that taught hard detachment.

The winter was cold and foggy. I was invited to a publisher's party—my first—in Whitehall Court. I knew no one there. A white-haired woman screamed at me: "What is the most exciting experience you have had in your life? I will tell you mine. I once swam over a volcano." One of the young partners of the firm said, looking up at the ceiling of his flat: "This room is very high." Another partner said: "This room is very large." I was glad to get out of the crush and went out into the fog to study the posters announcing Bodies Found, outside Scotland Yard, then walked back to my cheese-flavored room in Fitzroy Street. The book sold six hundred copies and was soon remaindered. Another innocent publisher issued it in a pocket edition in 1933; it was remaindered once more. Still, I was an author.

And I was an author with a contract. I was to have £25 for a volume of short stories and £50 for a novel, when I delivered them. But how in the next two years was I to live? I could not survive as the librarian of the Bath Club. I would have to be a spare-time book reviewer. It did not occur to me that there was any other solution. I was warned: "Once you use book-reviewing as a crutch you'll be on crutches all your life. You'll never be able to throw them away."

The brotherly Mr. Bassellthorpe, so uncertain of me, so fearful of my tendencies, but so indulgent, gave me what I needed. He gave me a small regular job of sending out two or three books to English reviewers every week or so, for his paper. I had also to do a review myself. I was paid £5 a week and kept the job for years. Indeed until in the thirties I wrote *The Saint* and was sacked for good. The task was easy: the paper's moral attitudes enabled it to find most of the important imaginative literature of the early part of the century unsuitable for review. Pound, Eliot, Joyce, Huxley, Lawrence were ignored. The imagination, especially the modern, upset Mr. Bassellthorpe. But history, biography, politics, travel and general literature were pretty safe. Many reputable English scholars and essayists—in my time—H. M. Tomlinson, E. H. Carr, Richard Church, Harold Hobson and some survivors of the nineties, contributed. Many still do. I imagine the paper has mellowed. Even so, though £5 a week was a godsend, it was not enough and, of course, I wanted to write something of my own. I had managed to get *Rain in the Sierra* published in *The New Statesman*. I asked to see the editor.

· · ·

In 1928 *The New Statesman* was edited in a shaky building only too conveniently next door to a little pub in Gt. Queen Street. The review had been founded in 1913 by the Webbs and by Bernard Shaw to propagate very seriously the new ideas of Fabian socialism: its circulation was small; it had lost money for fourteen years and its wealthy backers had to subsidize it: but Fabian socialism was the rising idea. Unlike modern tycoons who wish to buy a sudden respectability and who treat journals as commercial products to be played about with and quickly dropped, the backers of *The New Statesman* were firmly dedicated. But the payments to the writers were meager even when they were famous, and there were periods of crisis when from week to week one did not know whether the thing would close down: the pugnacious editor, Clifford Sharp, a domineering and hard-drinking man, was reckless of libel actions. The literary editor, Desmond MacCarthy, was noted for his charm and indolence and when I went to see him, he was not there. He had not been in the office for months.

I was taken to a shabby top room of the building where there was a third- or fourth-hand desk, a couple of chairs and a sofa with broken springs, on which people sometimes slept. The most solid object in the room was a gas meter. I met here the temporary editor, S. K. Ratcliffe, an impish middle-aged man, well-known in Fabian circles and who lectured at American universities. (He was a Scottish pedant too; for years he would send me post cards of praise or blame, but making a list of grammatical and printers' errors and of incorrect punctuation. If I talked on the radio he would send a card saying, perhaps, "Breathing rather heavy on second page.") Now, at our first meeting, he said: "What did you read at the University?"

"I've never been to a university," I said. I thought I was done for. Mr. Ratcliffe bobbed up gaily in his chair.

"Totally uneducated," he said. "Like me. I didn't go to one either."

That was a relief. We chatted, and presently he became mischievous. He left the room on tiptoe with me and said to a very severe Cambridge girl who sat in a little office like a lavatory: "How is he?"

The girl shrugged coldly. She was tall and stern and had corn-colored hair.

On tiptoe again Mr. Ratcliffe nipped across a passage to the editor's door and listened; then he went in and soon came jumping out like a naughty boy and whispered: "Go in. He'll see you."

Clifford Sharp was a massive man, red in the face, handsome, a glaring editorial chunk, full of drink. He sloped at his desk. On the wall was a poem in large letters; I think it was by Belloc:

> *Thank God you cannot bribe or twist*
> *The Honest British journalist.*
> *But judging what the man will do*
> *Unbribed, there's no occasion to.*

"You've been in Spain?" he said thickly. "There's a book by a young man called Pritchett. Will you review it?"

"I wrote it," I said. He grunted with anger and suspicion.

"Well," he said, "go away and talk to Mr. Ratcliffe."

Outside Mr. Ratcliffe gave a skip of delight.

"I've got just the thing for you. Do me a hundred fifty words on the history of the Coptic Church. Do you know anything about it? No? That's good. Look it up."

Ten shillings for that. A few months later I advanced to

six hundred words on Galdos and the Spanish novel. £1 for Galdos. The lure of book reviewing is that you can sell the books at half price—a matter that explained why one or two down-and-out journalists came in and did short notices on out-of-the-way volumes. In a year I had moved up to an expensive *Life* of Columbus, for I had read a good deal on the Spanish discoveries and on the opening up of the Americas. These became my specialities. But once more disaster threatened *The New Statesman*. Clifford Sharp's drinking made him reckless. He libeled the Commissioner of Police: the paper's sponsors, the Webbs, the Shaws and Arnold Bennett had to pay up. Ratcliffe went off to America. A rolling and eloquent boon companion of Sharp's (Clennell Wilkinson, who had lived in Egypt and Africa) became literary editor, a fellow with a husky voice who had written a *Life* of Dampier. He belonged to the group of older journalists who had taken up the tavern habits of Belloc and Chesterton. He arrived in the office with the martyred look of a man whom God had heartlessly appointed to save the whiskey business from bankruptcy; he had been cursed, he said, with an illness called "waking up in the morning two double whiskies under par." In his conversation strange protests would go off like gunfire. One I put into a story: "Bloody white women in Africa crawling about taking photographs of poor helpless wild animals. Damn cruel. Poor animals sooner be shot—what?"

That final "what?"—softened to a husky, injured "wha . . . ?" marked him as a surviving Edwardian. He did not last long. Sharp's final aberration—for he died soon after—was to appoint an Anglo-Catholic Fabian called Ellis Roberts. He was like a soft fat cooing priest. When Kingsley Martin became editor they soon quarrelled and he left. Kingsley hated religion.

The paper's most talented young man was G. W. Stonier,

who wrote about Flaubert, Kafka and Joyce and about films, under the pseudonym of William Whitebait. Stonier, a year or two younger than I, was a sharp and candid critic with an excellent eye for the delicate and bizarre in vulgar events. He was an eccentric who came into his own in the Blitz. He wrote the only comic book I know about it. He became a great friend. He astonished us all by going to live in Africa a few years ago.

I write here of *The New Statesman*'s early days. I saw little hope of more than a guinea or two now and then. For the next twenty years one had to work for other papers in order to afford to write for it. I managed to write for *The Fortnightly Review,* which published two or three short stories of mine. It was necessary to write a very long story to complete a book. Reviewing did not give me enough money for living in London, and so I moved to a cottage in the hills above Marlow. I became the novel reviewer for *The Spectator,* the rival weekly which in those days was far more prosperous than *The New Statesman.* My life became a shade less precarious.

And so I became a literary journalist of highbrow tastes who lives in a country cottage because it is cheap and who divides his time between reviewing and doing his "own work."

In the country one is outside literary circles, and I have rarely been intimately connected with them. There is a disadvantage in not being a paid-up member of a set in England, for one's continued existence is a surprise; and sets give their members publicity. But in the long run they become little parishes of mutual admiration; they corrode the independence of criticism, and the novelist or storyteller—unless he is satirical—is taken further and further away from the ordinary life he has sprung from. One advantage of country life is that it gives one time, for there is little distraction. One cannot pick and choose one's neighbors, and slowly, seeing them month in, month out, one sees them in the round; in the country people reveal themselves without intending to do so. Conversations are longer, and in this relaxed life it is easier to let the bucket down into the unconscious. For most novelists there is far too much opinion in cities: a little is necessary but it goes a long way.

The cottage where I lived was a little flint place about three miles up in the hills from Marlow. The nearest house was a bungalow which often changed hands—and some odd specimens occupied it from time to time. One of these, for a while, was a very dry young Scot, a classics master at Charterhouse. Most of the week he was alone and he would drop in and propound jokes about English history: he was tirelessly trying them out and refining them. They were the joint work of himself and a gay friend in London who sometimes came down. A pretty, chain-smoking girl with a rude tongue, a disturbing wink and an awful cough used also to come down to their parties. It emerged that the schoolmaster and his friend were writing a funny book together and quarrelled so much (the girl told me) that she had once thrown the manuscript on the fire. I don't know if this was true; but once when she was alone there she accidentally burned out some of the furniture when she had fallen asleep over a cigarette. The springs of the chair were thrown out on the lawn, which she dug up when she was burying tins. The book was 1066 *and All That.*

When my wife was away acting in a repertory company in the north of England we found a down-and-out sailor in London who came down to look after me. A long time afterward, years indeed, some of these events became the basis of a story called *The Sailor.* It was at Marlow that the evangelist in *The Saint* fell into the water.

These stories have been thought well of, but they were

written later in my life; in Marlow they were fermenting in my mind. My task was to finish a long story called *The Spanish Virgin* for my collection, and to go on to writing a novel. I had no wish to write a novel and did not know how to set about it, but the publishers insisted. To their surprise my book of short stories succeeded with the critics and readers; instead of selling the expected six hundred copies, it sold more than three thousand. It has been out of print since 1930, and so has the novel *Clare Drummer* which evokes, with a novelist's necessary translation of fact into fiction, my private Irish experience. It is a nervous attempt to come to terms, but I was trying to write autobiographically without portraying myself. There is a central blur in the book, and the mannerisms are shocking; I am on a seesaw in which I go erratically from awful hyperbole to good observation. The critics noted this and said I was writing off my nerves. *Clare Drummer* sold under a thousand copies and, like the other two books, has long been out of print.

If the reviewers were puzzled by my mixture of feverishness and amateur incompetence, Mr. Bassellthorpe—my benefactor—was totally shocked. He had had hopes of my moral character; they were dashed and we were drifting apart. Why were my people so unpleasant? Why were my tastes so morbid and why was I so pessimistic? I said one could only write as one was. Soon we went off to one of his pleasant lunches. One of my affectations, caught from the older generation, was to carry a walking stick. I carried it under my arm down Piccadilly. The spectacle embarrassed him and he murmured. It was a bamboo stick with a curious head like a polished root and I explained that it was a male bamboo: the bamboos with the crook were female. The shopkeeper had told me. Mr. Bassellthorpe was exasperated. "People have sex on the brain today," he said angrily. Our lunch was a failure.

But he was a man of scrupulous conscience. He wrote me a letter that evening saying that it had come to him that he had spoken of my writing in an un-Christian manner. He apologized, though his opinion remained, and he begged me to try and be a better man. I wished he had not apologized for, like so many people of conscience, he had had his cake and eaten it, with satisfaction.

To be young is painful but exhilarating: to be certain and to pass into uncertainty and on to new certainties; to be conscious of the changes from one hour to the next; to be intolerant of others and blindly interested in oneself. It is so hard to remember youth, simply because one loses dramatic interest in oneself. One is harsh; one is all sentiment. It is the time of friendships. I used to think of myself as more exposed than my friends, yet clearly I was not. At a moment when I felt wise an elderly and amused doctor said I looked like a bolting pony. A poet, older than myself, said I burned everything up, including myself. I was tame yet I was avid. I was shy and I was aggressive. Goodness knows what any young man is like except egotistical and perhaps fanatical. I was fanatical about writing: the word and the sentence were my religion; everything must be definite. I was rather snobbish about the need to be poor; and, I think, selfish. Not that there was much opportunity for people like myself to be better off. So when I look now at the excesses in my writing that break out without reason, I see they represent unsatisfied energies, inchoate desires, unresolved dilemmas. Signs of militant weakness. It is pretty certain that the effect of the violent quarrels in my childhood home was to close my heart for a long time. I used to feel, as young people do, older than my years. I had (I thought) seen too much. The trap was that I had not experienced it. I saw people as trapped in their own natures and divided into those who go for power and dominance and those who do anything to keep the peace and make secrecy their defense. There is a theory among psychologists which is less flattering: that an eldest child (and I was that creature) finds himself isolated, leaps at his freedom, becomes even adventurous and self-sufficient—but, untrained by conflict, breaks in a crisis, disperses himself and goes to pieces. I have certainly had to deal with that.

The year of the Wall Street crash I got £75 from my publisher and, under the common delusion that it would be easier to write in France, I went down to Cassis in the South of France to stay in the farmhouse kept by a Frenchman called Roger Nion. I did not know half Bloomsbury had the habit of going there. The peaches were ripe, the sun was hot, the red rocks of the Mediterranean burned against the peacock sea, the cicadas made a din all night in the pines and the dogs of the valley barked at the moon. It was all very gay and lazy. In the cafés the Gramophones played, over and over again, pleasant tunes like "The Sunny Side of the Street." The street would not be sunny again for many, many years. I was too sun-soaked to write.

Roger Nion was an absurd man. He had been a stage manager. He was an elderly dandy who wore a monocle and who went on long rides on a racing bike. He looked like a dragonfly as he whizzed to the beach. His favorite phrase was *tout s'arrange*. People thought him a bit of a fraud and a parsimonious French peasant dressed up, but I liked him. His unexpected gift was that he was a powerful and courageous swimmer. It was frightening to see his head bobbing up and down, a couple of miles out in a rough sea. His character came out in a small contraption he had invented for catching flies. It lay on his dining table: this was a small cylinder made sticky with honey, on which the flies that infested the place would alight; the cylinder slowly conveyed them to the glass death chamber attached. Roger used to watch this with satisfaction as he read detective stories. I mention this because it occurs to me that that was what my first three novels were like: machines for conveying my characters into a trap.

When I got back to England I ran into one nervous illness after another. I walked about with a knife sticking into my back by day; when I went to bed my nightmares were about air warfare. I was often sitting with the crowd of Out Patients at hospitals, waiting to be X-rayed. My duodenum twanged. I went into fevers. In Cornwall I got very ill. My habits of work cannot have been helpful. I rewrote and rewrote all day and half the night at some periods: the hours and my anxieties must have been hard on my constitution. Samuel Butler has some lines about Radicals having bad digestions. I must have been very Radical. What in fact eventually cured me was success in love, and in my work.

9

I must go back to the situation at Bromley after my return from Spain. My parents had moved by this time. I occasionally wrote to my mother but rarely got a reply. The lack of letters and of frequent meetings was, and still is, normal in our family; except for my mother, we all really liked to be "on our own."

I went down to Bromley. The shooting-box dream had gone; there had been others, but now I found myself walking up a respectable gravel driveway to a tall, double-fronted Edwardian house, a substantial place, in the best part of the town. The family had gone up in the world. There was a dinner gong in the wide hall, a barometer and Turkish carpets—signs of gentility. In the long drawing room there was a grand piano which, as I told in my earlier volume, Father had secretly bought. The famous picture called Limpets (by Mabel Lucie Attwell, I believe), of two naked children displaying their rosy bottoms on a rock by the sea, was in place; so was *Wedded*. They were now supported by half a dozen large landscapes of greenery, water and cattle, bringing to the house an appropriate note of the Lake District, for it was called *Rydal Mount,* as were also some 100,000 other houses in England at this time.

Mother was tidily dressed. There was, for the first time, a maid in the house, an elderly religious woman whose eyes gazed with searching eagerness: she was stone deaf—a shrewd move on Father's part, because family conversations had the remorseless candor of Yorkshire utterance. The family communicated with this gentle woman by a sort of semaphore and she lip-read. We had never had a housemaid in my time.

I was relieved to see we had so obviously bettered ourselves, although the dining room table, sofas and sideboard had enlarged their old silent war with each other; in fact I never remember a time when our furniture did not look like evidence of the class war more than anything else. Oak, walnut, cherry, mahogany, flashed their veneers sarcastically at one another. When I said to one of my brothers that we were going up, he said: "In smoke!" And, now that my other brother, the very successful one, had left home, he added (entirely without malice and as if metaphor alone could describe the situation), "Rats leave a sinking ship." The remark was an example of our family's poetic tendency. There was no sign of sinking. Indeed, the Divine Mind had wisely supplied a chauffeur to drive my father about. Father said: "I feel I can breathe here." But he did dreamily ask if I knew the pines and sandy commons near Hindhead. He asked, he said, merely because only the previous week he had been through there on his way to the South Coast on business.

My mother asked if I thought Queen Ena was really happy with King Alphonso. She was worried by my bony appearance. Noticing I had not brought pajamas for the night, she thought I must be short of money. She looked at me with suspicion: "Are you still doing the writing?" She always spoke of it as if writing were some unlucky thing—like rain—and that I was out in it without a coat. I was offered a glass of ginger wine.

"That's all you'll get," she said disloyally. Then switching to near-loyalty: "Of course, your father always buys the best."

Father said, in royal manner, "We always drink it."

The house, or rather the alterations to it, had cost a lot—and, in fact, the Divine Mind had shown that it was the duty of my remaining brother and sister, who were earning their livings, to live there and contribute to the upkeep. If they rebelled Father took this to mean they were trying to destroy him out of blatant ingratitude. There was a fear that Animal Magnetism or the false evidence of the material senses—Mortal Mind, in short—might suggest (and we know the danger of suggestion, don't we?) that they get married and leave home. My father did most sincerely feel that marriage was for him alone. Mine had caused consternation. Still, we were on good terms, so long as we skated past difficult subjects. Hearing that I was reviewing books, he was proud and enthusiastic. It suggested to him that he should buy new books. He did so. Delighted to get out of his factory, he was soon in the best London bookshops, buying on a large scale. Seeing a picture of John Stuart Mill at Bumpus's, he asked my advice on whether to get the works. He did not read these books; he stacked them up in a wardrobe in his bedroom which was already pretty full of the widely advertised ones. No one was allowed to take them out of the wardrobe. He loved stores and stock.

There was one small cloud. The Divine Mind—here, as usual, at variance with my mother—had brought our grandmother to live in the house: her husband, the minister, after some hard years in a rough factory town in Lancashire, had died. Our grandmother had not changed her opinion that my mother, if not still a harlot, had idle dirty London habits, and that our father would have done better "elsewhere." Mother occasionally spoke of "the old b——" and mocked her Yorkshire accent. But Grandma's tiny inheritance had timidly trebled itself in Courtauld's shares for thirty years. Father had pointed out the folly of letting money run lethargically to fat in this way. He persuaded her to transfer what would eventually be his share for a livelier career in his business. The career was indeed lively and brief; and there was already a faint notion that his brother in Canada might see the attraction of giving his share a canter too. He was a poor working man with a large family who had not made good in Canada and had to look to the future. One couldn't tell, of course, but the Divine Mind might show the way. Father never said this directly: he was opposed on principle to "voicing one's desires"; the Divine Mind hated you to "voice." You prayerfully waited for the Divine Will to "unfold." As Father said: "We must not outline what channel will open up." Mother, unfortunately, "voiced" and very frequently.

"Do you believe in this . . ." she said to me. Her face was torn by mistrust. The old story of her pawned engagement ring and other wrongs came out.

"No," I said.

"You're a wicked boy," she said. "Your father does."

· · · ·

I did not often visit my parents, for it was difficult to get an opportunity of talking alone with my mother. If one telephoned, Father always answered and one could sometimes hear her voice half whimpering in the background. She had wept when Mr. Shaves died; it brought to mind all the deaths in her family.

But each time I went home the situation had become richer. Serious matters in our family were always discussed at mealtimes. Someone was told to whack the gong in the hall, though we were already gathered. We filed in and started; beginning innocently with things like the best kind of stove to have. Presently there were allusions to deeper matters. And they were discussed before my grandmother, as neat, pretty and vain in her eighties as ever. It was safe. Like the maid, she too was stone deaf. Conversation was frank, especially if I was there. I will say this for us: we loved to put on a show.

"Will you have a little more, Grandma dear?" my mother would say.

"More?" one of my brothers shouted in her ear.

"Eh, ah fancy a bit of fat, Walter," my grandmother would say. She loved fat.

"Pass it up quickly, it may be your last chance," one of my brothers said. My father tried vainly to silence him.

"After all," the boy went on, "she paid for it. And it may be her last."

These episodes would end with some shy appeasing statement, at great length, from the jollier voice of the Divine Mind. The old lady went to her sitting room and, on her horsehair sofa, lay reading a love story in a religious magazine until she fell asleep, under a tapestry picture of Moses smashing up the Commandments at the time of the Golden Calf—a good picture for our family—and one she had woven herself when she was a girl. She had luckily brought a good deal of her furniture with her. We had not enough of our own for the four reception rooms.

Later someone would say: "You'd better go and see how she is."

"You never know," said my young brother.

(I have described some of this in a scene in *Mr. Beluncle,* for it oppressed my mind; the novel was very much influenced by Schchedrin's *The Golovlyov Family*.)

The implication was terrible, but so much had money come to obsess us that no one realized it. In her eighties, Grandma might easily pass "to another plane of consciousness" without warning. She had been heard crying out in the night for William, her dead husband. Or groaning: "Oh, God help me!" Yet, she got up brisk and early in the mornings, in her village fashion, and set to work. Once a week she would put on a cloth cap, kirtle her skirt, take up the carpet and linoleum from the floor of her sitting room and bedroom and, with a pail of water and scrubbing brush, she would be down on her knees scrubbing the boards. She suspected "London dirt" everywhere. When that work was done, she'd attack my mother for not doing the same to the rest of the large house. Then she'd sit demurely crocheting in her room, making one more doyley to add to her hoard. There were pretty well a thousand in her wardrobe. At other times, she would wrap up one or two of these in paper and slip out to the pillar box at the corner and post it to her son in Manitoba. Once she sent him a strip of linoleum in case he was "in want." The postman brought these things back because they were not addressed. When my mother said *she* would send them, the old lady suspected a plot, accusing Mother of wanting the doyleys and lino for herself, and took to making bigger parcels and throwing them out of the window when she saw the postman come up the drive. He used to bring them back to Mother at the back door. The old lady was shrewd enough to see that her little money had vanished.

"Eh," she would say to my mother, "this is what you've done to my son."

"Give it back to her. I'd sooner live in a shed than this," Mother would say. "I don't want her charity. I like things straight."

The story is too painful. But one day, the old lady (now bedridden) said out of her loneliness to my mother: "You're the only one who loves me. You're the only one." It was true; my mother looked after her to the end. The burden of dealing with the jealous old lady was hers.

In a year or two, she died. Father always lost his self-control in the large emotional matters of life. He wept. He became helpless. He had no notion of what to do; some bewilderment at the fact that other people existed, independently of himself, made him cling to the idea that events had not happened—perhaps one of his reasons for conversion to Christian Science. He invented excuse after excuse for delaying the funeral, one of the mad reasons being that Miss H. would be put out by his absence from the office. Perhaps the reason lay in a sort of Tolstoyan anger at the fact of death; it is certain also that he loved his mother passionately. There the body lay in the house. The result was horror. The dead woman's body burst in the coffin and was borne dripping from the bedroom.

His mother's death had saved Father financially. He wept often when he mentioned the little bits of jewelry she had left; and although he laughed, as we all did, at the hoards of crocheting and embroidery she left, he wept as he admired them. He had inherited from her a love of craftsmanship and of hoarding things.

The financial peace did not last long after his mother's

death. Father was on acrimonious terms with his partner. Desperate second mortgages, "borrowings" from my brother began. But a final break with the partner settled it all. I do not know the rights and wrongs of it, but the Divine Mind could do nothing about writs and about lawyers with serious cases. Explaining one of these Father said: "I told him he ought to have been old enough to know it was an ordinary business risk."

He said this arrogantly and shrewdly, yet immediately a glow would come on his prosperous and optimistic face, as if he had ascended to the Platonic condition of Risk, as if he were Divine Risk in person. He exuded the bliss of insolvency as an ideal to be aimed at; he captivated many. And, unable to share this light, we became, I'm afraid, cautious and were ashamed to feel we might be mean-minded and even guilty. How extraordinary it is that one feels most guilt about the sins one is unable to commit.

The news came one day in the winter that the firm had gone into liquidation. We were all wretched. My brothers had the delicate task of arranging the affair. I was told Father made a fine speech at the crucial meeting: he was not a minister's son for nothing, and several of those present were very moved. And, looking back on it, I see it *was* moving to see a man who had worked so hard and with scrupulous talent to be his own master, defeated. He was greatly respected in his trade; if he had turned from God to his admiring business friends, he would have succeeded. Inside him was an artist who had not been able to change his style.

In distress I went to see him at his office. I had always been proud of his nameplate on his factory and was shocked that "the business" which had so beglamored and harassed our lives was gone. He often said, in his disordered emotional moments, that, but for his religion, he would "end it all," and I feared that this might occur, forgetting that it was really one of his energizing self-dramatizing statements. So now I went up the stone stairs that had seemed like prison stairs to me so often, with self-reproach at my inability to rescue him, and with guilt in criticizing him. I felt very close to him. What an emotional state he could put me in! I entered his showroom, once so scented, but now smelling of floorboards, whitewash and empty showcases. He lead me to his office.

"They have to leave you a desk," he said, claiming his rights. "Have a cup of tea? The gas is on."

I have often thought how distressing this meeting must have been for him. I was his eldest son and he identified me with his own father, the minister and intellectual. My brothers in the business world could and did help him much more than I; but I, like his father, was an unsettling visitor from outside. He was beginning to wish he had had a life like his own father's. We were at the beginning of that phase so common in the lives of fathers and sons, when the father feels *he* is the son. This is a truth that is missing from a story called *The Fly in the Ointment* which I eventually wrote about our interview. It was one of those rare stories that require little more than total recall from the writer. My father was affectionate and was moved by my calling on him here, for his office and factory were his real home, where he had kept so many things private to himself: his Gramophone, his photographs, his special coffee cups, the motto containing words of Emerson's. I feared we would both weep; we were saved by a distraction. A large fly flew in from the showroom. Father detested flies: emissaries of dirt. He went at it with a copy of *The Draper's Record*. I went at it with an evening paper. We missed. A fury seized us. He got up on his desk to bash it on the ceiling and there, looking down at me, he said sternly: "You're going bald, my boy."

It made me feel I was the fly. He was very stern when

I helped him down. I asked him what he was going to do. I remember the afternoon sun catching his face as he said: "I feel" (he always said "I feel" rather than "I think") "I'd like to take a trip around the world."

"You want money for that," I said. I ought not to have said that. He was on to me at once. Scornfully he said: "Money! That is one thing this has taught me: I don't want money ever again."

It was I who went home in a suicidal state of mind and not an energetic one either. A bankrupt father would be costly.

These events in my father's life occurred at a time when my own affairs were in a state of emotional bankruptcy. There had been a sad flaw in my Irish marriage from the start and wounds can become too appealing and engrossing. My wife and I had both thrown over, long before, the religion that had deceived us, travel distracted but we had the sense eventually to be a good deal apart. It is bad when difficult marriages become too interesting. We separated finally and since we had no children this was simple.

I had gone to live in a studio in Hampstead. I wondered if I should ever be fully in love. I was excited by the company of women, but the excitement seemed never to go beyond the sexual to a love of the person. Obviously I was one of those who must wait for the *coup de foudre*. Better the certainty of instinct than the muddle of too much thought.

The coup came, of course. I knew my present wife scarcely at all before she came to my studio, but at the first passing sight of her I remember my eyes had filled with strange tears. My old, romantic landscaping of girls vanished. I loved instantly the voice and the way she laughed. I *knew* without asking any more. When I spoke to her I scarcely listened to what she said, nor do I think she listened to me. This evening in 1934—it was appropriately Guy Fawkes Night with the London sky starred by rockets, we skipped away from the door of a political meeting which (we were glad to hear from each other) did not interest us. A genius of some kind united us as we got away on a bus in Tottenham Court Road, and the genius has not left us since. We went up to Wales, where an amorous and eloquent Welsh farmer who came to her mother's house exclaimed that she "had the bloom on her." In 1936, when I was divorced, we were married in Hampstead Town Hall and set off to Paris. Everyone, it seemed to me, gazed at her in the cafés, the restaurants and cabarets we went to, and late at night we went laughing up the stairs of our hotel in the Rue Monsieur le Prince, not to the *cinquième* but something much better. The only bad omen was that there were only refugees from Germany in the Dome. We went back to a cottage by the sea in Dorset for a few weeks, where I finished a book and played dominoes as the October gales whacked at the roof. From now on I began to live: I became the father of a daughter and, two years later, of a son. Passion had brought out in me the repressed male instinct for responsibility, and I think passion alone among human feelings, is the root of this instinct.

I had told my parents of my coming divorce. Father put on his affronted look at first. (He had, I heard, been beside himself with rage when one of his secretaries had got married.) I believe he thought he alone had the right to be divorced. But he got over the offense quickly. He used to drop in at my studio unexpectedly. He felt *he* would like a studio. No young woman was there. He pointed out that until the divorce I would have to pay income tax as a single man. And another idea had occurred to him.

"Have you made a will?" he asked.

"No." I said.

"Well," he reflected a while and then brightened. "There's no need to. If anything happened to you it would come to me. I'm the next of kin now."

So he revealed, all innocently, one of the reasons for the fight he had put up against all marriages. He had a longing for his children to belong to him alone, and for himself to rest solidly but sublimely in being next of kin. When we all disappointed him, he moved ambitiously toward becoming next of kin to my aunt and uncle in Ipswich, a ticklish campaign that went on for years, but here he was to be out-maneuvered.

When he met my future wife her warmth delighted him. The country boy was glad she came from a family of Welsh country people and farmers; he felt vicariously reunited to the land. He mentioned old Yorkshire farmers he remembered; and, not to be chauvinistic, uttered the names of a few Welsh hotels he had stayed at when he was on the road, and named the big Welsh-owned shops in London. He felt at once that here was a young woman in whom he could confide certain discoveries he had lately made, certain truths which would be helpful to us. Within half an hour he was blushing with his latest revelation: "You see, dear, I have no income. And if you haven't an income, you've got nothing coming in. That's the point."

And to me, he said, in congratulation: "I like a girl I can put my arm round."

True to his emotions he did not come to our wedding in Hampstead Town Hall; nor, since she never moved without him, did my mother; there was no hostility in this though there may have been a sense of propriety.

10

In the thirties my life changed completely. I was no longer the industrious apprentice. Praise —so necessary to writers—gave me confidence. It surprised me. The act of writing excites, but I have little sense of the merits or demerits of my work, though I have been obliged to recognize its general limitations. All writers know the gap between aspiration and performance and it plagues them. But I am curious to know why I have written this way and not that. If I began to write better it was for two reasons: in my thirties I had found my contemporaries and had fallen happily and deeply in love. There is, I am sure, a direct connection between passionate love and the firing of the creative power of the mind. I am no believer in the moral of *La Peau de Chagrin* or Shaw's theory of the necessity of abstinence. The mind of the restrained or sexually discontented man wanders off into shallows. My mind had been abroad too long, in a double sense: not simply in France, Ireland or Spain, but in a manner that had used only half of myself. Finding my English contemporaries, I found myself.

I had always dragged behind and, in fact, I was a few years older than most of the writers who became well-known at this period. The social conscience of a generation had been aroused. The cause of our anger lay in our powerlessness in a society ruled by torpid old men. One could not go to an industrial town without seeing the terrible sight of unemployed men walking the streets, ten yards apart from one another and never speaking, wandering from shopwindow to shopwindow. I had known the smell of poverty in Camberwell and Bermondsey. Our powerlessness had a half-forgotten source in the huge casualties of the 1914 war. We who had been too young for it were left with few immediate elders to help us in our contacts with the old. We simply collided with those elders and got the worst of it. We began to feel our strength, though unavailingly, when the Spanish Civil War broke out.

I found myself making speeches at meetings on behalf of the Republican cause. Only three or four people in England —my friends Gerald Brenan and Franz Borkenau among them—knew anything at all about Spaniards or Spanish history, and we saw a new Spain imposed on the reality: this new Spain was not Spain but an export of European ideologies and conflicts across the Pyrenees: Fascism, Communism and European foreign policies. The Civil War on the Republican side was at first a traditional popular rising such as had occurred at the time of the Napoleonic invasion. It sprang from the popular hatred of the disastrous Moroccan war and the resentment in every town and village against conscription.

It was a characteristic example of the *furia española*, long expected during the lethargy of the twenties, and was doomed to disintegration, ecially when the foreigners intervened, for regionalism had for centuries been a force: the unity of the country existed only on paper. On the Franco side there was the traditional resort to the grim authoritarianism of the army and the Church. He intended the traditional coup d'état but, especially because he came from Morocco, he was felt to be an invader. The reformist ideas of the Spaniards I had known were swept away. Among those murdered I think of Melquiades Alvarez, briefly a Prime Minister. He was an Asturian lawyer with whom I used to sit talking in his garden in Madrid. He was, fatally, a liberal. I think of Lorca reading his poems to a small party of us—murdered too: Unamuno going out of his mind in Salamanca and other friends escaping into exile. The list is long. It was certain, as one set of intervening foreigners after another went through the process of disillusion, that the Spaniards would settle this civil war in their own violent and cruel way; and that for ourselves, this was the first act of the Second World War. In London clubs, usually so good-natured, there were violent quarrels, and they were mainly between those under forty and those older.

Spaniards came to our flat. Among them were two who brought a note of farce that ended during the Second World War in a sinister manner. One was a bouncing Spanish journalist who began working in the Spanish Embassy when the Civil War started, under Perez de Ayala, the Ambassador of the Republic. Ayala was an excellent novelist of the intellectual kind, comic, brainy and poetic by turns. He was one of the best talkers in Madrid. His portraits of members of the government were wickedly entertaining and I loved his novels and his company. He was a man of vocabulary. One of the pleasantest things in the Spanish life of that time for myself was the unaffected willingness of distinguished Spaniards to throw away hour after hour in good talk. No pomposity, no sense of their importance cut them off. They lived in their own fascination with being timelessly human.

I shall call the journalist Paco. He was young, fat and had a stentorian voice. He loved long cigars. He would make loud intimate remarks about his physical state wherever he was. In a club he would bawl across a crowded room a sentence like: "My testicles are blown up like footballs. I cannot sleep with anyone."

This Sancho Panza hated intellectuals and was always jeering at my views about Spain, but we were on affectionate terms. His constant companion was a rich and fashionable Spanish professor, a dandy and Anglophile who had houses in Spain, France and London. He had his yacht and his private aircraft and a notably upper-class English accent. These two friends were born to plague each other and used to drop in on us at late hours and stop half the night. Sometimes a very proper Englishman from the Foreign Office, with bowler hat and rolled umbrella, would drop in too and reveal an improbable side to his character. He was Rodney Gallop, one of the few Englishmen who could speak Basque. He could sing Basque songs. Paco would mock the professor's English accent.

"Do you hear that? He says he lives at Sevenucks. Say Sevenoaks." Blamelessly the professor said it.

"Do you hear—Sevenucks. Sevenucks." He chanted it. The professor countered now and then by making fun of Paco's sex life.

"Have you heard about his testicles? Typical Spanish puritan. All talk about sex, no performance."

In a few months a change came over Paco. I went to see

him at the Embassy. He locked the door: "I'm surrounded by spies."

Naturally: he had become a secret supporter of Franco. We had a violent quarrel about this and we ceased to be friends. I saw him once driving a Rolls-Royce down Piccadilly, the picture of happiness, with a long cigar in his mouth. And then, in the Second World War, I found him sitting next to me at dinner, where the professor was also a guest, and a young naval officer just back from the Russian convoy. The two Spaniards did their turn. Joyfully they accused each other across the table of being German agents. In the middle of this, Paco was called to the telephone and when he came back, he said to me, in a very changed way: "I wish we were friends again like we used to be."

Within a week he was deported to Spain. He was a German contact. Or so the professor said. The professor said he had turned him in. I've never seen Paco since; in Madrid I could never trace him after the war. I couldn't help enjoying his follies.

In the thirties those who came from the upper-middle-class and who had been to public schools and the old universities were easily drawn toward Communism because of the discipline, the training for leadership, the team spirit and élitism at these places. To some, Marxism was for a time a scripture, and not having met anyone in the working class up till then, they tried guiltily, masochistically and idealistically to get in touch with them, often making absurd declarations of feeling inferior. I was brought up very differently. I had been to school with working-class boys and girls. My parents and relations, my grandfather the bricklayer, my eccentric great-uncle, the cabinetmaker, my mother the shopgirl and my father the errand boy and shop assistant in Kentish Town, had belonged originally to this class. Marxism as a dogma could have no appeal to me, but as a way of analyzing society and of presenting the interplay of class and history, it stimulated. The fundamentalism and the totalitarian consequences of Marxism were naturally repugnant to one like myself who had been through this mill in a religious form. It would be impossible for me to become a Communist or a Roman Catholic after that; and, in any case, I was constitutionally a nonbeliever. Rarely have the active politicals had a deep regard for imaginative literature. Writers are notoriously given to ambivalence, and live by giving themselves to the free mingling of fact and imagination.

So although when the Spanish Civil War came I was ardent for the Popular Front, I was much less interested in "the People" than in the condition of individual people. I was particularly concerned with their lives and speech. In their misleading sentences and in the expressive silences between would lie the design of their lives and their dignity. Sometimes ordinary speech is banal and it is always repetitive, but if selected with art, it could reveal the inner life, often fantastic, concealed in the speaker. This was the achievement of Henry Green in novels like *Living* and *Back;* and in Hemingway's best stories. Up till now in English literature the "common" people had been presented as "characters," usually comic. I had a curious conversation with H. G. Wells about this. I asked him to tell me about Gissing, who had taken his working-class and lower-middle-class people seriously, so that to my mind he was closer to the Russian tradition than ours. Wells began, in his sporty way: "The trouble with Gissing was that he thought there was a difference between a woman and a lady, but we all know there is no difference at all."

But when I asked if it were possible to present, say, a

lower-middle-class man or woman seriously and not as a comic character, he reflected and said "No." My opinion was and is that it is, of course, possible; and that the essence of comedy is not funniness but militancy. I have rarely been interested in what are called "characters," i.e., eccentrics; reviewers are mistaken in saying I am. They misread me. I am interested in the revelations of a nature and (rather in Ibsen's fashion) of exposing the illusions or received ideas by which they live or protect their dignity. On the other hand, in the preoccupation with common speech which I suppose I owe to my storytelling mother and to listening closely to Spaniards and others abroad, I did not follow more than I could help the documentary realism that was fashionable in the thirties. The storyteller either digests or contemplates life for his own purposes. It is a flash that suddenly illuminates and then passes.

I write this to explain how I came to write a story called "Sense of Humour," the first one of mine to make a stir and give me what reputation I have as a writer of short stories. It has appeared in dozens of anthologies and has been broadcast in many languages. The tale had long been in my mind. I had written two or three versions, including one long explanatory one in the third person. None of these seemed right to me. They suffered from the vice of exposition or explanation. I put them aside and eventually saw there was another method; it is pretty obvious, but it had not occurred to me. A now-forgotten Welsh writer, Dorothy Edwards, had written a story, in the first person, in which a character unconsciously reveals his obtuseness by assuming an air of reasonableness and virtue; and, in Hemingway, I found the vernacular put to similar use. The words spoken were so arranged as to disclose or evoke silently the situation the people were trying in their awkward way to conceal. The main source of my tale was that commercial traveler I had met in Enniskillen ten years before, who took his girl for rides in his father's hearse. My task was to make him tell his fantastic tale as flatly and meanly as possible, and to see his life through his eyes alone. The tale was written almost entirely in dialogue. I had little recollection of my original but I had known many salesmen of his kind, in whose minds calculation plays a large part. The couple are followed everywhere by a young man on a motor bike, the previous lover of the girl; he crashes and is killed during one of these pursuits. The salesman and his girl travel in the hearse with the youth's body. On a simple level the story contrasts the humorless young man with the childish and cruel "sense of humour" of the girl: but I hope I may say there is far more to the story than that. It brings out (I think) my notion of the militancy and symbolism that underlie comedy. I think, also that I gave the vernacular of that period a role it had not had up till then. I have often been asked to explain the tale; some people found it shocking and cruel, others poetic, others deeply felt, others immoral and irresponsible, others highly comical. The most intelligent interpretations came from French and German critics, thirty-five years after it was written. (I am pretty sure that although I am often described as a traditional English writer, any originality in my writing is due to having something of a foreign mind.) My own suspicion is that the tale is a "settling" of my personal Irish question; and I am certain that if one is writing well, it is because one is at a point where one is able to define things hitherto undefined in one's own mind or even unknown to one until then.

I am more interested in the question of the "foreign" strain. Questions of class were very important in the thirties and in giving my uncouth character a voice I was consciously protesting against the dominance of the voice of what is called the high bourgeois sensibility. My narrator was not a "char-

acter"—in the traditional sense—though he was extraordinary.
The world he lived in was one of the vulgar push and self-
interest that was changing the nature of English society. In the
next twenty years one would see that England was packed with
people like him and his rootless friends. His emergence as a
type is commonly misunderstood by literary critics who, owing
to the stamp that Dickens and Wells put upon him in their
time, have thought of the lower-middle-class or petty bourgeois
as whimsical "little men." But in this century all classes have
changed and renewed themselves; they have certainly released
themselves from the cozy literary categories of the nineteenth
century, and carry inside them something of the personal anarchy of unsettled modern life. Since my own roots are in this
class and I know people who belong to it like the palm of my
hand. (The standard view that they are inevitably Fascist is
crude and untrue.) In the writing, American influence—particularly of Hemingway—is clear; and both from a literary
point of view and a social one, this was natural.

I do not write this to claim any great merit for the tale. I
am clinically concerned with it as something new in my own
life which was brought about by the times and the emancipa-
tion my new marriage had given me. I had become real at last.
I worked for months on this story, for in writing there is a
preliminary process of unwriting, and ideas are apt to be
dressed in conventional literary garb in the first instance. (In
considering the character of Prince Myshkin in *The Idiot*,
Dostoevsky seriously considered Mr. Pickwick as a starting
point.) A good story is the result of innumerable rejections of
one's own attempts. Also, very often, of rejections that are more
painful. "Sense of Humour" was turned down by all likely
publications in England and America. I put it away with the
feeling that I had made one more bloomer. Then, at last, John

Lehmann's *New Writing* appeared and he published it. I got
£3 for the story. I cannot say that I woke up to find myself
famous but I had modestly arrived. It is a pleasant and also
curious experience. I loved being congratulated, especially
publicly in restaurants! One admirer, only an acquaintance at
the time, and a comically shamefaced womanizer, begged
me to introduce him to the girl in the story, for whom he had
fallen. I had drawn her from several models, but chiefly from
a girl I had glanced at in the desk of an Irish hotel. The important thing for me was that the story woke me up. It led me
on to "The Sailor," "The Saint" and "Many Are Disappointed," which became far better known.

When I was writing for *The New Statesman* in these
early days, David Garnett was the literary editor, and in one
of our talks about writing novels he said that when one could
not get on with a book, one should create an extra difficulty.
That did not help me because difficulty of all kinds surrounds
me in writing, and writing has always seemed to me the result
of being able to throw innumerable temptations from the
mind. I have an impatient character; for every page I write
there are half a dozen thrown away. The survivors are criss-
crossed with deletions. I went through a long period of talking
to myself when I went for a walk, and again and again I
would catch myself saying, with passion, two words: The End.
Not necessarily the end of a story or an essay, but the end of
the confusion, the end of the statement or sentence. My weakness for images was caused by the poet's summary instinct. I
have had to conclude that I am a writer who takes short
breaths and in consequence the story or the essay have been
the best forms for me and early journalistic training encouraged this.

Because of its natural intensity the short story is a memorable if minor literary genre. There is the fascination of packing a great deal into very little space. The fact that form is decisive concentrates an impulse that is essentially poetic. The masters of the short story have rarely been good novelists: indeed the short story is a protest against the discursive. Tolstoy and Turgenev are exceptions, but Maupassant wrote only one novel of any account: *Une Vie*. Chekhov wrote no novels. D. H. Lawrence seems to me more penetrating as a short-story writer than as a novelist. An original contemporary, Luis Borges, finds the great novels too loose. He is attracted to Poe's wish for the work of art one can see shaping instantly to the eye: the form attracts experiment. It is one for those who like difficulty, who like to write a hundred fifty pages in order to squeeze out twenty. At the time of the Spanish war, when I had to go to a protest meeting in an industrial town, one of the speakers interested me. I wrote two pages about her and gave up. From year to year I used to look at this aborted piece. No difficulty: no progress. Suddenly, after twenty years I saw my chance. When one is making a speech one is standing with one's body and life exposed to the audience: the sensation is frightening. Write a story in which a woman making a speech in her public voice is silently telling by the private voice her own life story *while* she declaims something else. To do this was extremely difficult. One learns one's craft, and craftsmanship is not much admired nowadays, for the writer is felt to be too much in control; but, in fact, the writer has always, even if secretively, to be in control. And there is the supreme pleasure of putting oneself in by leaving oneself out.

I have written six volumes of short stories and many others that have never appeared in book form. I am surrounded, as writers are, by the wreckage of stories that are half done or badly done. I believe in the habit of writing. In one dead period, when I thought I had forgotten how to write, I set myself a well-known exercise which Maupassant, Henry James, Maugham and Chekhov were not too grand to try their hands at. It is the theme of the real, false or missing pearls. I was so desperate that I had to say to myself: "I will write about the first person I see passing the window." He happened by ill-luck (for I thought I knew little about this trade) to be a window cleaner. The story is "The Necklace." Whatever may be thought of this tale—I myself do not like the end, which should have been far more open—it revealed to me as I wrote two things of importance in the creative imagination. The first: there is scarcely a glint of invented detail in this tale; it is a mosaic that can be broken down into fragments taken from things seen, heard or experienced from my whole life, though I never cleaned a window or stole a pearl. The second thing—and this is where the impulse to write was *felt* and not willed—is the link with childhood. To write well one must never lose touch with that fertilizing time. And, in this story, some words of my mother's about her father came back to me. He was a working gardener and coachman. It was part of the legend of her childhood that one morning his employer's wife called: "Lock the drawers: the window cleaner is coming." I did not write about my grandfather but about the universal preoccupation with theft.

The Irish, the Italians, the Russians and the Americans have an instinctive gift for the short story. Alberto Moravia once told me that the Italian successes in this form and their relative failure in the novel is due to the fact that the Italian is so conceited that he dare not look long and steadily at his face in the mirror. I would have thought that the gift is due to the Italian's delight in the impromptu. Frank O'Connor used to say that the form is natural to societies where the element of anarchy is strong and the pressure of regard for society is weak. In English literature we indeed had to wait for the foreign rootlessness and rawness of Kipling before we had a master. Once discovered, this quickly appeared in Saki, in D. H. Lawrence, in the pastorals of A. E. Coppard and T. F. Powys, in Walter de la Mare, Max Beerbohm, H. E. Bates, Elizabeth Taylor, Frank Tuohy, James Stern and Angus Wilson. Later starters, we have done well.

Toward the end of the prewar time I wrote one more novel. It was called *Dead Man Leading*. The subject was the search for a missing explorer. I had avidly read the lives of Livingstone, the African missionaries, the account of John Speke and Sir Richard Burton. One particularly, the experience of a Frenchman, René Caillié, on the Niger—he got to Timbuktu—especially interested me because of his almost comical masochism. I had detected this characteristic, I thought, in Captain Robert Scott, in Vilhjalmur Stefansson, whom I had met, and in others who seem to have chosen hardship. The Fawcett story—Fawcett vanished in Brazil—offered a suggestion, though mine had nothing to do with it. I attempted a psychology of exploration. I chose the Amazon for my expedition because I knew the literature of the Amazon well. I constructed a small model of my bit of the river in the garden of a cottage we had rented in Hampshire—my explorers were ants struggling through the long grass—and, for the rest, consulted a large number of missionary diaries in the British Museum. Missionaries always write down the practical detail. I was stuck at one moment for some items about Manáos which I could not find in books or photographs. One evening when I was returning from London with a drunken businessman in the train, he told me all about the city. He had just come on leave from a bank there. This novel was more imaginative than my earlier ones; but it came out not long before the war started and that killed it.

More than ten years passed before I wrote another.

At the time of Munich we were living in a flat in a large house overlooking the canal close to London's "Little Venice." Strings of painted barges went by, bearing the water gypsies who were still part of London life. I worked in what had been the linen room of this Victorian house, and there I helped a young Jewish boxer rewrite his novel about prize-fighting in the East End. In addition to reading for a publisher, I reviewed books. I wrote a story which indicated my angry political mood: it was a satire about a country which was suddenly abandoned by the public statues of its great men, who were disgusted by the decadence of its government. The story was too clumsy to be published in any of my collections and I long ago lost the manuscript. I was also working on a short documentary film which was never produced but which introduced me to the extraordinary language of film directors. I was told someone had "alibied his idealism over onto documentary." The early documentaries were the first attempt to put a real England, as distinct from the phony American version, on the screen.

After Munich we saw war was inevitable. Our daughter was a year old; my wife was pregnant again. We wisely went to live in the country. I got out my bicycle, for we did not own a car and pedaled over Berkshire until I found an empty, isolated farmhouse in the Lambourn valley, eight miles from Newbury—horse-racing country. Owing to the long decline of English agriculture at the beginning of the century such houses were cheap. I paid £1 a week for a sedate, solid, ivy-covered Georgian house of the spacious farming kind, a place with a large walled garden and apple orchard. The garden ran down to the spring-fed Lambourn river, which flooded when the white water buttercups came out. This pleasant place was called Maidencourt—a misspelling of Midden-court, I suppose. It lay down a blind lane ending at the railway crossing of the little Lambourn branch line; and then continued as a footpath across the Downs behind us to the Roman Ridgeway above Wantage. From the top there, on a clear day, we could see the spires of Oxford. My wife and I often cycled to Oxford —a good fifty miles there and back—during the war when clothes were scarce in search of things for our children. I mention this footpath—it can easily be identified in Thomas Hardy's *Jude the Obscure*—for Hardy's topography is always minutely exact and is part of his concern with human circumstance. Jude followed it on his journey to Oxford. I once saw something close to one of the scenes in this novel enacted in the farmyard behind our house. There were shouts and laughter one afternoon and when I went out to see what was happening I found a girl chasing the farm lads with castrating scissors.

There had always been a farm on our site since Domesday. We had no gas or electricity; our water was pumped down by a windmill on the hill. By hard work in the coal shed, cutting wood, using paraffin stoves, and wearing thick clothes we kept warm. We set about growing huge quantities of vegetables. When Chamberlain finished his short announcement that war had been declared, I solemnly sowed two long rows of turnip seeds. The first winter of the war was fierce. The trees, the blades of grass, the cattle in the fields, were encased in a glaze of ice for nearly three months. One seemed to be walking on breaking glass. Our old-fashioned pump broke down and when my son was born we had no tap water for weeks. We got dozens of buckets from the frozen stream and our pond, and from a house half a mile away. The first water-carrying journeys exhausted me, but soon I got uncommonly strong and carried my load as easily as any farm hand does. All telephone wires were, of course, down and one had to walk for miles to get the doctor. I must say I enjoy things going wrong; later on, when the war made every simple act of living difficult, so that I seemed perpetually bicycling to Newbury or Hungerford and back with shopping swinging from the handlebars, I was in excellent health. Domestically, the hardships of the war were felt most heavily by the women, especially by young mothers, like my wife.

We spent the next seven years or so at Maidencourt, the longest time until then I had ever lived in one house. In the war period I kept a diary, as bleakly factual as I could make it, but I am not a natural diarist. I lack the secretive, snaillike temperament, and I was also so busy writing and reading all day that there was little energy left for making notes. It is all second-rate stuff, but I am surprised by my political outbursts about the state of English society. The war was most of the time a siege for us; we were imprisoned; and I found myself expressing the general view that English society must be revolutionized. English country life is utterly different from urban life. Because elections were suspended in local government and because I lived in a house of some consideration locally, I found myself obliged to become chairman of our Parish Council and had to represent it at the District Council in Hungerford: absurd appointments for an unpractical townee like myself. When the owner of the local Big House, a charming retired colonel, was about to leave the district he invited me to become Chairman of the local Conservative Association. I said I could not do this because I was a Socialist. He replied: "I don't see that makes any difference." He sincerely meant it.

The war, it is true, did revolutionize life in the dying life of the countryside eventually. In the Lambourn valley when I first went there, I found many older laborers who could speak Spanish. When sheep-farming collapsed around 1900 they had been forced to emigrate to the Argentine and Patagonia.

My diary noted these things, but it is mostly a mixture of groans, observations about the weather, the crowd of people who came down to get out of London for a night's sleep, and war incidents. A parachute comes floating down from the sky "with no man attached." Spent bullets hit the wall. Bombs fall miles away but in the country sound travels and you think the bomb is in the garden, because every nail in the floorboards gives a jump. I find a comic entry.

> Nov. 22nd. A gale all night walloping about *inside* the roof as well as bumping outside the windows and bringing down branches onto the cowshed. Awakened at 5 a.m. by two loud ringing explosions as hard as pick on stone. Lay, heart beating violently, rigid, listening if the children had been woken up. They were not, at least they didn't cry. Then I got out of bed to see what I could out of the window. Stubbed my toe. My curses woke up everyone. The baker said "they" dropped at Kintbury and killed two cows and a horse.

And another entry, too long to quote here, describes one of those short fierce air raids on London of the last year of the war. I sat at the top of a house in Hampstead recording the fantastic firework display of the London barrage, the sky rippling with magnesium rain, and the carrot-colored fires. Every object in the house, every cup and saucer, jumped and rattled, and spent shrapnel—or whatever it was—came rattling down against the walls. Sometimes one was excited, sometimes careless in these raids. Sometimes angry or scornful. Once Louis MacNeice and I wandered down the streets in St. Johns Wood and tried, unsuccessfully, to carry away a stone lion from the garden of a destroyed house. The thing was too heavy. But in the raid I was describing our fears were allayed by John Betjeman, who kept us laughing by assuring a teddy bear he had kept from his childhood that he and the bear were all right because they had been to confession, whereas the rest of us, as non-Christians, would certainly be in hell any moment. After a couple of hours the raid was over and then I discovered how terrified I had been: I could not speak clearly because one end of my upper lip had risen up and was stuck to my right nostril. I was not a man who could keep a stiff upper lip. I must have been looking like a rabbit.

There is another note about an evening with George Orwell, who in the melancholy way of one who had been trained for duty when he was young and was inured to suffering, rather liked the war, for he saw it as a fight against the governing class as well as a fight against the Nazis. I went to a flat he had taken at the top of an apartment block; the beauty of the place (to him) was that one could more easily get out onto the roof to put out fire bombs if one lived on the top floor. His health had been ruined by the wound he had got in Spain and he had the strange lonely detachment and fevered half-laughing energy of the sick.

My life was harassed but prosaic. My business was to stop farmers from letting their cows out, getting the waterweed out of the stream when the springs rose, and making plans for the burial of the dead when the Germans invaded us. I joined the Local Defence Volunteers, later the Home Guard, and armed with a tin hat, a Winchester and ten rounds of ammunition, sat up in a thresher's hut at night, waiting for parachutists and

listening to the bombers grinding over, after 1940. We were
thankful to be out of London, for the flats behind ours in
Maida Vale had been blown to bits. The hut on the Downs
belonged to our sergeant, whose father had been a traveling
thresher. He loved the hut because he had had measles in it
when he was a boy. It was sacred to him; we were defending
not the nation, but the hut and his childhood, and his feeling
epitomized what everyone felt about this depressing and un-
wanted war. The hut had bunks, a stove for making tea—our
strong point. One night a drunken roadster tried to get in: four
of us marched him away for a mile while he sang army songs
to us and started to show us the scars on his chest. He was our
only invader.

In our squad there were the thresher, a shepherd turned
gardener; a farmer whose child was dying, a baker's boy who
later fought in Burma and an eager simple youth who lived
with a blind couple. When we were issued with bayonets he
was in ecstasies: he practiced bayonet thrusts in the parlor of
the cottage while the blind couple sat in the room with him.
There was a bit of a row at the hut one night at a time when
German aircraft were passing over, because the gardener and
I went out on guard and gathered glowworms, which he
arranged round the brim of his hat so that it was like a phos-
phorescent halo. Our sergeant said a German plane could
easily see them. If the invasion came we were supposed to join
up with the Lambourn troop, mainly stable boys; but our lot
all agreed they wouldn't do anything to defend Lambourn, a
delinquent little place, but would rush home to defend their
wives. One summer evening we took turns at trying a very
long shot at a hare that sat with its ears pricked up in a cornfield. We fired twenty rounds but got nowhere near it. We
were as touching a rustic group as any out of Thomas Hardy.
I read Gibbon's account of his time in the militia in 1759; his

was a drunken regiment. It was difficult for us to get a glass of beer in the country during the war. I grew to have a deep affection for the villagers. The experience stirred me and I wrote a radio play about Gibbon's farcical conflicts with his drunken father in the militia. Like Elizabeth Bowen, Louis MacNeice, Rayner Heppenstall and others, I wrote several radio plays during the war. Before the war the B.B.C. did not care for left-wing people; and indeed I saw in a producer's list a note about myself. It said: "Embittered left-wing intellectual."

Among my wartime obligations was to do fire watching on the roof of *The New Statesman* every now and then. I was fortunate. There were no air raids on that battered neighborhood on the nights I was there, but I had arrived one morning at the beginning of the Blitz to discover the office was one of the only buildings left in Great Turnstile. I climbed through fallen ceiling rubble and glass, to be ordered out by a policeman who said two unexploded bombs were lying outside. I was trying to deliver my weekly article. The editors had moved off to the top floor of a printing works, under a glass roof. I had to walk to the south of the river to it. Under all that glass one's proof corrections got jumpy when the sirens went and one's stomach turned over.

The war, as I have said, was an imprisonment. It brought me into touch with my fellow prisoners in an England I knew little about: the England of factory workers. I went for weeks to shipyards, to engineering works, marshalling yards, and railway control centers. I became a documentary reporter. I spent a short time in an aircraft carrier off the coast of Scotland. It is fascinating simply to see strange things, though I saw so many that each experience wiped out the one that preceded it. I was very conscious of being thinned away to the condition of voyeur. One particular experience sums up my role. Just after the

Rundstedt offensive I was sent for a week or two to the front-line radio station in Luxembourg, when the Germans were only ten miles away. Since I had been too young for the 1914 war and was too old to serve in this one, I had the common, romantic civilian guilt, and it was appeased in the nights when the Germans sent small rockets into the town and made the air smell of burned rubber. It was further appeased when I cadged a lift off a truckload of American technicians who were going up to Trier, which had just been captured. I described the experience in a long article which was published in *The New Statesman* and often reprinted, so I will say little more, beyond telling the one ludicrous incident.

We seemed to be traveling, as we got near to Trier, under an arcade of mild shellfire. We arrived in the town, which was mostly a mound of stinking damp rubble. The technicians soon revealed their real purpose. We were really on a semi-looting expedition: the idea was to dig motorcycles out of a ruined factory. We were all afraid of snipers—I especially—and of the Military Police. As we got to the factory, one of their jeeps went by: on the bonnet they had set the town drunk as a mascot. They had put an opera hat on his head: with his simpleton's grin, he added to one's horror of the destruction. When the M.P.'s had gone we got into the courtyard of the factory. The weather was wet: the crew were encumbered with sten guns, rifles and other weapons. They had to get rid of their arms while they clambered into the ruins. I was the solution to their difficulty. They asked me to mind their guns. They hung them on me. I stood there in the rain for an hour, a human coat stand, a grotesque and passive human explosive. The expedition failed and we went on to other likely spots. I came away with a couple of bottles of Moselle, a copy of *Le Grand Meaulnes* which I took from a wrecked house—an apposite and healing fantasy and a characteristically literary choice on my part. Writers always steal books. The only time I was ever singled out as a target in the war was back in Luxembourg: a trigger-happy American fired a couple of rounds at me after curfew. I heard bullets sing past my ears, as in books writers say they do. I fell flat. I took the shots as an uninvited compliment.

There is not much more to say about the war. In one of Elizabeth Bowen's stories a character is made to say of the Blitz—and by extension of the war itself: "It will have no literature." In that sense it was like a car smash or pile-up. English writing did not vanish, but for years the experience exhausted us mentally and physically. And then, there is nothing as dead as a dead war and, as the pace quickens, the latest war kills the one before it quickly. One is ridiculous to be still alive and the best thing is to keep one's mouth shut. Looking at the war egotistically from a writer's point of view, it was a feverish dispersal and waste of one's life. It is often said that this was a good time when all private defenses gave way, especially the defense of class differences, and that we all came together for once; and one hears regrets that after the war this revolution spent itself and that we went back to our traditional privacy. We did; though not to the old kind. I am not sure that to be so drowned in the mass was good for the act of writing, for the kind of humanity required of artists is not the same thing as the united public humanness we felt as citizens. A writer soon finds himself wondering how large a helping of human beings his talent can manage, without being swamped by the huge amount of social reality that is forced upon him. The unconscious benefits may be deep; the anarchy of war is a release for a time: the ultimate effects are indirect.

I felt my own case to be uncommonly like my father's when he was taken away from his business by the 1914 war.

From that he did not recover. I was luckier: I think I can say, without conceit, that I did recover, but I too was changed. I became a literary critic and in the bizarre circumstances I have described. I had, of course, been a reviewer, but now a more reflective kind of criticism took up most of the time the war left to me. Although my criticism has been praised, I am not sure that the change was totally for the good. I shall glance at some of the circumstances.

Younger contributors to *The New Statesman* were called into the services and government organizations, so it became my job to write the leading literary article for the paper, almost every week. Since few new books were published, Kingsley Martin and Raymond Mortimer decided that the article must deal with a rereading of the classics. I had to sandwich this task between my war jobs. Maidencourt was a good quiet place for long blinding spells of reading and writing; and though I was often dragged out of it, the long, slow train journeys—it often took five hours to get from Newbury to London—gave more time for reading. The trains were crowded but usually people were too stunned to talk. So, one week the subject might be Walter Scott, the next Dostoevsky, after that Benjamin Constant, George Fox, Zola, Gil Blas and so on. When I look now upon the list of the scores of such essays from this pen, they seem to fly about or droop like washing on a clothesline. Two thousand words was the limit. In the first year the tone was nervous: my writing is filled in with hesitant or forensic phrases. I was writing against time. I had read widely but I had never "done" Eng. Lit., French Lit. or Russian Lit. I had no critical doctrine—a shock later on to the platoons of New Critics and later regiments—for critical doctrine is of little interest to the novelist, though it may mean something to the poet. The tendencies of the thirties persuaded me to the historical situation of the writer who was being enjoyed first and *then* examined. We were fond of calling ourselves victims of an age of transition; but it seemed to me that this has been the lot of every writer of any distinction at any time. I was moved by attitudes to social justice; but presently I saw that literature grows out of literature as much as out of a writer's times. A work of art is a deposit left by the conflicts and contradictions a writer has in his own nature. I am not a scholarly man; and I am not interested for very long in the elaborate superstructures of criticism. Some of my critics speak of insights and intuitions; the compliment is often left-handed, for these are signs of the amateur's luck; I had no choice in the matter. Anyone who has written a piece of imaginative prose knows how much a writer relies on instinct and intuition. The war added to my knowledge of human nature. I appear as a disarrayed stoic, a humanist with one wall of his room missing—an advantage there, I think, for all writing has one of its sources in the sense of a moral danger to which the writer is sensitive.

So a critic emerged from the hack. I attained a reputation in England and America and found that I was seriously split in two. I had the advantage of being an heir to the long and honorable tradition of serious periodical journalism; and of having, in a minor way, written imaginatively: I am aware of the novelist's moves. I cannot help putting myself in his position as he faces the empty page. I have always thought of myself—and therefore of my subjects—as being "in life," indeed books have always seemed to be a form of life, and not a distraction from it. I see myself as a practicing writer who gives himself to a book as he gives himself to any human experience.

I am very conscious when I am praised of what I owe to two friends who were of great help to me. The first is Raymond

Mortimer, a brilliant literary editor who put me on to many writers I knew little about. When I am complimented on having dug up some forgotten author the compliment should go to him. In French and English he has read everything. He is sharp with the careless sentence. My tastes were not always his, but his tolerance and friendship have always been valuable. My other stand-by was one of the best talkers and letter-writers in England: Gerald Brenan, who was writing his two great Spanish books at Aldbourne during the war. His village was about twelve miles from ours, and we would bicycle over to see each other and have long conversations. He was and is an original, as diverting and yet as serious about life as he is about literature. He lives in a streaming imagination, yet he can be a very stern critic. He is a piquant mixture of the military man, the poet, the scholar and the traveler, and for him life exists to be turned into writing; and when one is with him, one seems to see this happening before one's eyes.

Beyond these two friends was the fatherly figure of Kingsley Martin, the complete and very histrionic puritan, handsome, masochistic, a restless prophet who contained the fluctuating conscience of the Left and the most impressive if most infuriating editor of an English paper in our generation. He was tactless, affectionate, and (we used to say) was only cheerful when the news was bad. I could never draw the portrait of a man so complex; and there is no need to. He drew his own portrait very honestly and vividly in his own autobiography. He was Meredith's Dr. Shrapnel to the life, for under his pacifism was a very violent man and a headlong rationalist.

I am appalled by the amount I have read. This reading has certainly distracted me from original work of my own: for myself—if not for the reader—one or two good stories are worth all the criticism in the world: the best criticism of a story is another story, of a play, another play. In my criticism, perhaps even more than my stories, I am self-portrayed. When I reread those essays written in such numbers over the last thirty years, I am surprised to see how much they are pitted with personal experience, and how much reaction to life itself, either nettled or expansive, has been packed into an epigram or an aside. In penetrating to the conflicts of authors, I have discovered and reflected on my own.

One thing the war did for me was to introduce me to gout. The country doctor glanced at my agonized big toe that looked like a red tulip and said I was suffering from a lack of vitamins. Since we finished our small meat ration in the first two days of every week, we lived plainly. Drink appeared only on Mondays and Tuesdays at the pub, and I rarely was able to get a glass of wine. The disease recurred and it was not until a devastating attack when the war was over that it was diagnosed. I was on my way to Spain when I was crippled with it. I was told to take aspirins every two hours. I have always been ignorant about medicines for I have had good health, except in my occasional psychosomatic periods, so I unknowingly overdosed myself. I got to my hotel room in Barcelona, flopped on the bed and woke up twenty four hours later with my hat and overcoat still on. Modern drugs have cured me. For a time I blamed my maternal grandmother, the gouty and bibulous old lady from Kentish Town, who had begun her life as a barmaid in Oxford. I supposed I had inherited the weakness from her; but I discovered that the cause lay, among other things, in living off liver and other offal during the war in order to make the meat ration go round. The disease used to attack me when I was about to take some long journey or start some large piece of work. It drives one to contortions that make people laugh. It is said to stimulate the imagination and intellect and certainly, just before it occurs, one is in a state of startling illumination and euphoria, as happens—according to Dostoevsky—before an attack of epilepsy.

11

I must go back to 1936 and the crisis in my father's life when his business went into liquidation. One does not expect one's father to fail; he is the hero. When, through weakness, he does so, one is shocked and, for some reason, guilty before the revelations that come out. It was awful to find out that the seeds of this downfall were sown long, long before and to suspect the taint was in oneself. My severity when I was young was due to dread of this. In one way the old gentleman was responsible for fathering a set of merciless prigs, and I think only our mother softened us with her strange alternations of disloyalty and decency. She knew her lot would always be a losing gamble and relieved the tedium by fits of vituperation.

What alarmed the rest of us was that this vigorous man

was about to be let loose on the world or into a vacuum in which we would have him and his debt-creating genius on our hands. Our mother was ill and in a wretched state. His spry feats and deeply shaded intrigues had one good effect on us: we were all scrupulous about money; but there was a bad effect. We were not exactly mean, but we had become liable to fits of unimaginative caution and mockery. We became wry-minded. We were relieved to have gone up in the world; but the more we knew or guessed about Rydal Mount, that solid looking double-fronted villa in Bromley, the more it looked like a piece of Lake Poetry that had gone wrong. Was the house paid for? How was it paid for? I did not see my parents often, and if they came to stay with us in London or at Maidencourt my father talked only about food or God. Every two hours he needed nourishment, so between the three large main meals of the day, there had to be a sandwich or a plate of cakes to keep him going in his deck chair in the garden, where he dozed off over his religious pamphlets and woke anxiously listening for the sound of plates and cups. He needed food as he needed credit. As a guest he ate up the day and got very irritable because I worked. He wanted, he demanded, the whole attention of my wife and myself. He would break into my study and with falsely whimsical voice would say: "Haven't you done it, old boy?" He always complained that I was a pedestrian fellow; a shower of energizing Biblical remarks used to be thrown at me. He would close the door and go away sadly. And then pretend to be fascinated when my wife typed what I wrote.

For my brothers and sister, who lived near to him and who saw him often, the matter was different. They were closer to atmospheric changes in his financial life. My brothers were in trades connected with his own. They had known of bank's threats and court orders.

It was obvious that his salvation lay in converting his house into flats. But how could more money be raised and where would he live while the conversion was taking place? We trembled. My successful brother had been called to the rescue several times: the rest of us were poor and careful.

Father did *not* tremble. He was exhilarated, for—and we were too stupid to realize this—the conversion would mean that he would have *two* dream houses and that the conversion itself would be a superb opportunity for expense. He got himself a temporary job at £4 a week in a Christian Science Reading Room and left the task to the Divine Mind. I need hardly say the Divine Mind turned up trumps. Down came the manna; in came the architect and builders. The next job for the Divine Mind was to find "alternative accommodation." It has struck me since that this modern phrase sums up my father's lifetime ideal. He was fond of quoting the Scripture: In my Father's house are many mansions.

In one of my earliest returns to the house, Father casually mentioned (as I have related) the pine trees, the heather and the gorse of Hindhead in Surrey. Unknown to us, it had long been his secret intention to live there. The Divine Mind, for once, did nothing. Or, if you prefer it, the Divine Mind produced one of its genuine miracles, a miracle so wonderful to the point of farce, so tragic in essence that I was bitter when I heard of it.

My mother, who never spent a penny on herself all her life and hated to go to the door of the house for fear of what legal document would be pushed into her hands, answered the door one day and, clean out of character, went mad and bought a vacuum cleaner from a doorstep salesman. The event is incredible in itself. It amazed, it frightened, it enraged my father when he came home. Having bought the thing she must have suddenly become frightened herself, for she hid it behind her dressing table. When Father spotted it he was stupefied: he saw he had a rival spender. He was even more put out to hear she was not in debt. She had paid for the machine out of her own pocket.

Where did she get the money? She told some fib about a little present she had had from her well-off sister, who often slipped her a pound or two. Father was almost satisfied with this tale, but he was a meddling, ferretting, examining kind of man and, feeling certain that the cleaner was a swindle of some kind at the expense of an ignorant woman, he got behind the dressing table to look at the machine. In doing so he stubbed his toe. I have mentioned in my earlier volume the sensibility of my father's hands: his feet were no less sensitive. They were sentient and thinking feet. He discovered the kind of thing that always annoyed him in a house, some small imperfection which my mother, not having been born in a Yorkshire manse, would carelessly let go. He bent down. Monstrous: the carpet had been incorrectly laid. There was a lump in it. In a minute he had the corner of the carpet up and in his mother's plaintive voice complained of the dust. Under the carpet was a heap of silver coins. Eighty-three pounds, I have been told. My mother's secret savings of a lifetime. She mistrusted banks.

I know this story because my father himself told me it. He was laughing uncomfortably, red in the face, like a boy, abashed, ashamed, almost weeping: not with guilt but with admiration that out of the mouth of such a babe and suckling as our mother, such praise should come. As for herself, she was defeated. It was she who felt guilty, even dishonest. She wept. She confessed. Then after his emotion had died down, Father asked the shrewd Yorkshire question: "Is there any more?" Mother, gratified by his display of feeling and destroyed by guilt, admitted there was. He had relied so much on the money of the detested Miss H, of *A Cab at the Door;* now jealousy had its victory.

"Where?"

I am glad I did not witness the scene. My father had the habit of hiding silver articles he had bought secretly among his underclothes. Mother had stuffed another £300—it is said —in notes between sheets and blankets and in drawers all over the house. I doubt if there was as much. It was with this money that they set out for Hindhead—Father's heaven—and found a pleasant little house there.

All conifers, heather, gorse, commons and hills my mother hated and Father deeply loved, especially the pine-smelling air. He would stand by the Golden Valley entranced, taking it all into his exhilarated lungs. He loved the name itself: "Golden Valley." He said it aloud and he would brace his strong frame as if absorbing some mystical gold. Or because the name sounded like an advertisement, for he liked advertisements too. There was a richness in the air of this high Surrey region, for half-hidden in the firs and coppices of birch were the houses of prosperous businessmen. His local church had many well-off people.

He had moods when he was profoundly amused by himself, particularly by his brash or pushing adventures—the salesman who has taken all by surprise or thought of an ingenious way to keep a foot in the door. He blushed when he told of these things—a blush of modest wonder at his genius; or at his disasters when the push landed him in trouble. He dwelled, for example, on a tale of going to see a Mr. Y, whom he didn't know, the chairman of a building society or a bank; and having been refused an appointment, he decided to turn up at his private house, timing his arrival for about five-thirty, when the gentleman would be home. How lovingly he told of the maid who asked him in to wait; how he appraised the furnishings of the library; how inquisitively he began to study some photographs on a desk, after half an hour; how suddenly he saw an alarming portrait. By accident, he had come to the wrong house. He had come to Mr. X's not Mr. Y's. There was Mr. X's picture—and Mr. X had firmly told him some weeks before that if he didn't pay some debt or other, there would be another court order. Father got out of the house as quickly as he could, unseen, as Mr. X's car passed him at the gate. A narrow squeak.

Or again, at Hindhead, this aromatic spot, there was the incident of Lord G's hat. My father's attitude to lords was more north-country and American, than the rather snobbish, respectful indifference of the south: if he saw a lord, his way was to go up and shake his hand in a brotherly way. He had gone to a party which seemed to offer opportunities for one who aspired to the Christian Science "practice," and there stood Lord G. Whether, from his account of it, my father ever shook Lord G by the hand I cannot say; but it is certain that Lord G was a very tall man with a small head who wore a sporting kind of trilby hat. My father was a short fat man with a large head. As he left the party, my father looked at the hats in the hall and decided by a mixture of accident and design to try on the hat of Lord G. He liked it. He left the party and walked home in it. Mother opened the door to let him in and there he was, modestly triumphant, with this absurd little hat on his head. I say no more. I do not know whether Lord G was in need of prayer at that time, but contact had been made. With extreme shyness, my father said: "You never know."

The interlude at Hindhead, beginning as it did with my mother's private miracle, was uncommonly restrained in one way: the villa was small. Here something odd happened, to Mother, too. She was in poor health; but worse, she was desperate and bored. She was a London girl. She hated Nature. She could not, as I have said, stand conifers; the only acceptable trees for her were the moody, changeable and deciduous. She hated quiet. She knew scarcely anyone in the neighborhood and indeed my father was terrified that she would make a friend and let her tongue wag. It did wag when it got a chance.

So there was Mother, stuck among a lot of well-off stockbrokers and Commons. A few whimpering telephone calls got through to us; but it became increasingly difficult to speak to her if one rang. Father owned the telephone and rarely were we allowed speak to her. His egotism was so much more powerful and commanding than hers. She also feared the telephone as she feared the front door. Father commanded us one day to come down at once: she was terribly ill, he said. My wife and I hurried down. She was not ill at all. She was soon rocking with laughter. She was driven to tricks by his enormous righteousness. Obviously they had had one of their weekly rows and he wanted a breather, for her response to his righteousness was always a wild theatrical scene. She loved "dragging up everything." She got my father out of the room, gripped my wrist, stared frantically into my eyes and slyly pulled down some quantities of cloth from a cupboard. It was heavy, expensive material used for upholstering sofas and chairs, in gaudy colors and with a cobbled surface: it had what looked like threads of metal in it. She held up a piece, then another piece and another. She had been a shopgirl and shopgirls have their fancies when they are bored. While my father was in London Mother had made up this cache of valuable material into a dozen pairs of her obsessional garment: bloomers. She slipped from the room and came back wearing a fantastic pair in bright orange; then she pulled them off and tried on pair after pair. They looked like sofas on her. The stuff was so heavy that they stood almost upright on the floor for a second or two before they collapsed. She screamed with laughter.

"They ought to have had me in the business," she said. "I used to be in the millinery." She looked at me with her always questioning look, half serious, half inviting me to join her fantasy of Father recovering his fortunes by manufacturing upholstered bloomers. She sat down exhausted.

"You've got to do something in this hole or you get driven out of your natural," she said and her gray-green eyes filled with tears.

This happened at the time of Munich. That year the flats were finished, but had only one tenant. Anyone who could was getting out of London. Father and Mother did the opposite: they returned to face the Blitz.

The town of Bromley was badly bombed during the war. A lot of the High Street and several churches went up in flames. Some of the suburban streets looked like jaws with rotting gaps in them. There were thousands of missing windows and cracked ceilings among the surviving houses. Here, to our consternation, my parents sat out the whole war. They refused to move. They did come and stay in the country with us but only in the mid-war lull when the raids moved to the coast and provinces. They had great courage. Or was it courage? My first urgent invitations to come down were answered sharply by my father. "We can't leave the house." And from my mother, whimpering: "He doesn't want to leave the house with all these things." I was angry. One of the traditional explanations of why we never went for holidays when I was a child was: "We can't leave the house here on its own, empty." Now the house was sacred. It seemed to me that Father's passion for property and things—his capital!—had become as mad as his mother's, and that he was obstinately risking our mother's life and health, not to mention his own.

I went down several times to persuade them to move. It was always an eerie experience. One walked up the silent and empty hill in the dusk to the blacked-out place, where Mother clung to me and then pointed to the long crack in the ceiling with a timid pride: "Look, Vic, our crack! That was the land mine." And Father said: "We've got the water back now."

During a raid it was my father's habit to go into another room and pray: he called this spiritual or protective fire-watching. He refused to have a shelter. Mother, in her irrational way, would sit in her nightdress on top of the stairs—instead of sheltering underneath them as one was advised to do. "I want to get out quick," she said and saw herself taking a fast slide down to the door.

One night, when she had sent him out of the room to take the kitchen rubbish to the dustbin (it was astonishing to hear *her* ordering him about—he had never done housework in his life), she put her familiar grip on my wrist and after leading me to the windows to peep through the blackout to see if "he," i.e., "that old Hitler," was coming, she took me on a fast, furtive tour of Father's bedroom, opening the drawers and saying in an excited rage: "Pants. Shirts. Socks. Collars," and occasionally revealing the bits of silver he had hidden there. It was an hysterical protest against the hoard for which, she slyly conveyed, he was risking their lives. She loathed possessions more than anything else. She seemed to me like a trapped animal at that time and she was in a bad nervous state. Yet when he came back, she was in awe of him.

And a strange thing happened perhaps briefly typical of other families in these times. The "wicked" Miss H who had quarrelled bitterly with my father—the quarrel that led eventually to the break-up of his business—had been bombed out of her house in Dulwich. What passions blew to nothing in that explosion I do not know; but now the elderly Miss H came and sheltered with my parents. The two frightened women got on well and supported each other; my mother spoke well of her. But, lest I should think there had been nothing in the old jealous scenes she had made regularly in our childhood, Mother maintained just a shred of the respectability of that passion and said, as she passed the door of the bedroom where Miss H had slept before she moved out: "She *always* left the door open at night and called 'Goodnight' when he passed."

It was a matter of pride with Mother to keep the passions going.

One knows little about the inner lives of one's parents. They were in their late sixties and there was a sort of complicity in their battles. The appalling things they said expressed the fascination of their knowledge of each other and of the undoubted passion that had, at some time, entangled two temperaments so disastrously different. And then, time had brought about an ironical turning of the tables. My father had thought that by becoming a Christian Science practitioner he had liberated himself and found his true vocation. (Incidentally the Christian Science Church refused to recognize him— I don't know why.) What he hadn't realized was that he had lost his freedom: the "practice" had to be carried on in his own home. No more shopping trips in the West End, very few ritual "hair cuts" at Harrods now. The more she had him in the house, the more adroit she became at preventing him leaving it. He was as housebound as his own father, the minister, had been.

It was a pity that Father never took her to the cinema; with its fantasies her own would soon have become identified.

As it was, she took up reading. I was astonished to find her reading Dickens, and the Brontës. It was about this time that she decided she had cancer—this, of course, was a fantasy that served as a weapon directed at her husband's religion—and she would sit rubbing her skirt at the stomach. The habit began as a sly taunt; but gradually became set and then frantic, so much so that in the next fifteen years she had worn a patch away in many of her skirts. She did not have cancer. It was my father who eventually died of it—but that was a long way off. Her nervous illnesses were real enough, but he and we knew how much she could put on, in order to hold him.

"I hold him back, I know I do. I've always held him back," she would say. But, in fact, he was mystified by his failure to be one of the "big" practitioners and, since at last he earned only a few guineas once in a while there was nothing to hold him back from. The invalid on the couch controlled him.

Why did he fail in this chosen vocation? So long as they practice in the wealthy parts of big cities, many Christian Scientist practitioners prosper, if prosperity is the test; and in view of the general materialist tendency of the religion it must be. One of his friends, a shrewd fellow from Newcastle who had been on the road, succeeded, and Father often went to find out the secret. The secret of Father's failure was his drastic and egotistic nature. He was more exacting than the holiest. He did not, (like his own father, the minister,) believe in hellfire and damnation, but he had the same rigid and pleasureless spirit of domination. The Newcastle fellow was a good man, but he used to beg Father to stop dragging the Divine Mind into everything. He urged him to relax. But Father was an absolutist, a fanatic. He moved from group to group among the many schismatics which, in others, might have been the sign of an independent spirit; but in him, I'm afraid, it was due to his intolerant compulsion to "put people in their right place," i.e., to contradict them flatly. His religion was a book religion and he was afloat in a sea of abstract nouns that flowed meaninglessly into one another. He thought everything and everyone outside his religion was a waste of time; he often said he wanted God, more and more of God. In the end people felt they were drowning in his unending talk.

"You bore people. You go on too long," Mother would say from the sofa where she lay, longing for respite. The fact is that life had been so totally translated into words for him that it had become meaningless. As a writer, I am uncomfortably aware of the warning in this.

12

The war was over. Several times I had tried to get on with a novel, but I had had to put it aside. We were turned out of Maidencourt because farming had become prosperous, and the farmer wanted his house back. We tried London, but London was a sordid and miserable place. For a year or so I was literary editor of *The New Statesman,* but I disliked the job. It gave me little time for writing. Once more we returned to the country, on the edge of Savernake Forest. The Americans who had turned down all my stories now published what they had rejected. I wrote a successful novel, on my obsessive subject: *Mr. Beluncle.* I traveled again. I wrote *The Spanish Temper,* lectured at Princeton and went to South America. The diversity of my interests seems to have killed off the novelist, but it was good for a short-story writer, who needs restlessness. The writer had almost completely absorbed the valet.

But the valet had his difficulties.

My brothers and I had always given money to our parents but now they needed more solid support. Debt forced the sale of Rydal Mount. The small profit soon went. Our parents now shared a tiny villa in a depressing street of little houses, with a widow—another stone-deaf woman, an exaltée. When I went to see them she used to greet me with words like: "Victor, go on giving your good tidings to the world." She had heard I had been broadcasting.

It was always a gloomy journey to Sundridge Park, for from London Bridge to this place I passed through the bitter scenes of my adolescence. What would my life have been if I had not got that train to Paris so many years before? I remembered my clerkly self with the stiff wing collar, the spot on his chin (I had imagined I had caught anthrax), his nose in a book. I remembered the lowered spirits—after the brief escape into literature in the train—when I walked home to the family quarrel. I saw the golf club Father had joined forty years before and where he had never played—one of his daydreams. Now the roles of father and son were reversed. It was I, now, who resembled a stern but worried Father going to see an unmanageable son. And I felt sad that my Father's ambitions (which had seemed, at one time, so admirable if fear-inspiring) had come to failure. And this led me to think that, for all my travels and books, I was a failure, too, trapped in a character I could not escape. Was I, in my own way, as self-deluded as he? Some words of my mother's come back to me: "All your life you hope, but in the end you find you have to live without even hope."

What had she hoped for? Simple security. No more.

The house which my parents shared with the widow

was small. Its only distinction was an overgrown hawthorne tree that darkened the sitting room window. The widow's husband had planted it as a tiny bush, donkey's years before. Father opened the door eagerly and Mother would be half-creeping behind him: they had gone to the door a dozen times to see if I was coming. I was taken into the back room where, what with a desk, a table, armchairs and sofa and a sort of chiffonier belonging to the widow, three people hardly had room to move. Old people cling to their possessions, and my parents had imposed theirs on the widow's with comic effect: their carpet covered hers, there were two fenders, two coal buckets, two lots of fire-irons, two sets indeed of most objects. Meals were doubled, for the widow was beginning to fail and could not cook for herself. There was a spare room upstairs stacked from floor to ceiling with the leftovers from Rydal Mount. The usual war was going on between my father's religion and my mother's disbelief in it. They were united in a mild battle with the old lady, who would take her bath at three in the morning and remain there so long that my parents lay awake fearing she had drowned. Mother enjoyed these eccentricities. The widow had been known to rush out to a passing coalman and cry to him fervently: "Thank you for all you did for us in the war."

My father, the exasperated healer, found himself with two invalids on his hands. I must say he showed great patience, especially with the widow, who eventually became incapable of looking after herself. Indeed he became a nurse to her. In her exalted way she gave him the Biblical name of David. Father glowed. He was not displeased. He had become a Saint. Mother twitched a bit with her old jealousy and slyness, but laughed it away. She was in her eighties, too. Her resource was her gift for comic observation: Father observed nothing except the price of things. It amused her that she who had had to endure a stone-deaf maid and a stone-deaf mother-in-law, should now be living with a stone-deaf widow. She laughed even more because the two quarrelling old odd-job men who came in to sweep the leaves and "do" the little garden were stone-deaf also and accused each other of stealing, by dumb-show and lip-reading. In place of hope in her life, Mother wavered between fear and a sustaining sense of farce. I give a sad account which is shadowed by my own sadness but I was not a frequent visitor. My brothers and sister used to visit the old couple very regularly and bring a grandchild or two. This livened them.

Father occupied himself with reading the Bible and writing quotations and thoughts from it on slips of paper which he arranged on his desk or tucked into his wallet. He occasionally had a patient and (if he heard unmistakably from the Divine Mind that his work had been well done) would get into an aggressive state and send out preposterous bills. This led to the inevitable quarrels about money that marked his whole life. He owed some of these patients to one of the Big Men of the religion, but here too an appalling thing happened. The Big Man, famous in London and Boston, strayed from the path; there was a revolt which, characteristically, my father followed. But the revolt turned to a scandal. The awful word "women" was mentioned; Father was horrified. Worse, the Big Man dropped dead.

At this point, Father heard of another saint, a woman, of course, who sent out garrulous additions to the revelations of Mrs. Eddy from Arizona or California, in the form of expensive newsletters. Here, he told me, was the Truth at last, and his salvation. I was called in to subscribe for them. I gladly did. We dreaded that he was running up huge bills. This turned out not to be so and shows how mean or, at any rate, how calculating I had become. I was alarmed to meet a celebrated bookseller in London who said: "I met your father the other day. What an interesting man. And what a book buyer!"

The fact was that, rather touchingly, his new dream was to play a part in my kind of life. My success as a writer had an exhilarating influence on him.

There occurred what I ought to have realized would soon happen. Seeing my name in print so often, he thought he too would turn author: he wanted to be like me. I was called to Sundridge Park, and he said he had met a second Big Man, who was offering him a large sum of money if he would write a popular book on "*true* Christian Science," i.e., not on Eddy-olatry. Father was agog to do this. He bought a desk, a new typewriter, quantities of paper, but when he sat down to write the book, he couldn't get his thoughts together. Would I help him? The book (he said) was to be "the crown of his life." What he meant, he said, was Would I ghost it for him? Or, as weeks went by, Would I not only write it for him but publish it under my name? The money would be huge. I was very embarrassed at having to turn the idea down. I said he knew I did not believe in his religion.

"I know that," he said. "And I know you've written that novel about it, *Mr. Beluncle*, with me in it. I glanced at it. I couldn't read it. I don't mind at all. But," once more his fierce sentence came out, "let me tell you that without my religion I would have finished myself years ago."

He was about eighty. But this new Big Man dropped dead too.

In this sad little house, except for the flash of the old rage, his character softened, to our contentment. My wife and I were offered a glass of gin and vermouth—he had always set up as a strict teetotaller—and I was sent to a little room to get the bottles. "They're on the far side under the bed." I came into a room piled with furniture they had not been able to squeeze in with the widow's in the other rooms: there I saw what his last burst of buying had been. It had occurred during the war. He had stored—fearing to starve—hundreds of leaking packets of soup powders, cheeses, biscuits, spaghetti, packets of things now rotting away and enough to keep mice going for years; and, sure enough, under a couple of stacked beds and tables there was a long row of gin, whiskey, vermouth and port bottles he had bought years before—waiting for a rise in the market. I crawled in and got a couple out. He himself took a sip of port and so did my mother. We were very cheerful and gossiped our heads off. I think he read an occasional review I wrote and was very proud when I was praised. He was carried away by the title of one of my books of criticism, *The Living Novel*, which of course he did not read.

"I like that. Living. Life," he said. "That's what the world wants. Mrs. Eddy says . . ."

The only story of mine I know he read was one published in *The Listener* about two drinking women talking about a flea. It is called *Things As They Are*. The thought of fleas disgusted him. Fleas were obscene and lower class. If, in earlier days, Mother suddenly started unhitching her skirts and half-undressing, crying with the fever of the hunt: "Walt, Walt, I've got a flea. I've got a flea"—he would turn green with sick anger. He denounced me for writing a story so vulgar and indecent.

But Mother was slowly fading. She crept to the door to greet me no longer, but lay on the sofa scratching her skirt and saying furtively to me: "It's cancer." We forced him to get a doctor who regularly saw her while Father argued with him about the errors of medicine. My poor mother did not have cancer; she was suffering from the humiliating ills of old age. Almost toothless, for she either refused or was not allowed to go to a dentist, she could digest nothing. She was worrying, too, about what would become of Father if she died.

Early one morning Father rang me up, howling—there is no other word—and in tears.

"Your mother has just died. Five minutes ago. I was downstairs making her a cup of tea. I heard a shout. I turned off the kettle and when I got upstairs she was dead."

I caught the train and was down at the house an hour later. His grief was awful. He moaned and swayed, without control. When his own father, the minister, died (my brother told me) Father had stood in the cemetery and had given out an animal howl of "Father, I love you," and had tried to throw himself into the grave. His nature was primitive. My wife followed me down to the house and, on sound instinct, made egg sandwiches for him. Grief does indeed create physical hunger, and two or three years later he always spoke of my mother's death and egg sandwiches in one breath.

I had gone at once to see my mother's body. She lay, a tiny figure, so white and frail that she looked no more than a cobweb. I stood there hard and unable to weep. Tears come to me only at the transition from unhappiness to happiness; now I was frozen at the thought of her life. She had been through so much and I had been so much outside it. My father said that a week before she died she suddenly became very young looking, even her hair seemed golden to him, as it had been when he had first seen her in Daniel's shop in Kentish Town.

My mother's laughter is what remains with me; everything turned into a tale in her talk—a tale she would tell, with her despairing work-worn fingers spread over her face, with her laughing eyes peering through the gaps between.

. . .

After her death, Father stayed with my youngest brother for a long time and was easily managed so long as he could watch Westerns on television. But presently the old restlessness came back. He declared it was morally wrong for old people to live with their children and went back to the widow's house. She too had died in the meantime. She had left him a little money and considering his care and nursing of her, it was deserved. Capital at last.

So once more he set out to prospect the south coast of England for a new house, a place where he could breathe, and where the water was soft and the fish good. We nervously watched his departure to seaside resorts and country hotels. He would return to us to discuss the brochures he had got from house agents. They were always lists of large houses at high prices. These discussions were long. They were in fact not discussions but monologues; he explained that since he lived alone he talked a lot. He did. One monologue, I remember, began at midday; after an hour or so he paused when he was interrupted by grandchildren who looked upon him as a wonder; he continued through two more large meals until one in the morning, in which no one but he said anything. One saw a man fulfilled: he had seen a place in the West Country by the sea with four or five bedrooms, three reception rooms, a large garden, near a town noted for its Dover Sole such as he and my mother used to eat after a couple of dozen oysters near Liverpool Street station when they were courting. The cost of this place was £9000, add another couple of thousand for alterations.

"But you'll be lonely there on your own. And it's far too big. You ought to live near us or your friends."

He was about eighty-two. He looked austerely at me.

"I have no friends. They are all dead."

"And where would you get the money?"

"It will 'unfold.' *You* could raise it." He wanted us to buy him the house. There was a family council. The idea was mad. It was agreed that I would explain to him that none of us could "raise" such a sum. I wrote to explain this, for he never listened. He never forgave me, though by now he had changed his mind and thought the East Coast might be more bracing.

"I feel I want to be braced."

He went to live in lodgings on the East Coast and every day went house-hunting. But he got a cold which turned to flu. My youngest brother had an agitated message from his landlady and drove over to fetch him back. They drove the forty miles to my brother's house outside London and arrived in the shopping street in the late afternoon. He asked my brother to slow down so that he could see what the season's "new lines" were, in the shopwindows. The old commercial traveler woke up in him. "I like this contemporary" was his phrase. "It's modern." They drove on to my brother's house and Father collapsed as he got out of the car. They got him to a chair and called for a doctor.

"Not the knife. I won't have the knife," he gasped. He said he was hungry. Then he died. It was not my mother but he who, without pain, died suddenly of cancer.

He had wanted to be buried in Kirbymoorisde, his birthplace, but neither he nor any of us knew anyone there. His Yorkshire relations had scattered and gone. A new crematorium, very modern, almost contemporary—his word again—had just opened in the new suburb near my brother's house. My father's body was one of the first to be cremated there. That was a distinction: a new house. He did not believe in the reality of death. He believed that he would "pass on" to another plane of consciousness and would die and die again until he was the perfect image of the Divine Mind.

The astonishing thing was that he left no debts. He left us all his egotism, as our mother left us her racing tongue. I loved seeing the sad voluptuous pout of his lips as he carved a joint and the modest look on his face when, at my house, he passed his plate up and said, as his own mother had before, "Just a little more."

It should have been his epitaph.

Now in my turn I have become an old man, though no one would think of telling me I am. And this is not out of consideration, but is due to the frantic cult of youth nowadays. Better doctoring helps. In fact one's age goes up and down, round and about, all one's life. I am seventy, and in my father's phrase, "I would like a little more." I shall never be as old as I was between twenty and thirty when with its deceitful energy, my young body carried a pained, fogged and elderly mind across France, Ireland, Spain and the Tennessee mountains on foot. I am impatient about the time I so dreamily and indecisively wasted then. I am glad that after thirty I got back into touch with my childhood; this gave me my vocation, and doing what one wants to do lightens the burdens of life. A writer is more fortunate than most people in being able to carry his work with him. He pays for this happy independence by having to work much harder than the mass of employed people and indeed, today, his profession is not only precarious, but seems to be vanishing. It has been in my nature to work hard but hard work can lead to the idleness of the time-and-motion mind. When the profession dies out it may be possible for the writer to do better the few things he ought to do, instead of the hundred things that are a distraction from it. The cost of literature is far, far higher than the public who get it free in the libraries imagines, and it is getting higher. Once he has proved himself, a writer or any artist needs to be relatively rich, subsidized or in some way kept—think of Goya, Velasquez, El Greco, of Shaw—his leisure does not consist of lying on beaches in the Caribbean, but in a labor delightful because it is fanatical. Scott and Balzac desired wealth recklessly, acquired huge debts, and debt is a kind of wealth to those who work furiously within it as these men did. I often wish I had had the guts to get into debt.

I have done, given my circumstances and my character, what I have been able to do and I have enjoyed it.

V. S. PRITCHETT was born in England in 1900. He is a short-story writer, novelist, critic and traveler. His short stories have appeared in collections in the United States under the titles *The Sailor and the Saint, When My Girl Comes Home, Blind Love* and as individual contributions in *The New Yorker* and *Holiday*. Among his novels are *Mr. Beluncle, Dead Man Leading* and *The Key to My Heart*. Random House has also published *The Living Novel and Later Appreciations,* a collection of critical essays, most of which appeared originally in *The New Statesman,* and his Clark Lectures, *Meredith and English Comedy*. He has been a lifelong contributor to this paper and is now a director. His memoir, *A Cab at the Door,* was published by Random House in 1968.

Mr. Pritchett's extensive sojourns in Europe, the Middle East, and South America have led to the writing of several books on travel, among them, recently, *The Offensive Traveller*. With photographs by Evelyn Hofer, Mr. Pritchett has written *London Perceived, Dublin: A Portrait* and *New York Proclaimed*.

Mr. Pritchett has visited the United States, where he gave the Christian Gauss Lectures at Princeton, was Beckman Professor at the University of California in Berkeley, and has been writer in residence at Smith College, and Zisskind Professor at Brandeis University. He is a foreign Honorary Member of the American Academy of Arts and Letters and the American Academy of Arts and Sciences.

VINTAGE BIOGRAPHY AND AUTOBIOGRAPHY

V-658   ALINSKY, SAUL D.   *John L. Lewis: An Unauthorized Biography*

V-250   BURCKHARDT, C. J.   *Richelieu: His Rise to Power*

V-725   CARR, E. H.   *Michael Bakunin*

V-746   DEUTSCHER, ISAAC   *The Prophet Armed*

V-747   DEUTSCHER, ISAAC   *The Prophet Unarmed*

V-748   DEUTSCHER, ISAAC   *The Prophet Outcast*

V-617   DEVLIN, BERNADETTE   *The Price of My Soul*

V-225   FISCHER, LOUIS (ed.)   *The Essential Gandhi*

V-132   FREUD, SIGMUND   *Leonardo Da Vinci*

V-147   GIDE, ANDRE   *If It Die*

V-499   GOODMAN, PAUL   *Five Years*

V-449   GRAY, FRANCINE DU PLESSIX   *Divine Disobedience*

V-268   JUNG, C. G.   *Memories, Dreams, Reflections*

V-50   KELLY, AMY   *Eleanor of Aquitaine and the Four Kings*

V-728   KLYUCHEVSKY, V.   *Peter the Great*

V-581   KRAMER, JANE   *Allen Ginsberg in America*

V-215   LACOUTURE, JEAN   *Ho Chi Minh*

V-677   LESTER, JULIUS   *The Seventh Son*, Volume I

V-678   LESTER, JULIUS   *The Seventh Son*, Volume II

V-280   LEWIS, OSCAR   *Children of Sánchez*

V-634   LEWIS, OSCAR   *A Death in the Sánchez Family*

V-92   MATTINGLY, GARRETT   *Catherine of Aragon*

V-490   MYRDAL, JAN   *Confessions of a Disloyal European*

V-624   PARKINSON, G. H. R.   *Georg Lukacs: The Man, His Work, and His Ideas*

V-373   PAUSTOVSKY, KONSTANTIN   *The Story of a Life*

V-133   STEIN, GERTRUDE   *The Autobiography of Alice B. Toklas*

V-100   SULLIVAN, J. W. N.   *Beethoven: His Spiritual Development*

V-287   TAYLOR, A. J. P.   *Bismarck: The Man and the Statesman*

V-256   WILDE, OSCAR   *De Profundis*

V-106   WINSTON, RICHARD   *Charlemagne: From the Hammer to the Cross*

V-158   AUDEN, W. H. and C. ISHERWOOD   *Two Great Plays: The Dog Beneath the Skin and* The Ascent of F6

V-601   AUDEN, W. H. and PAUL TAYLOR (trans.)   *The Elder Edda*

V-673   BECK, JULIAN and JUDITH MALINA   *Paradise Now*

V-342   BECKSON, KARL (ed.)   *Aesthetes and Decadents of the 1890's*

V-271   BEDIER, JOSEPH   *Tristan and Iseult*

V-321   BOLT, ROBERT   *A Man for All Seasons*

V-21   BOWEN, ELIZABETH   *The Death of the Heart*

V-48   BOWEN, ELIZABETH   *The House in Paris*

V-294   BRADBURY, RAY   *The Vintage Bradbury*

V-670   BRECHT, BERTOLT   *Collected Works*, Vol. I

V-207   CAMUS, ALBERT   *Caligula & 3 Other Plays*

V-2   CAMUS, ALBERT   *The Stranger*

V-223   CAMUS, ALBERT   *The Fall*

V-245   CAMUS, ALBERT   *The Possessed*, a play

V-281   CAMUS, ALBERT   *Exile and the Kingdom*

V-626   CAMUS, ALBERT   *Lyrical and Critical Essays*

V-135   CAPOTE, TRUMAN   *Other Voices, Other Rooms*

V-148   CAPOTE, TRUMAN   *The Muses Are Heard*

V-643   CARLISLE, OLGA   *Poets on Streetcorners: Portraits of Fifteen Russian Poets*

V-28   CATHER, WILLA   *Five Stories*

V-200   CATHER, WILLA   *My Mortal Enemy*

V-679   CATHER, WILLA   *Death Comes for the Archbishop*

V-680   CATHER, WILLA   *Shadows on the Rock*

V-140   CERF, BENNETT (ed.)   *Famous Ghost Stories*

V-203   CERF, BENNETT (ed.)   *Four Contemporary American Plays*

V-127   CERF, BENNETT (ed.)   *Great Modern Short Stories*

V-326   CERF, CHRISTOPHER (ed)   *The Vintage Anthology of Science Fantasy*

V-293   CHAUCER, GEOFFREY   *The Canterbury Tales*, a prose version in Modern English

V-142   CHAUCER, GEOFFREY   *Troilus and Cressida*

V-723   CHERNYSHEVSKY, N. G.   *What Is to Be Done?*

V-146   CLARK, WALTER VAN T.   *The Ox-Bow Incident*

V-589   CLIFTON, LUCILLE   *Good Times*

V-173   CONFUCIUS (trans. by A. Waley)   *Analects*

V-155   CONRAD, JOSEPH   *Three Great Tales: The Nigger of the Narcissus, Heart of Darkness, Youth*

V-10   CRANE, STEPHEN   *Stories and Tales*

V-531   CRUZ, VICTOR HERNANDEZ   *Snaps: Poems*

V-205   DINESEN, ISAK   *Winter's Tales*

V-721   DOSTOYEVSKY, FYODOR   *Crime and Punishment*

V-722   DOSTOYEVSKY, FYODOR   *The Brothers Karamazov*

V-188   ESCHENBACH, WOLFRAM VON   *Parzival*

V-254   FAULKNER, WILLIAM   *As I Lay Dying*

V-139   FAULKNER, WILLIAM   *The Hamlet*

V-282   FAULKNER, WILLIAM   *The Mansion*

V-339   FAULKNER, WILLIAM   *The Reivers*

V-381   FAULKNER, WILLIAM   *Sanctuary*

V-5   FAULKNER, WILLIAM   *The Sound and the Fury*

V-184   FAULKNER, WILLIAM   *The Town*

V-351   FAULKNER, WILLIAM   *The Unvanquished*

V-262   FAULKNER, WILLIAM   *The Wild Palms*

V-149   FAULKNER, WILLIAM *Three Famous Short Novels: Spotted Horses, Old Man, The Bear*

V-130   FIELDING, HENRY *Tom Jones*

V-45   FORD, FORD MADOX *The Good Soldier*

V-187   FORSTER, E. M. *A Room With a View*

V-7   FORSTER, E. M. *Howards End*

V-40   FORSTER, E. M. *The Longest Journey*

V-61   FORSTER, E. M. *Where Angels Fear to Tread*

V-219   FRISCH, MAX *I'm Not Stiller*

V-8   GIDE, ANDRE *The Immoralist*

V-96   GIDE, ANDRE *Lafcadio's Adventures*

V-27   GIDE, ANDRE *Strait Is the Gate*

V-66   GIDE, ANDRE *Two Legends: Oedipus and Theseus*

V-656   GILBERT, CREIGHTON *Complete Poems and Selected Letters of Michelangelo*

V-473   GOODMAN, PAUL *Adam and His Works: Collected Stories of Paul Goodman*

V-402   GOODMAN, PAUL *Hawkweed*

V-654   GOODMAN, PAUL *Homespun of Oatmeal Gray*

V-300   GRASS, GUNTER *The Tin Drum*

V-425   GRAVES, ROBERT *Claudius the God*

V-182   GRAVES, ROBERT *I, Claudius*

V-717   GUERNEY, B. G. (ed.) *An Anthology of Russian Literature in the Soviet Period*

V-255   HAMMETT, DASHIELL *The Maltese Falcon* and *The Thin Man*

V-15   HAWTHORNE, NATHANIEL *Short Stories*

V-476   HOROWITZ, ISRAEL *First Season*

V-489   HOROVITZ, I. AND T. MCNALLY AND L. MELFI *Morning, Noon and Night*

V-305   HUMPHREY, WILLIAM *Home from the Hill*

V-727   ILF AND PETROV *The Twelves Chairs*

V-295   JEFFERS, ROBINSON *Selected Poems*

V-380   JOYCE, JAMES *Ulysses*

V-484   KAFKA, FRANZ *The Trial*

V-683   KAUFMANN, WALTER *Cain and Other Poems*

V-536   KESSLER, LYLE *The Watering Place*

V-134   LAGERKVIST, PAR *Barabbas*

V-240   LAGERKVIST, PAR *The Sibyl*

V-23   LAWRENCE, D. H. *The Plumed Serpent*

V-71   LAWRENCE, D. H. *St. Mawr and The Man Who Died*

V-315   LEWIS, ANTHONY *Gideon's Trumpet*

V-553   LOWENFELS, WALTER (ed.) *In a Time of Revolution: Poems from Our Third World*

V-537   LUKE, PETER *Hadrian VII*

V-673   MALINA, JUDITH AND JULIAN BECK *Paradise Now*

V-136   MALRAUX, ANDRE *The Royal Way*

V-479   MALRAUX, ANDRE *Man's Fate*

V-180   MANN, THOMAS *Buddenbrooks*

V-3   MANN, THOMAS *Death in Venice and Seven Other Stories*

V-86   MANN, THOMAS *The Transposed Heads*

V-496   MANN, THOMAS *Confessions of Felix Krull, Confidence Man*

V-497   MANN, THOMAS *The Magic Mountain*

V-36   MANSFIELD, KATHERINE *Stories*

V-137   MAUGHAM, SOMERSET *Of Human Bondage*

V-78   MAXWELL, WILLIAM *The Folded Leaf*

V-91   MAXWELL, WILLIAM *They Came Like Swallows*

V-221   MAXWELL, WILLIAM *Time Will Darken It*

V-489   McNALLY, T. AND *Morning, Noon and Night*

V-562   McNALLY, TERENCE *Sweet Eros, Next and Other Plays*

V-489   MELFI, L., I. HOROVITZ, T. McNALLY *Morning, Noon and Night*

V-593   MERWIN W. S. (trans.) *The Song of Roland*

V-306   MICHENER, JAMES A. *Hawaii*

V-718   NABOKOV, V. (trans.) *The Song of Igor's Campaign*

V-29   O'CONNOR, FRANK *Stories*

V-49   O'HARA, JOHN *Butterfield 8*

V-276   O'NEILL, EUGENE *Six Short Plays*

V-18   O'NEILL, EUGENE *The Iceman Cometh*

V-165   O'NEILL, EUGENE *Three Plays: Desire Under the Elms, Strange Interlude and Mourning Become Electra*

V-125   O'NEILL, EUGENE JR. AND WHITNEY OATES (eds.) *Seven Famous Greek Plays*

V-586   PADGETT, RON AND DAVID SHAPIRO (eds.) *An Anthology of New York Poets*

V-478   PARONE, EDWARD (ed.) *Collision Course*

V-466   PLATH, SYLVIA *The Colossus and Other Poems*

V-594   PROUST, MARCEL *Swann's Way*

V-595   PROUST, MARCEL *Within A Budding Grove*

V-596   PROUST, MARCEL *The Guermantes Way*

V-597   PROUST, MARCEL *Cities of the Plain*

V-598   PROUST, MARCEL *The Captive*

V-599   PROUST, MARCEL *The Sweet Cheat Gone*

V-600   PROUST, MARCEL *The Past Recaptured*

V-714   PUSHKIN, ALEXANDER *The Captain's Daughter*

V-24   RANSOM, JOHN CROWE *Poems and Essays*

V-732   REEVE, F. (ed.) *Russian Plays*, Vol. II

V-297   RENAULT, MARY *The King Must Die*

V-564   RUDNIK, RAPHAEL *A Lesson From the Cyclops and Other Poems*

V-16   SARTRE, JEAN-PAUL *No Exit* and Three Other Plays

V-65   SARTRE, JEAN-PAUL *The Devil and the Good Lord* and Two Other Plays

V-238   SARTRE, JEAN-PAUL *The Condemned of Altona*

V-586   SHAPIRO, DAVID AND RON PADGETT (ed.) *An Anthology of New York Poets*

V-330   SHOLOKHOV, MIKHAIL *And Quiet Flows the Don*

V-331   SHOLOKHOV, MIKHAIL *The Don Flows Home to the Sea*

V-153   STEIN, GERTRUDE *Three Lives*

V-85   STEVENS, WALLACE *Poems*

V-141   STYRON, WILLIAM *The Long March*

V-63   SVEVO, ITALIO *Confessions of Zeno*

V-178   SYNGE, J. M. *Complete Plays*

V-601   TAYLOR, PAUL AND W. H. AUDEN (trans.) *The Elder Edda*

V-750   TERTZ, ABRAM *The Trial Begins* and *On Socialist Realism*

V-713   TOLSTOY, LEO *The Kreutzer Sonata*

V-202   TURGENEV, IVAN *Torrents of Spring*

V-711   TURGENEV, IVAN *The Vintage Turgenev* Vol. I: *Smoke, Fathers and Sons, First Love*

V-712   TURGENEV, IVAN *Vol. II: On The Eve, Rudin, A Quiet Spot, Diary of a Superfluous Man*

V-257   UPDIKE, JOHN *Olinger Stories: A Selection*

V-605   WILLIAMS, JOHN A. AND CHARLES F. HARRIS, (eds.) *Amistad 1*

V-660   WILLIAMS, JOHN A. AND CHARLES F. HARRIS, (eds.) *Amistad 2*

V-580   WILLIAMS, MARGARET (trans.) *The Pearl Poet*